FICTION HOUSE PRESS
PRESENTS

TRUE MYSTERY

August 1957
Vol. 7, No. 4

This reprint edition is a facsimile of the original magazine. Variations in printing and quality can be attributed to the original magazine which was printed on pulp paper. No attempt has been made to politically correct any language deemed inappropriate to the modern reader.

New Material
© 2021 Fiction House Press

ISBN 978-1-64720-362-7

www.FictionHousePress.com
fictionhousepress@gmail.com

MAIL ORDER BUSINESS

Your Big Opportunity!

34-lesson course on proved, tested, up-to-date, **profitable** methods. Amazing treasure-house of the best mail order plans and practices. How to start your mail order business on a small one-man scale . . . how to keep it growing more and more profitable month after month. Money-making facts. Full price only **$9.95**. Satisfaction guaranteed or refund. Circle below **No. 40** for Mail Order Course.

5 ACRES and INDEPENDENCE

How to Buy a Small Farm and Run It PROFITABLY!

SECURITY is yours when you own a few acres and use them wisely. You supply your own food requirements and possibly enough extra to enjoy a comfortable cash income. Teaches you practical things you want to know about livestock, farming, poultry, orchards, etc. Only **$4.95**. Order "Farming" **No. 4** in coupon.

ART SCHOOL *Self-Taught*

No previous Art training necessary. These excellent lessons guide you step-by-step. You train yourself for a fine career in Art by following these logical, easy-to-understand instructions. More than 700 illustrations included! Lessons cover industrial design, fashion drawing, painting, lettering, typography, packaging, photography, etc. Entirely PRACTICAL and commercial throughout. Satisfaction or refund guaranteed. Full price, only **$9.95**. Order "Art School Self-Taught." **No. 1** in coupon at bottom of page. Rush order today.

How to Run a RESTAURANT...

Get into a Good MONEY-MAKING BUSINESS of *Your Own!*

Virtually a complete self-instruction course on starting and operating profitable lunch-eonettes, cafeterias, diners, tea rooms, etc. Teaches you the all-important facts about leases, licenses, equipment, furnishings, decorating, kitchen arrangement, menu-planning, etc. How to make money!

FULL PRICE, Only $6.95, Postpaid This could be your BIG chance! Satisfaction guaranteed or money back. Order "How to Run a Restaurant," **No. 2** in coupon below.

PUBLIC SPEAKING FOR SUCCESS

HOW TO HANDLE PEOPLE

Oratory and public speaking is an art which **must be learned.** Don't you believe bunk about "natural born" speakers! For your greater personal advancement let this excellent course teach you the fundamentals of influencing people; how to make them laugh, cry and ACT. Only **$6.95**. Circle **No. 3** in coupon below. Satisfaction or refund.

PIANO TUNING

Experienced piano tuners charge up to $10.00 for a job they finish in about an hour. Repeat business, too! You can start training for this profitable field **right now**. It is NOT necessary that you play piano . . . you don't even have to understand music at all. **SELF-INSTRUCTION COURSE — only $4.95 complete price.** This excellent home-study course includes instructions on piano regulating, repairing—other servicing operations every good piano tuner knows. Also covers electric organs, tuning by Stroboscope, etc. Good, clear, helpful illustrations to guide you step-by-step. Money-Back Guarantee. Order "Piano Tuning". Only **$4.95**. Circle **No. 7**.

HOW TO BUY, SELL, TRADE OLD GOLD, ETC. A new to-the-point Technical Bulletin to teach you how to make money dealing in precious metals—broken jewelry, old gold, silver, platinum, etc. Enormous opportunities for those with experience. Only **$1.00**. Order "Old Gold," **No. 20** in coupon below. Guaranteed!

HOW TO GET A GOOD JOB

Shows you step-by-step the successful techniques of up-grading yourself into a better position in any field. Teaches you how to SELL yourself to a new employer for the highest price. A Practical 36-Lesson Course. Full price only **$4.95**. Satisfaction or refund guaranteed. Circle **No. 43** in coupon for 36-lesson course.

AMAZE Your Friends

Let music develop your personality—increase your popularity. You'll enjoy learning this tested, short-cut way. You'll learn by playing REAL music, with BOTH hands, right from the very FIRST lesson. This is NOT a trick system—but it IS a genuine piano course that's lots of FUN. Satisfaction or refund guaranteed! Complete price only **$6.95** postpaid. Circle **No. 53** in the coupon below.

How to be a BARTENDER and the Art of Mixing Drinks

Professional information for the liquor trade and man-about-town. Details on mixing and serving 300 most popular drinks. PRACTICAL instruction for working behind the bar. How to handle and use spirits, wines, beers. **Trade secrets** on the care of bottles, glassware, mirrors, utensils. How to make syrups; bottle in bulk, prepare fruit. Excellent illustrations. Also includes appropriate toasts for good fellows. Only **$1.95**. Order 'Bartender' **No. 32.**

LOCKSMITHING & Key Making

PRACTICAL UP-TO-DATE COURSE!

ONLY $5.95 COMPLETE—Teaches you the **professional** "secrets." How to pick locks, decode, make masterkeys, install and service key systems, etc. Step-by-step detailed, illustrated instructions make every operation crystal clear. Money-making information for carpenters, mechanics, hardware dealers, gunsmiths, cycle shops, maintenance men, etc. 55 lessons! Satisfaction guaranteed or your money back. Order "Locksmithing Course," **No. 6** in coupon. Only **$5.95**. Mail coupon today!

Learn YOGI! The Art of SELF MASTERY

Practical Course — ONLY $5.95 Complete Yogism aids your self-confidence, will-power, self-control. Helps your personal efficiency. Points out time-tested methods for a happier, more **successful** life . . . based on modern scientific discoveries plus ancient Yoga Secrets for releasing your deeper powers. Practical, valuable for everyday use by busy, level-headed Americans. **Send No Money.** Pay postman $5.95 plus C.O.D., or send **$5.95** for postpaid shipment. Satisfaction or refund guaranteed. Send for this "Practical Yoga Course" **No. 22** in coupon.

Make the Most of What You've Got!

STOP FORGETTING!

How To Develop Your Memory And Put It To Practical Use

Teaches you how to remember by teaching you how to do CLEAR, ORDERED thinking, speaking and working. Not a "trick system" but virtually a self-instruction course in **concentration** and straight thinking. Learn how successful people retain, recall and USE information, knowledge and facts. This information worth its weight in gold. Full price only **$4.95**. Order "Memory Course," **No. 23** in coupon!

How to Use BETTER ENGLISH in Your Letters and Conversation

Daily YOU are being judged by the language you use. Your other abilities, however great, are generally discounted if your English is faulty. So don't let your shaky English hold you back in business or social life. **Improve your speech and writing** by studying these interesting, PRACTICAL lessons. Teaches you how to increase your vocabulary—learn new words and use them right. How to spell and pronounce correctly. Secrets of good letter-writing and entertaing conversation. Full price ONLY **$4.95**. Satisfaction or refund guaranteed. Order 'Correct English.' Circle **No. 30** in coupon below.

HAPPINESS IN MARRIAGE Written by a physician! Intelligent men and women can now get the modern, helpful, scientific facts they want about sex and the love life. Virtually an encyclopedia of Sex, the Journal of the American Medical Association says it "ranges the entire gamut of sex subjects from birth, thru adolescence, marriage, sexual aberration and disease, and rejuvenation." A really **great** work! Order "Sex Happiness in Marriage." Only **$3.95.** Just circle **No. 24** in the coupon.

How to Write Songs—

A PRACTICAL COURSE IN LYRICS—MUSIC—SELLING

Best selling hit songs often are written by those who know only the special "techniques" or **secrets.** You don't have to spend long dreary years studying theoretical music in order to do popular songs the public goes wild over. If you have the stuff inside of you to begin with . . . this **practical** course will teach you how to **get it down on paper** and will teach you exactly how and **where to offer it** for sale. ONLY **$4.95.** Satisfaction or refund guaranteed. Order "Song Writing." **No. 26** in coupon.

HYPNOTISM

REVEALS to you the fundamentals of **Practical** Hypnotism. Amazing illustrated lessons. Big 280-page treatise jam-packed with fascinating information. In simple understandable language you will enjoy. Full price only **$3.95.** Satisfaction or refund guaranteed. Order "Hypnotism" today. **No. 27** in coupon below.

EUGENE FEUCHTINGER'S HINTS ON VOICE DEVELOPMENT

Basic exercises designed to *strengthen* your vocal organs and *improve* your voice. These new self-instructions include the most important parts from the world-famed voice course put out by the Prefect Voice Institute. Full Price, only **$2.95.** In coupon below circle **No. 28.** Order "Voice Development."

HOW TO SING FOR MONEY—Teaches you the art and business of singing popular songs professionally. **Practical** course written by ASCAP-member Charles Henderson, one of Hollywood's top-flight vocal coaches—who has worked with Bing Crosby, Dinah Shore, Frances Langford, Kenny Baker, etc. These short-cuts to success teach you how to make the most of what you've got! Full price, ONLY **$4.95.** Order "How to Sing for Money." Circle **No. 29** in coupon below.

SWEDISH BODY MASSAGE

Course of instruction in the Art of Body Massage and Hydrotherapy. Contains information on fundamentals of anatomy, physiology, procedure for complete massage, approved exercises, etc. Includes business advice. This valuable study may open door to a basic knowledge of the profession. Only **$9.95,** complete. Order "Body Massage." **No. 15** in coupon. Satisfaction guaranteed.

JEWELERS & WATCHMAKERS Cyclopedia

Packed with trade secrets, manufacturing processes, little-known formulas, etc., for opticians, stone setters, engravers, case makers horologists, photographers and others. 1001 money-making ideas for the practical man! Only **$2.49.** Order "Jewelers Cyclopedia." **No. 18.**

watch and clock repairing

PRACTICAL COURSE IN HOROLOGY

Learn at home spare time. How-to-do-it lessons for beginners as well as those already in the trade. Thorough self-instruction training in the fundamentals of American and Swiss timepieces. Contains a wealth of helpful photos, drawings, diagrams, charts, etc. Only **$7.95** for everything! Order "Watch & Clock Repairing." **No. 5** in coupon. Satisfaction or refund guaranteed.

World-Famous HEALTH & MEDICAL TEXTS

by Dr. Joseph F. Montague, M. D.

Troubles We Don't Talk About—Learn from an eminent specialist what should (and should not) be done about hemorrhoids or piles, abscesses, fistulas, itch and other common rectal ailments. Ethical and most helpful! Only **$4.95.** Circle **No. 55** in coupon below.

Nervous Stomach Trouble—A useful manual written in an interesting, helpful way . . . written for victims of high tension modern living. Satisfaction guaranteed or your money back! Only **$4.95** postpaid. Circle **No. 58** in coupon below.

Constipation—How To Combat It—Tells you in plain language things you should know about this nearly universal trouble. Debunks the claims of many high-powered advertisers! Explains what is considered proper treatment, and warns you against certain harmful patent medicines and "health" foods. This wonderful manual worth its weight in gold! Only **$4.95.** Circle **No. 59** in the coupon below.

HOW TO *WIN* . . . WHAT YOU WANT

Workable, usable formula by Kenneth Goode, big-time advertising man & top-level merchandising executive. Shows you how to guarantee your success in almost any field. Proved secrets explained for first time! Includes details of "The Planned Success Method." Brass tacks, not blue sky! Full price only **$4.95.** Circle **No. 57** in coupon.

Learn UPHOLSTERING

Start by doing work on your own furniture to save money & beautify your home. Then branch out as you gain experience. You'll learn quickly and enjoy these step-by-step illustrated lessons. Easy-to-follow instructions on how to create, repair and remodel practically all kinds of upholstered furniture. You get everything for only **$8.95,** complete. Satisfaction or money back. Order "Upholstering." **No. 9** in coupon.

Cure SELF-CONSCIOUSNESS

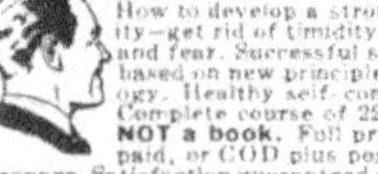

How to develop a strong, positive personality—get rid of timidity, bashfulness, shyness and fear. Successful self-instruction lessons based on new principles of practical psychology. Healthy self-confidence can be yours! Complete course of 22 home-study lessons, **NOT a book.** Full price only **$8.95,** postpaid, or COD plus postage. Mailed in plain wrapper. Satisfaction guaranteed or refund. Order "Curing Self-Consciousness Course" today. Circle **No. 41** in coupon at bottom of page.

HOW TO GET ALONG IN THIS WORLD . . .

Put YOURSELF in THIS PICTURE — SUCCESS

Boiled down, **practical** tips on Success! Here, gathered together for the first time, are 5,000 gems of worldly wisdom on how to live fully, joyously, successfully . . . how to handle people, make money, be happy. Most interesting—and useful. Only **$1.95** complete. Order "How to Get Along in This World." Circle **No. 33** in coupon below.

APARTMENT HOUSE MANAGEMENT Wonderful field for ambitious men and women, especially those over 40. Experienced managers have steady work, good pay and SECURITY. Satisfaction or money back guaranteed. Complete, only **$8.95.** Course **No. 8** in coupon below.

POULTRY RAISING

Practical, workable instructions on how to start a chicken flock in your back yard or on a small farm. Teaches you how to do egg farming efficiently, pleasantly—**and profitably!** Explains every detail of poultry raising, step-by-step. Only **$4.95** complete. Order "Poultry Raising." **No. 13** in coupon. Satisfaction or refund!

BUILD IT YOURSELF Be a practical handyman! Save time and money using these professional TRICKS-OF-THE-TRADE. Carpentry now made easy. New self-instruction course in one handy volume, complete with full-page photographs, etc. Teaches practical woodworking, painting & decorating, upholstering, power tools, cabinet making, etc., etc. COMPLETE PRICE ONLY **$3.95.** Order "Build It Yourself." **No. 17** below.

SHOE REPAIRING COURSE

New, well-illustrated, step-by-step series of lessons on how to rebuild shoes. Written for the beginner who wants to go into business or the family man who wants to save money by doing his own shoe repairing. Full price, only **$6.95.** Satisfaction guaranteed. Order "Shoe Repairing Course." Circle **No. 44** in coupon below.

Complete Practical Blueprint Reading Course

Interesting, simplified self-instruction lessons for builders, mechanics, electricians, etc. 24 volumes, including over 60 actual blueprints, diagrams and step-by-step drawings. FULL PRICE ONLY **$11.95.** Unusual bargain! Satisfaction or refund guaranteed. Order "Blueprint Reading Course." **No. 16** in the coupon.

MASTER MIND!

Learn Short-Cut Mathematics

Juggle figures, do baffling number tricks. Make people gasp at your marvelous **lightning-quick** mind. Multiply 4 figures by 4 figures without using old-fashioned multiplication! Big cloth-bound volume: fully illustrated course. A fascinating study.

Sharpen Up Your Brain Power Includes worked-out problems, answers, etc. Sensational bargain, only **$3.95,** postpaid—or C.O.D. plus postage. Satisfaction guaranteed or refund. Order this amazing "Short-Cut Mathematics" today. Simply circle **No. 11** in coupon. Then clip and mail.

IT'S EASY TO ORDER In coupon draw a circle around the number of each course you want us to send you. Print your name and full address clearly, then mail coupon right away. Send full payment with your order and we'll prepay all postage charges—on C.O.D. shipments you pay charges. Satisfaction or refund guaranteed . . . you take no risk.

FREE!! Select two or more courses from this page and we will include an **EXTRA** educational item as a special bonus . . . without any additional cost to you! You may ***keep*** this excellent Dividend Item, as your own, even should you send back for refund the courses you order. We reserve the right to withdraw this unusual offer when present limited stock is gone. Don't lose out—***mail coupon today!***

NELSON-HALL CO., *(Established 1909)*
210 S. Clinton St., Dept. GT-87, Chicago 6, Ill.

MAIL THIS NO-RISK COUPON TODAY!

NELSON-HALL COMPANY, Dept. GT 87 — N
210 South Clinton Street, Chicago 6, Ill.

Please rush me the practical concentrated courses I have circled below. I understand each is complete and that this is the full price, nothing more for me to pay. I have the right to examine everything you send me for 10 full days. Then if I am not ***more*** than satisfied in every way I will return the material and you ***guarantee*** to make complete immediate refund, without question or quibble. (Draw a circle around the number of each course you want.)

1	2	3	4	5	6	7	8	9	11	13	15
16	17	18	20	22	23	24	26	27	28	29	30
32	33	40	41	43	44	53	55	57	58	59	60

☐ I enclose $ ______________ in full payment. Ship entirely postpaid.
☐ Ship C.O.D. for $ ______________ plus postage.

NAME ______________________________

ADDRESS ______________________________

CITY ______________ STATE ______________

☐ Check here if above order is for two or more numbers. In this case we send you, **without extra charge,** a fine educational volume as a bonus. You'll be delighted with this excellent gift. And it is yours to keep, free, even if you return the courses after inspection. MAIL this coupon NOW—this special bonus offer is subject to cancellation when our present stock runs out.

Earn BIG MONEY

Learn **ELECTRIC APPLIANCE REPAIRING At Home In Your** *Spare Time!*

WE FURNISH YOU THIS AMAZING ELECTRONIC KIT

WE GIVE YOU ALSO THE CERAMIC HEATER KIT

START YOUR OWN BUSINESS

There are millions of electrical equipment units in daily use in factories, homes, office buildings and on farms. Skilled electrical technicians are needed to keep this equipment in good running condition. Learn at home in your spare time.

$5.00-$6.00 PER HOUR

is often charged for making ordinary repairs. We show you how to repair refrigerators, vacuum cleaners, washing machines, motors, factory equipment, electrical farm equipment, do house wiring, etc.

BEGIN IN YOUR OWN KITCHEN, BASEMENT OR GARAGE. You don't need elaborate fixtures or expensive equipment to be a successful repairman. Work as many hours as you wish. The Electrical Appliance Technician is his own boss!

IF YOU ARE MECHANICALLY INCLINED, can hold and use tools, we will give you the training and time saving kits—a multi-purpose CHRISTY ELECTRONIC KIT whose dials show you exactly where the trouble lies with electrical equipment that does not work properly—a CERAMIC HEATER KIT that enables you to wire your own heating elements and pocket all of the profits for yourself—LESSON MANUALS written in simple, easy-to-understand language profusely illustrated showing step-by-step repair shortcuts—all of which give you the Know-how for making more money and how to get financial security.

"All CTS graduates are entitled to CTS lifetime advisory service."

R. S. Frazer, President

YOU ALSO LEARN how to build power tools from spare parts, how to solicit business and keep business coming in, what to charge your customers, etc. Thousands of CHRISTY graduates in all parts of the world prove the value of CTS Training. WRITE FOR SPECIAL PAY LATER FORM.

CHRISTY TRADES SCHOOL, 4804 N. Kedzie Ave., Dept. D-2482, Chicago 25

SEND FOR OUR NEW 32 PAGE CATALOGUE!

MAIL THIS COUPON TODAY!

CHRISTY TRADES SCHOOL, Dept. D-2482
4804 N. Kedzie Avenue, Chicago 25, Ill.

Gentlemen:

Please rush me your FREE ILLUSTRATED BOOK about Electrical Appliance Servicing, facts on your Electronic Kit and Special form for paying later from earnings while learning.

Name ________ Age ________

Address ________

City ________ Zone ________ State ________

NOW! Turn Your Waste Gas Into Blazing SUPER POWER!

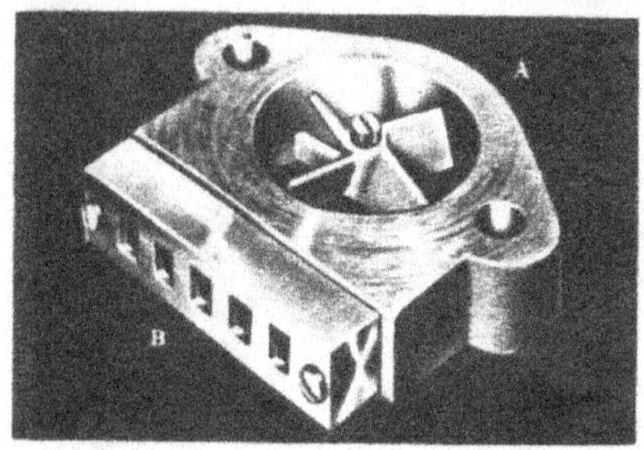

Up To 15 More Horsepower, 6 More Miles Per Gallon . . .

Or It Doesn't Cost You a Cent!

It's true! Now you can get the breath-taking acceleration . . . jack-rabbit starts . . . blazing new power that you've dreamed about for years — *simply by harnessing the raw, unburnt gasoline that your engine is wasting today!*

Get performance from your car that will make friends gasp with astonishment — and save $25, $50, and even $75 a year on gas bills doing it!

Yes! You, *yourself* can fit this amazing gasoline atomizer onto your car in as little as 20 easy minutes! Then simply turn on your ignition — and *a modern miracle of engineering science — comes to life under your hood!*

Test It 100 Different Ways!

Use it to flash away from other cars . . . spurt up the steepest hills! Feel the new, life-saving *reserve power passing* power you get at 50-60-70 miles an hour *with your foot still only halfway down on the pedal!*

Actually SEE for yourself the enormous gas savings it gives you! *Savings that must pay you back its full purchase price in the first 3 to 4 months that you use it.* or YOUR FULL MONEY BACK! Here's why!

This Power Booster is patterned after superchargers selling for as high as $600. It SUPER-MIXES . . . SUPER-VAPORIZES . . . SUPER ATOMIZES your gas . . . mixes that gas with much greater volumes of air . . . makes that gas *more explosive* in your engine . . . squeezes the *hidden power* out of that gas! No wonder dozens of leading car magazines call this the "money-saving discovery of the year."

Try It Entirely At Our Risk!

This MINI-SUPERCHARGER (U.S. Patent No. 2,409,937) sells for only $11.95 for most cars — or $14.95 if your car comes equipped with a special four barrel carburetor. This is *your total cost — there is no installation fee!* You have nothing to lose. You must be amazed and delighted or your full money back! ACT TODAY!

FREE: AMAZING DIAL-O-MAGIC TROUBLE SPOTTER! Saves you up to $250 on repairs! Lets you *dial your trouble* with a flick of your finger! BUT ACT TODAY!

We Guarantee Your Gas Savings!

Yes! This device must save you — on gas alone — EVERY SINGLE CENT OF THE MONEY YOU PAY FOR IT—OR YOUR FULL MONEY BACK! This offer is good for a full four months! ACT TODAY!

MAIL NO-RISK COUPON TODAY!

NORTH AMERICAN STEVENS, INC.
31 West 47th Street, New York 36, N. Y.
DEPT. RP-8

IMPORTANT: *For Fast Service Be Sure Coupon Is Completely Filled In. (Please Print)*

Yes, I want to try your amazing MINI-SUPERCHARGER *entirely at your risk!* I will pay postman only amount checked below plus low C.O.D. charges.
☐ $11.95 (My car does not have a four barrel carburetor.)
☐ $14.95 (My car is equipped with a special four barrel carburetor.)
I understand that it must do everything you say or my full money back! Also send me as your Extra Gift Premium, the Free DIAL-O-MAGIC Trouble Spotter I may keep it even if I return the MINI SUPERCHARGER.

MAKE OF CAR ____ YEAR ____
MODEL ____ 4 DOOR OR 2 DOOR ____
4 CYLINDERS ____ 6 CYLINDERS ____ STRAIGHT 8 ____ V-8 ____
STANDARD TRANSMISSION ____ AUTOMATIC ____
NAME ____
ADDRESS ____
CITY ____ ZONE ____ STATE ____

☐ CHECK HERE TO SAVE MORE! Enclose check or money order and we pay all postage and handling charges! You save as much as $1.06! Same money back guarantee, of course.

© Copyrighted 1956 by North American Stevens, Inc.

AUGUST, 1957 A SKYE PUBLICATION VOL.7, No. 4

TRUE MYSTERY

The Magazine of Actual True Life Crime Cases That Are Stranger Than Fiction!

Editor, BILL GUY

Asst. Editor, PAT GRUBBS — Art Editor, WALTER PINKAVA

CONTENTS

FULL-LENGTH MYSTERY CASES

MYSTERY FEATURES

SPECIAL DEPARTMENT

The photos on pages 8, 26, 30, and 36 were specially posed by professional models.

Cover color printing by the Regensteiner Corporation, Chicago, Illinois.

TRUE MYSTERY, Vol. 7, No. 4, August 1957. Published quarterly by Skye Publishing Co., Inc., executive and editorial offices at 16 East 55th Street, New York 22, New York. Arthur Bernhard, Publisher; Alan Sills, General Manager; Bob Salomon, Circulation Director. Ray Peck Co., 545 Fifth Ave., New York 17, N. Y., YU 6-7995, Advertising Representatives. Annual subscription (4 issues) $2.50 in the U. S., Canada, and P.A.U.; $3.00 foreign. Twenty-five cents a copy. Manuscripts and art material accompanied by stamped, self-addressed envelopes will be carefully considered, but the publisher and editors will not be responsible for loss or damage. Copyright 1957 by Skye Publishing Co., Inc. All rights reserved. Re-entered as second-class matter at the Post Office at New York, N. Y., under the act of March 3, 1879. Member Audit Bureau of Circulation.

HERE IS IMMEDIATE COMFORT FOR YOU WITH

Patented

RUPTURE-EASER

T.M. Reg. U.S. Pat. Off. A PIPER BRACE TRUSS

For Men! For Women! For Children!

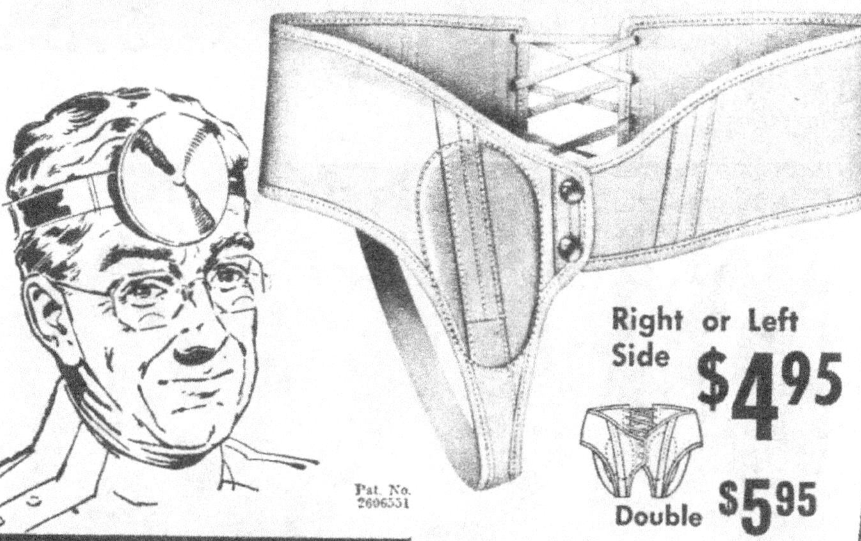

Right or Left Side **$4.95**

Double **$5.95**

A strong form-fitting washable support designed to give you relief and comfort. Snaps up in front. Adjustable back-lacing and adjustable leg straps. Soft flat groin pad — **no steel or leather bands.** Unexcelled for comfort, **invisible under light clothing.** Washable and sanitary. Can be worn under girdles and corsets. Also used as after-operation support. Sizes for men, women and children.

NO FITTING REQUIRED!

A MOST EFFECTIVE SUPPORT FOR REDUCIBLE INGUINAL HERNIA

Rupture-Easer is a highly effective support. Hundreds of thousands of hernia sufferers have discovered wonderful relief, comfort and protection in Rupture-Easer. Rupture-Easer is easy to wear.

RUPTURE-EASER IS SANITARY

Unlike steel and leather trusses, Rupture-Easer is comfortable and sanitary. It can be washed without harm to the fabric. You never offend when you wear Rupture-Easer.

EASY TO ORDER

Just measure around the lowest part of the abdomen and state right or left side or double.

10 DAY TRIAL OFFER

Money-back guarantee if you don't get relief.

PIPER BRACE COMPANY Dept. BD-87
811 Wyandotte Kansas City 5, Mo.
Canadian Orders—
Mail to: PIPER BRACE (Canada)
1242 McGill College Ave. Montreal, Canada

OVER 1,000,000 GRATEFUL USERS!

Unsolicited Testimonials From Our Thousands on File:

Minnie LaJeunesse, Minneapolis, Minn., writes: *". . . the RUPTURE-EASER is very comfortable and almost a miracle as to the way it holds one in place, and am very much pleased and satisfied with the belt."*

Harley Decoteau, Montpelier, Vt., says: *. . . "The last brace you sent me was wonderful. I have been ruptured for 30 years. I am now 36, and in 30 years, I have never been more pleased."*

Stanley C. Forbes, Rockville Center, L.I., N.Y. writes: *". . . What a Godsend it is to me now as I wear my RUPTURE-EASER. I can sleep with it. It feels so wonderful I will more than recommend it to everybody . . . I am now able to go back to work."*

Joseph A. Parks, Orlando, Fla., thanks us and writes: *". . . I have five of various kinds and prices, but yours up to this time is the most satisfactory yet. Its simplicity amazes me; it is so light and comfortable on me, I don't know I have it on."*

Juanita Addington, Twin Falls, Idaho, writes: *". . . I would like to have another RUPTURE-EASER. It really has helped me. I can do practically anything with the RUPTURE-EASER on."*

THERE'S NO SUBSTITUTE FOR PROVED PERFORMANCE
ORDER TODAY!

NO STEEL OR LEATHER BANDS!
GET NEW WONDERFUL RELIEF WITH PATENTED RUPTURE-EASER!

MAIL THIS HANDY COUPON TODAY!

Be Sure to State Size and Side When Ordering! Order two for change-off when laundering.

Delay May Be Serious! ORDER NOW!

PIPER BRACE CO., Dept. BD-87
811 Wyandotte, Kansas City 5, Mo.

Please send......RUPTURE-EASERS by return mail.

Right Side ☐ $4.95 Measure around lowest
Left Side ☐ $4.95 part of my abdomen is
Double ☐ $5.95 ....INCHES.

(Note: Be Sure to give Size & Side when ordering)

Enclosed is: ☐ Money Order ☐ Check for $...... ☐ Send C.O.D.

We Prepay Postage Except on C.O.D.'s

Name...
Address...
City and State....................................

NEW BODIES FOR OLD!

I've Made New Men Out of Thousands of Other Fellows . . .

"Here's what I did for THOMAS MANFRE . . . and what I can do for you!"

—Charles Atlas

GIVE me a skinny, second rate body and I'll cram it so full of handsome, bulging new muscle that your friends will grow bug-eyed! . . . I'll wake up that sleeping energy of yours and make it hum like a high-powered motor! Man, you'll feel and **look** different! You'll begin to **Live!**

Let Me Make YOU a NEW MAN—IN JUST 15 MINUTES A DAY

You wouldn't believe it, but I myself used to be a 97-lb. weakling. Fellows called me "Skinny." Girls made fun of me behind my back. THEN I discovered — **"Dynamic Tension,"** and it turned me into such a **complete** specimen of MANHOOD that today I hold the title "THE WORLD'S MOST PERFECTLY DEVELOPED MAN."

My Secret— "Dynamic Tension"

When you look in the mirror and see a healthy, strapping fellow smiling back at you—then you'll realize how fast **"Dynamic Tension"** GETS RESULTS!

"Dynamic Tension" is the easy, NATURAL method you can practice in the privacy of your room—JUST 15 MINUTES EACH DAY —while your chest and shoulder muscles begin to swell, ripple . . . those arms and legs of yours bulge . . . and your whole body starts to feel full of zip and go! And **you'll** be using the method which many great athletes use for keeping in condition—prize fighters, wrestlers, baseball and football players, etc.

FREE MY 32-Page ILLUSTRATED BOOK Not $1 or 10c—But FREE

Send NOW for my famous book showing how **"Dynamic Tension"** can make you a new man. 32 pages, crammed with photos, valuable advice, answers to vital questions.

This book is a **real prize** for any fellow who wants a better build. Yet I'll send you a copy absolutely FREE. It may mean the turning point in your life! Rush coupon to me personally: **CHARLES ATLAS, Dept. 164-H, 115 East 23rd St., New York 10, N. Y.**

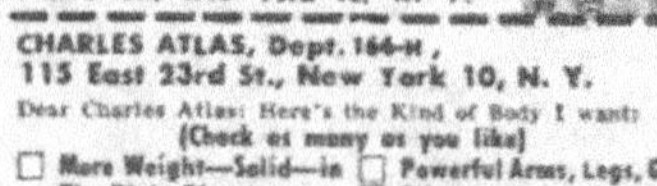

CHARLES ATLAS, Dept. 164-H, 115 East 23rd St., New York 10, N. Y.

Dear Charles Atlas: Here's the Kind of Body I want:
(Check as many as you like)

- ☐ **More Weight—Solid—in The Right Places**
- ☐ **Broader Chest, Shoulders**
- ☐ **Powerful Arms, Legs, Grip**
- ☐ **Slimmer Waist, Hips**
- ☐ **Better Sleep, More Energy**

Send me absolutely FREE a copy of your famous book showing how "Dynamic Tension" can make me a new man—32 pages, crammed with photographs, answers to vital questions, and valuable advice. No obligation.

NAME.......................................AGE..........
(Please Print or Write Plainly)

ADDRESS..

CITY.................................STATE..........

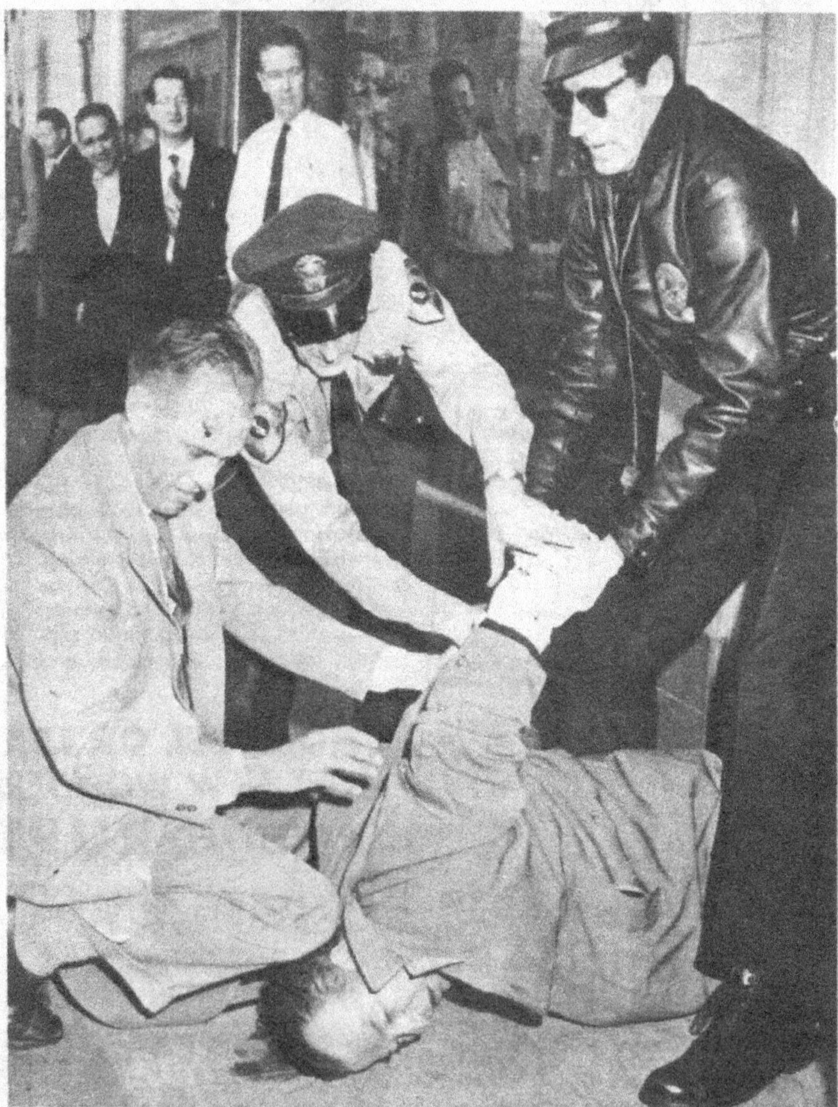

FLYING TACKLE foils a would-be robber, identified as Harry Kepple of Kansas City, after an attempted holdup of a jewelry store in crowded downtown Los Angeles. Police also captured a second suspect. Photo was made by AP staff photographer Hal Filan who happened by the scene on his way home from work.

EARNING LESS THAN $100 A WEEK?

I'll Set You Up In A Money-Making Business You Can Run From Home—A Business That Can Pay You As Much As $1,000 to $2,500 EXTRA!

Caught in a squeeze between high prices and low wages? Then listen to this: J. Kelly, of New York, followed my advice . . . earned $93.55 in four hours! T. Worley, of Michigan, paid off the final notes on his farm, financed a two-week vacation for his family—all with the money his Mason Shoe Business brought him in! C. Tuttle of California averages well over $80 weekly in spare time!

There's no reason why YOU shouldn't be adding $1,000 to $2,500 to YOUR INCOME . . . if you really want to make money. Send me the coupon below—and I'll send you—ABSOLUTELY FREE—the same powerful Starting Business Outfit that can add this kind of extra cash to your income!

Think for a moment what $1,000 to $2,500 a year EXTRA can mean to your way of living. With it, you could buy *ten* $100 suits . . . make a Big down payment on a powerful new car . . . Live in luxury for a month in Florida . . . Pay off your bills . . . or do almost anything you *can't* afford to do right now!

WHAT MUST YOU DO TO GET THIS KIND OF CASH?

"Sure," you say, "I could do all sorts of things with money like that. But what do I have to do to *get* it?" (This is the part I like to tell about—because it's so amazingly *easy!*)

Whether you realize this or not, you are an important fellow in your community. You have friends . . . relatives . . . neighbors . . . fellow workers. These people respect you, have confidence in you.

I want you to tell these people about Mason Shoes. I want you to take their orders. No pick-ups, no deliveries—just show them the styles, take their orders, and send the orders to me. And, for doing this, I'll see that you get commissions of from $2.00 to $4.00 on each and every pair—*plus* generous bonuses. One Mason man recently sold 38 pairs in just 4 hours! That's how good these shoes are!

WHAT MAKES SUCH EARNINGS POSSIBLE?

You ask, "How can I make money selling shoes, when anyone can buy shoes in stores?" Ask around, my friend, and you will discover this amazing fact: Many people do NOT buy their shoes in stores! Why is this so? Because the average shoe store, with its small stock of just a few hundred or thousand pairs, cannot possibly have all the styles, for both men and women, in all the hundreds of size and width combinations. As the Mason Man in your community, you draw on our stock of more than 250,000 pairs of shoes—sizes all the way from hard-to-find 2½, through the "ordinary" sizes, up to big 15 . . . widths from extra-narrow AAAA to extra-wide EEEE . . . 195 dress, sport, work styles for men and women!

YOU OFFER SOMETHING NO STORE CAN HOPE TO MATCH

What's more (and this is important), you can bring your wide selection *to your customer* . . . in his or her home or place of business. Stores can't do that! And Mason Shoes are *super comfortable* . . . they feature foamy-soft Velvet-eez air cushion innersoles . . . plus 3 *exclusive* comfort features. Mason Air Cushion Shoes are *good* shoes. They bear the famous Good Housekeeping Guarantee Seal! They're Nationally Advertised . . . yet never sold by stores, so folks *must* buy from you. That's why your Mason Business is a steady repeat business with regular profits rolling in right from the start, and growing each month.

TAKE THIS SIMPLE STEP TO INCREASED INCOME

There's no earthly reason why any first-rate man should be tied down to second-rate wages . . . not when extra cash comes as easy as this! You never invest one cent . . . because I send you EVERYTHING you need to get started . . . FREE. So don't suffer from "money shortage" another day. Rush the coupon below for *your* FREE Starting Business Outfit and start adding as much as $1,000 . . . $2,000 . . . even $2,500 to your income . . . NOW!

MASON SHOE MFG. CO.
Dept. 670
Chippewa Falls, Wisconsin

APPLICATION FOR INCREASED EARNINGS

MR. NED MASON, Dept. 670
Mason Shoe Mfg. Co., Chippewa Falls, Wisconsin

You bet I'm tired of "second-rate" earnings . . . I want to add $1,000 . . . $2,000 . . . even $2,500 to my paycheck during the next twelve months. Rush FREE Starting Business Outfit to me today!

Name____________________

Address____________________

Town________________ State________

The more the beautiful young girl struck at her killer, the less chance she had to survive . . .

THE TOUCH OF DEATH

By Harold Helfer

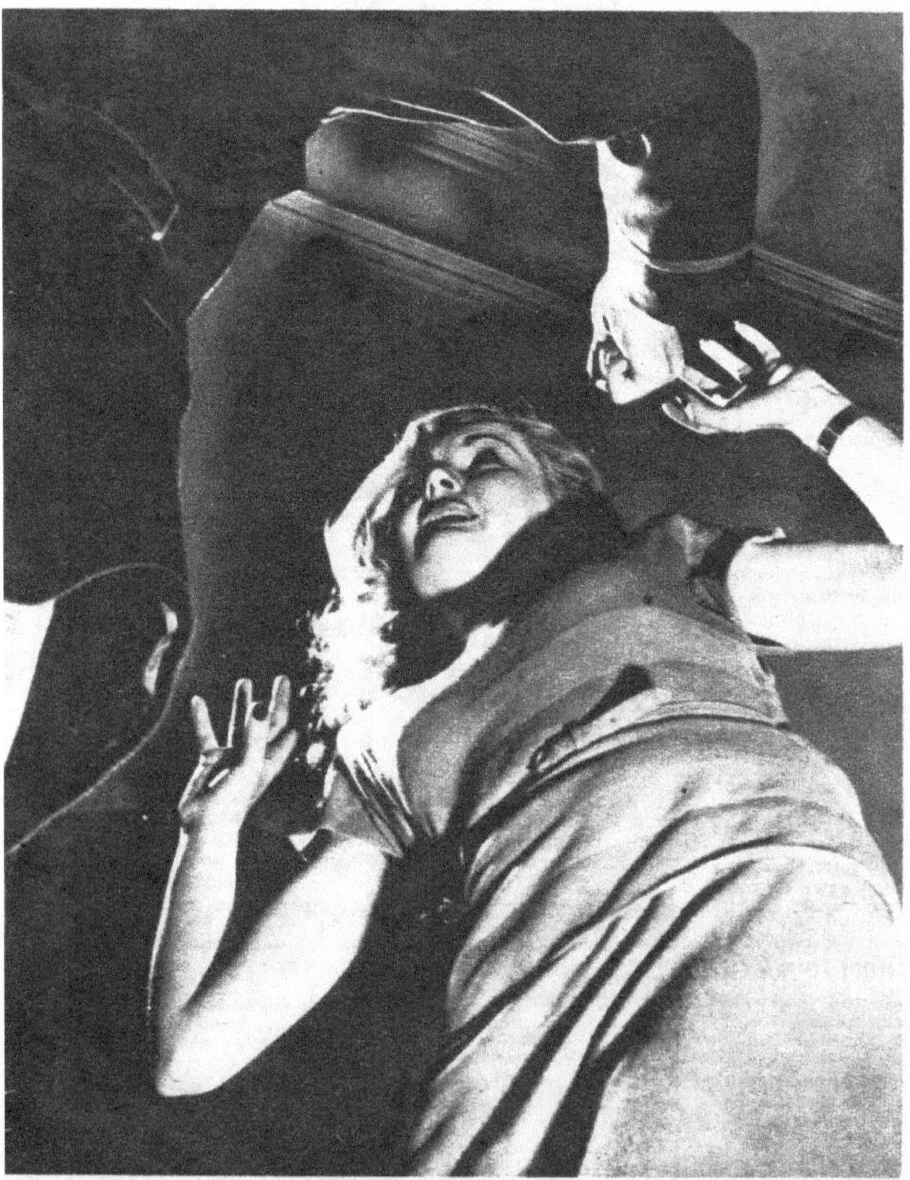

In a fury of rage and hate, the attractive Marie taunted her would-be lover.

ONE OF THE strangest cases in the annals of European criminology revolves around Marie Stanovich, a pretty Czechoslovakian girl.

In the first place, there was the baffling nature of the illness that overtook her. There was her growing gauntness and there were the strange fits into which she would lapse.

Doctors were, frankly, extremely puzzled by it all. Marie had been such a healthy, normal girl all along and then strangely, unexplainably, almost weirdly, she began having fantastic reactions, unlike anything they'd run into before.

After numerous examinations, they decided that she was suffering from some kind of chemical poisoning. But that made everything seem that much more mysterious. Because, although Marie worked in a chemical plant, she was a stenographer and never came in contact with the laboratories or with any of the chemicals. Furthermore, she was the only one in her office who had become so afflicted.

Poor Marie tried to work as long as she could. But – and this was perhaps tne weirdest part of all– it was plain that somehow she was receiving more and more poison in her body, despite the fact that now a constant watch was being kept on her as she worked and even as she walked through the corridor of the plant, to and from her office.

It was incredible that it could be so – and yet the poisoning continued and Marie finally had to give up her job and go home. As she went to bed, gaunt and gimlet-eyed, her doctors feared the worst.

It might very well be that Marie would have died if it were not for a simple circumstance that no one could have foreseen as having any bearing on this strange case.

Two employees in Marie's office had to work overtime one night, no doubt partially because the capable Marie was no longer able to be there. At any rate, the pair worked on until late in the evening. And, as it began to grow dark, they became aware of a peculiar phenomenon . . .

WHAT DID THEY SEE?

Can you identify this new development that gave police the source of Marie's poisoning and led them to her would-be killer? For the correct answer, turn to page 65

WILL YOU SPEND $2 TO SAVE YOUR HAIR?

How many hard-earned dollars have you spent to save your hair? How many hair tonics, gadgets, restorers, electrical devices, have you tried in the last few years — with no success? How many times after an unsuccessful hair-growing attempt have you sworn not to spend another cent on another hair treatment?

Yet, you buy the next product that comes on the market with hair-growing claims.

Stand in front of a mirror, take a long hard look at the top of your head. What have you to show for the money you spent on hair restorers? Do you have as much hair as one year ago? Do you see any signs of new hair, or new hair growth? Why the failure?

CAN YOU GROW HAIR?

Doctors who have spent a lifetime studying hair and hair growth have concluded that nothing now known can grow hair on a bald head. So, if you are bald, prepare to spend the rest of your life that way. Accept it philosophically and quit spending hard-earned dollars on hair growers.

If you can't grow hair — what can you do? Can you stop excessive hair loss? Can you save the hair you still have? Can you increase the life expectancy of your hair? Probably. Please read every word in the rest of this statement carefully, since it may mean the difference to you between *saving your hair* and losing the rest of it to eventual BALDNESS.

HOW TO SAVE YOUR HAIR

Itchy scalp, hair loss, dandruff, very dry or oily scalp, are symptoms of the scalp disease called seborrhea. These scalp symptoms are often warnings of approaching baldness. Not every case of seborrhea results in baldness, but doctors now know that men and women who have this scalp disease usually lose their hair.

Seborrhea is believed caused by three parasitic germ organisms (staphylococcus albus, pityrosporum ovale, microbacillus). These germs first infect the sebaceous glands and later spread to the hair follicles. The hair follicles atrophy, no longer can produce new hairs. The result is "thinning" hair and baldness.

Many men and women suffer needless worry and heartache as they peer into the mirror at their retreating hairlines. Worse, they suffer needless loss of hair because today seborrhea can be controlled—quickly and effectively—by treating your scalp with the amazing scalp medicine called Ward's Formula.

DOUBLE MONEY BACK GUARANTEE

In seconds, Ward's Formula kills the three parasitic germ organisms retarding normal hair growth. This swift germicidal action has been proven in scientific tests by a world-famous testing laboratory (copy of laboratory report sent on request). Ward's removes infectious dandruff, stops scalp itch, brings hair-nourishing blood to the scalp, tends to normalize very dry or oily scalp. In brief Ward's Formula corrects the ugly symptoms of seborrhea, stops the hair loss it causes. Ward's Formula has been tried by more than 350,000 men and women on our famous Double-Your-Money-Back Guarantee. Only 1.9% of these men and women were not helped by Ward's and asked for their double refund. This is truly an amazing performance.

Why not join the men and women who have successfully ended their troubles? Treat your scalp with Ward's Formula. *Try it at our risk.* In only 10 days you must see and feel the marked improvement in your scalp and hair. Your dandruff must be gone. Your scalp itch must stop. Your hair must look thicker, more attractive, and alive. Your excessive hair loss must stop. You must be completely satisfied — in only 10 days — with the improved condition of your scalp and hair, or simply return the unused portion for Double Your Money Back. So why delay? Delay may cost your hair.

Ward Laboratories, Inc., 19 West 44 Street, N. Y. 36, N. Y. © 1956

Doctors and hospitals can obtain professional samples of Ward's Formula on written request.

Ward Laboratories, Inc. Dept. 5908H
19 West 44 Street, New York 36, N. Y.
Rush Ward's Formula to me at once. I must be completely satisfied in only 10 days or you GUARANTEE refund of DOUBLE MY MONEY BACK upon return of bottle and unused portion.

Name ....

Address ....

City .... Zone ..... State ....

☐ Enclosed find $2, send postpaid (check, cash, money order)

☐ Send C.O.D. I will pay postman $2 plus postal charges. Canada, foreign, APO, FPO, add 50¢ — No C.O.D.

DOUBLE MONEY BACK GUARANTEE

TRUE MYSTERY HEADLINE CASE

By E. R. Trauts

Damned by forbidden desire, and waited for lovely Vicki—now

PROWLING SAVAGE OF LOVERS

Smiling suspect: "He's a twenty-three year old teenager. A little fish who wanted to be a big whale. He's basically a nice kid, but very mixed up," said neighbor.

THE blond-haired young man sat in a straight chair rocking dreamily on its back legs as he watched the pretty teen-age girls hanging around inside Robbie's Corral in Ramsey, New Jersey. Edgar Smith looked a few years younger than his actual 23 and maybe that was why quite a few of the 16-year-old girls gave him the eye as they went by him to their tables. Eddie wasn't catching the admiring glances at his handsome profile because he was concentrating on Vickie Zielinski, 15, sitting a few feet from him and talking to friends.

Vickie, a Mahwah, New Jersey high school student, was not entirely unaware of Eddie's glances in her direction. A couple of her classmates had whispered that Eddie was sizing her up and that made her feel excited and wanted. She knew the 23-year-old youth was not only married but was also the father of an infant daughter and that was why she didn't encourage him. Yet it was flattering to her teen-age heart to get direct and unashamed attention. It was only natural for a pretty young high school girl to feel this way.

Vickie and her friends had seen the young man a few times before in Robbie's Corral. He was always alone, and always sitting against the wall so that the chicks in the place could see his well-shaped nose and jutting jaw. One look at Edgar Smith was enough to see that he was a man who thought a lot of himself.

Maybe it wasn't Eddie's fault that he thought he was top-dog among the girls and women in his life. His young wife, 19-year-old Patricia, loved him deeply, had borne him a child, and was pregnant with a second. During Eddie's high school days he was a dancing Romeo with fellow students. Every girl had been ga-ga about him and so it followed that Eddie thought a lot about himself.

But Eddie wasn't going to rush things and scare Vickie away. It was enough that she had finally noticed him. Next time he'd talk to her, and after that matters would take their natural course. He got up from his chair and walked past Vickie's table. Their eyes met for a moment and Vickie blushed. Eddie smiled

someone watched his chance had come!

LANE

knowingly. "So long," he said confidently to her but Vickie didn't answer.

When the door of the teen-age hang-out closed the girls with Vickie gathered about her. "Did you see how he looked at you, Vickie?" one asked.

"Yes," she replied.

"Yeah, well, you better watch out, Vickie," a second said. "I know him. He's married. His name is Eddie Smith and he's got a wife and baby."

"I know all that," Vickie said heatedly, "and, anyway, I don't care because I don't intend going out with a married man."

But 15-year-old Vickie Zielinski didn't reckon on the persistency of a hot-blooded young man who saw a girl he wanted badly. Eddie in a deliberate take-it-easy method made several visits to Robbie's Corral and gradually won Vickie over to him. They started to exchange greetings and then got into talks over cokes.

Vickie told him a lot about herself. She was a lower junior at Ramsey High School. Her father, Anthony Zielinski, was a truck driver for Ramsey County, and she had two sisters, Mary, 18, and Myrna, 13. Once they lived in Pennsylvania. Honesdale was the name of the small hometown. Her father and mother were married there, and it was a pretty place.

Eddie wasn't shy about talking, either. He told his new friend that he was married but his wife didn't like going out and that was why he enjoyed hanging around Robbie's place. "I guess you saw me looking at you all those times I came, didn't you?" he questioned her.

"Yeah," she admitted.

"That's because I think you look great and I'd like to take you out some day."

"I wouldn't go out with you because you have a wife."

"I'm not going to do anything to you. I just like talking," he answered soothingly.

"That's what all you fellows say," Vickie said laughing.

After that conversation, Eddie attempted to make further advances. A couple of times he met Vickie on her way to school and gave her a lift in his car. Then

Partially clad body of Vickie Zielinski was discovered by her father in pool of blood in Mahwah, N. J. sand pit.

Vickie introduced him to her sisters one afternoon at the hang-out.

"You sure have a terrific sister in Vickie," said Eddie to Mary, the oldest girl.

"I know but she's only fifteen," Mary replied wisely.

But Eddie was not to be put off and he begged Mary a few times after that for her to fix him up with Vickie. "I think she's swell. One word from you, Mary, and she'd date me."

Mary lost her patience with him then and said angrily, "Why don't you stay home and pay some attention to your wife. Quit bothering my sister. She's too young for anything you got in mind."

Eddie tried to laugh her remark off, saying, "What do you think I'm going to do—attack Vickie?"

"I don't know what you want but don't try to get me to help," Mary said finally.

A little angry, Eddie left Mary and drove home to wife and child. The young couple lived at Bogert's Trailer Ranch in Mahwah, N. J. They owned a comfortable $4,500 trailer that contained two bedrooms, a living room, kitchen and bath. Eddie maintained his home and family by being a jack-of-all-trades in near-by towns. At present, however, he was unemployed and that accounted for all his free time, those hours he spent idling around the

Prosecutor Galda holds victim's school books and bag, as tousled-haired suspect explains the details of his story.

towns and flirting with teen-ager Vickie.

When Eddie got home, his pretty wife, Patricia greeted him with a kiss and the announcement that the kerosene heating stove had broken down. "So you better keep your jacket and coat on. I want you to drive me over to my mother's house. The baby won't be able to take this cold."

"Okay, okay," Eddie said sullenly.

Patricia noticed her young husband's sour mood and figured it was because of ill-luck in looking for work. She had no idea that he was angry over being rebuffed by Vickie and discouraged by older sister Mary.

Inside the car Patricia asked, "Do you think Bill will mind you keeping his car so long?" She referred to Bill Wallace, a close friend of the Smiths who lived in Mahwah.

"No. He said I could use it until I get a job. But I have to bring it back tonight," Eddie answered.

They drove over to Patricia's mother's house in Ridgewood, New Jersey. It was not an unpleasant ride. They talked of many things and had a couple of laughs over something funny Patricia remembered. Eddie stayed only a half hour at his mother-in-law's place and then said good night.

He arrived in Ramsey and started for the kerosene service store to pick up a couple of gallons and to arrange for repairs of the stove. As he cruised along the road he saw Vickie. She was on the other side of the road, walking with her school books held tightly against her. He blew the horn. She looked up and waved. Eddie stopped the car and Vickie crossed to it. He opened the door. "Hop in," he invited and she got in. "Where you going?" he asked as they drove off.

"I just came. I was at my girl friend's house. We were studying up on German for a test," she said.

"You want to drive around a bit or go right home?" he asked.

"I don't care," she said. "But if we drive around, make it short because I got to get home."

So he drove out to the sand-pit, a favorite spot for lovers who wanted to escape prying eyes. He felt a little excited sitting next to her. Her small but nicely shaped body was revealed to him by her open coat. Vickie was five feet tall and weighed 104 pounds but she already had the grace of a young woman. Eddie long ago had recognized her beauty. He decided not to waste time and so after a few innocent remarks about her school work, Eddie made a pass at her. He put his arm around her shoulder and drew the surprised girl to him. "How about a free kiss?" he asked, moving his hand downward.

"Come on, Eddie," she protested laughing nervously. "You better start the car. I have to go home."

"Yeah, sure," he said, kissing her and grabbing.

She pulled away from him. "I'm going to tell my father," she warned.

He reached for her and they started to struggle. They fought silently, viciously. Somehow they both realized something terrible was about to take place. Vickie grabbed for the door and flung herself out to the ground. He followed her and they continued fighting and then a blackness came over Eddie. It seemed like he was in a room and the room was closing tight around his head. He suddenly blacked out, but continued the weird battle with Vickie. Eddie hit and hit, knowing only blind fury.

Later, when he left the sand pit, he was alone. There was blood on the floor rubber mat. Blood was on his pants, too, and on his shoes. He could not remember where the blood had come from. All he recalled was a lot of running. He had run a lot and fought bitterly with some one. Who? He could not remember. Then he asked himself, what's your name? Edgar Smith. Where do you live? In a trailer camp in Mahwah. What date is it today? Tuesday, March 5th, 1957. Where are you going? And then Eddie remembered that he was returning the car to Bill Wallace.

The nature of his errand somehow sobered him and when he got to Bill's house the fear and trembling had left him. He gave the car to Bill and said, "Thanks a lot."

Edgar Smith went home to his wife and child that Tuesday night, but 15-year-old Vickie Zielinski never made it to the house of her parents who waited fearfully for her return. The Zielinski's finally called the police and a search was started for the young girl.

Vickie's father joined the all-night search. He insisted that something

(continued on page 14)

MEN PAST 40

Who are Troubled with *Getting Up Nights*

Pains in Back, Hips, Legs, Nervousness-Tiredness, Loss of Physical Vigor

The Cause may be Glandular Dysfunction

Men as they grow older too often become negligent and take for granted unusual aches and pains. They mistakenly think that these indications of Ill Health are the USUAL signs of older age.

This negligence can prove Tragic, resulting in a condition where expensive and painful surgery is the only chance.

If you, a relative or a friend have the symptoms of Ill Health indicated above, the trouble may be due to Glandular Dysfunction.

GLANDULAR DYSFUNCTION very commonly occurs in men of middle age or past and is accompanied by such physical changes as Frequent Lapses of Memory, Early Graying of the Hair and Excess Increase in weight . . . signs that the Glands are not functioning properly.

Neglect of such conditions or a false conception of inadequate treatments cause men to grow old before their time . . . leading to premature senility, loss of vigor in life and possibly incurable conditions.

The Excelsior Institute is completely equipped to give the latest and most modern scientific Diagnostic and treatment services.

The highly trained Staff of Doctors and Technicians is so extensive that your physical condition may be thoroughly checked during the day you arrive here.

Treatments Are Particularly for Men

The Excelsior Institute is an institution devoted particularly to the treatment of diseases of men of advancing years. If you were to visit here you would find men of all walks of life. Here for one purpose —improving their health, finding new health in life and adding years of happiness to their lives.

During the past few years men from over 3,000 cities and towns from all parts of the United States have been successfully treated here at the Excelsior Institute. Undoubtedly one or more of these men are from your locality or close by . . . we will gladly send you their names for reference.

Facilities for the Non-Surgical Treatment of Rectal and Colon

Rectal and Colon disorders are often associated with Glandular Dysfunction. These disorders if not corrected will gradually grow worse and often require painful and expensive surgery.

We are in a position to take care of these troubles either with or without Glandular Dysfunction treatments.

The proper treatment of such disorders can very easily change your entire outlook on life.

NON-SURGICAL TREATMENTS

The non-surgical treatments of Glandular Dysfunction and other diseases of older men afforded at the Excelsior Institute have been the result of over 20 years scientific research on the part of a group of Doctors who were not satisfied with painful surgical treatment methods.

The War brought many new techniques and many new wonder working drugs. These new discoveries were added to the research development already accomplished. The result has been a new type of treatment that is proving of great benefit to men suffering from Glandular Dysfunction or Rectal and Colon trouble.

COMPLETE EXAMINATION AT LOW COST

On your arrival here we first make a complete examination. The Doctors who examine you are experienced specialists. You are told frankly what your condition is and the cost of the treatments you need. You then decide whether or not you will take treatments recommended.

Definite Reservations Not Necessary

If your condition is acute and painful you may come here at once without reservation. Complete examination will be made promptly.

Select Your Own Hotel Accommodations

Treatments are so mild that hospitalization is not necessary so the saving in your expense is considerable. You are free to select any type of hotel accommodation you may desire.

DO SOMETHING TODAY

Taking a few minutes right now in filling out the coupon below may enable you to better enjoy the future years of your life and prove to be one of the best investments you ever made.

Non-Surgical Treatment of DISEASES of MEN
EXCELSIOR INSTITUTE

The Excelsior Institute has published a New FREE Book that is fully illustrated and deals with Diseases peculiar to men. It gives excellent factual knowledge and could prove of utmost importance to your future life. It tells how new modern non-surgical methods are proving successful. It is to your best interest in life to write for a FREE copy today.

Excelsior Institute.
Dept. 7043
Excelsior Springs, Mo.

Gentlemen: Kindly send me at once your New FREE Book on Diseases peculiar to men. I am .... years old.

Name ....

Address ....

City .... State ....

The Opportunities That Await YOU *NOW*

In Scientific Crime Detection Work

Follow in the steps of this successful career man . . . start to train now for a responsible, steady, well-paying position in the field of criminal investigation. If your job is dull, routine, without future . . . then here is your opportunity to forge ahead in an interesting career where trained men are always needed. For 36 years we have opened the "door to success" for hundreds of men in scientific crime detection . . . and now we will train you to take advantage of these same opportunities *if* you act immediately!

We will train you in your spare time through step-by-step home study lessons. I.A.S. training is neither expensive nor difficult to learn.

Over 800 American Bureaus of Identification

Employ I.A.S. students or graduates . . . factual proof of what I.A.S. training can do. Every one of these men learned FINGER PRINT IDENTIFICATION, FIRE-ARMS IDENTIFICATION, POLICE PHOTOGRAPHY AND CRIMINAL INVESTIGATION—the economical I.A.S. home study way.

So don't delay! Cash in on the increasing opportunities for finger print technicians and criminal investigators.

FREE! "BLUE BOOK OF CRIME"

Packed full of thrills. Reveals "behind the scenes" facts of actual criminal cases. Tells how scientific investigators solved them through the same methods you learn at I.A.S. Explains, too, how you can get started in this profession at low cost. Don't wait . . . mail in this coupon today.

INSTITUTE OF APPLIED SCIENCE
(A Correspondence School Since 1916)
Dept. 525C 1920 Sunnyside, Chicago 40, Ill.

CLIP AND MAIL COUPON NOW

INSTITUTE OF APPLIED SCIENCE
1920 Sunnyside Ave., Dept. 525C
Chicago 40, Illinois

Gentlemen: Without obligation, send me the "Blue Book of Crime," and list of Identification Bureaus employing your students and graduates, together with your low prices and Easy Terms Offer. No salesman will call. (Literature will be sent ONLY to persons stating their age.)

Name....................................

Address........................RFD or Zone......

City..................State...........Age....

(continued from page 12)

"terrible" must have happened to her. "She always let us know where she was going. Like tonight, she went to study with her friends. I know something bad has happened."

Anthony Zielinski did not work side-by-side with the police but trusting his intuition, went directly to the sand-pit where he knew couples often visited. He drove his car among the deep pits and got out.

Suspect's impassioned plea: "I don't know. I don't remember. I blacked out."

The sky was becoming light, although the sun was not yet up. Zielinski walked about with a fear that he would find what he prayed not to discover. And then, to his horror, he saw the body of his daughter, Vickie. She lay with her head crushed, her body partially undressed. A pool of blood glistened in the purple light of dawn.

After the report that the girl's body had been found beaten to death a wide search for clues was begun by investigating officers. One squad car found blood-stained trousers and shoes in a field on Oak Street in Ramsey, a short distance from the home of Edgar Smith's parents. A section of police investigators began questioning friends and class-mates of the slain teenager. But it was Bill Wallace, who led detectives to Edgar Smith.

Wallace, upon entering his car, which he had loaned Smith, saw several blood spots on the floor mat. He knew of the police hunt for the killer of the Zielinski girl and so he immediately reported the tell-tale signs to authorities. The hunt closed in on Edgar Smith, ex-marine, and young father.

The arrest of Smith immediately followed when he, under questioning, denied knowing the girl but collapsed in tears when confronted with the blood-stained shoes and trousers.

"Yes, I know Vickie," he admitted through his sobs.

He reenacted his encounter with the school-girl, but when a detective asked him about the actual killing at the sand-pits the ex-marine cried, "I don't know—I don't remember. I blacked out."

Patricia Smith, wife of the suspect, when informed of her husband's arrest for the slaying of Vickie Zielinski, wept and repeatedly uttered, "I don't believe it, I don't believe it."

The truck driver father of the dead girl closed his fists as police told him of Edgar Smith and said, "Just turn him over to me. Only let me give him full treatment for what he did. Then I'll be satisfied."

Mrs. Zielinski, mother of the girl, said softly, "I'd like to see him receive all that's coming to him. If I had my say, I would like to give him all that he gave our daughter."

And said Bergen County Prosecutor Guy W. Calissi, "Smith is a cool customer. I can't say he admitted anything—but he signed a statement. Let's put it that way."

While the suspected slayer of Vickie hugged the newspaper headlines, police authorities delved into his background. It was learned that Smith had no police record and that he had been a marine who was discharged for medical reasons. He had a spotty employment record and at the time of his arrest was not working. The slain girl's sisters reported that he had frequently talked with them to encourage Vickie to liking him. A neighbor of the young man remarked, "I knew Eddie quite well. He's a twenty-three-year-old teenager, so to speak. A little fish who wanted to be a big whale. He's basically a nice kid, but very mixed up."

Young Edgar Smith waived a preliminary hearing when Magistrate J. Frank Young entered a mandatory not guilty plea at the brief hearing of the alleged killer.

The slender but wiry blond youth looked grave as he asked, "Is there any bail?"

"No," the court said.

Smith swayed as if he would faint but the strong arm of an attendant held him steady. He seemed to lift his eyes in a prayerful manner and was heard to whisper, "Help me."

A police guard led the broken-hearted youth to a cell.

And at the Zielinski home, in an atmosphere of great sorrow, as the family prepared for the burial of Vickie, dressed in her favorite blue gown and blue matching slippers, Mrs. Zielinski had one final statement to make. She said, "I was hoping he would be caught, but I didn't think it would be so fast. Thank God."

EDITOR'S NOTE: *To protect the innocent, the name Bill Wallace is fictitious as used here.*

THE END

Make Her Over...
to please
YOU!
in
frederick's
Hollywood
Fashions
Champagne Loungers
#1310 CURVES ADRIFT
Copy of expensive French triumph! A skin-clinging, high halter, low back creation. Deep V-back, daring high slash thigh line, floating boned inner bra. Acetate Lastex. Black with White trim, white with Black trim. Sizes 32 to 36 $8.98
#1310
#1327 SHOCK WAVE
Hollywood's newest, most sensational shocker in glittering Metallic Lurex! Wicked little pants feature self drape climaxing in ring right over your tummy. Both bra and top fully lined, and elasticized for fabulous fit. White or Black Lurex. Sizes 32 to 38 $13.18
#1327
#781
#781 SCARLET HOUR
Sheerest nylon, and daringly short robe is fabulously trimmed with genuine marabou. Completely alluring, and a must for the glamorous boudoir wardrobe. Black, Red or Turquoise. Sizes 10 to 20 $12.98
#779
#779 WHIPLASH
The most daring of bikini sets in sheer nylon. Rows and rows of nylon ruching frost bra and merest whisper of a bikini panty. Alluring little bows add to the fabulous effect. Black, Aqua and Shocking Pink. Sizes 32 to 38 $6.88
#782
#782 SECOND SKIN
Favorite of Hollywood stars for glamour posing! Rich rayon satin with slit, slinky skirt. Siren Black, Radiant Red. Sizes 32 to 40
Free Merchandise Certificate with every single order.
Iron clad money-back guarantee.
Flirty Funsters
#765 GLAMOUR-ALL
Glamorous quilted TV Lounger. Stunning mid-calf length 1 piece charmer in gleaming rayon and acetate taffeta, all over quilted. Red, Black, White, Green. Sizes 10 to 18 Just $6.86
#24 "TERRY TREAT"
Elasticized to drape in dozens of figure-molding ways: turtle neck, off shoulder, cuffed, etc. Terry cloth. Black & Gold; Red & White. Sizes 10 to 18 $5.98
#765
#24
French Lines
#144 BETTER HALF
Imported French bra that isn't a bra at all! Only the under bust is covered but gives up lift with gleaming satin under cups, lightly boned. Perfection with plunge necklines. White or Black. Sizes 32 to 36. Will fit A and B cups $5.00
#144
#811
#811 SWEETHEART
Heart-shaped nylon with nylon lace heart inset. Thrilling gift idea! In Black or Red. 22 to 30" waist $3.98
Center of cup forms point for young natural look
Circular stitching lifts bust up and out
Firm 100% Nylon Crepe for wear
#96
#96 UP AND OUT
Nylon crepe for young, pointed uplift. Stitched cups give young firm lines to sagging breasts. Perfect bra under snug dresses or sweaters. In Black or Gardenia White. Low-priced. Sizes 32 to 38 B, 34 to 40 C cup $3.50
#107
#107 "FRENCH LINES"
Satin. Daring pointed lines make this a Hollywood favorite! Cups are satin lined for perfect uplift. Black, White. Sizes 32 to 38 B, sizes 34 to 38 C. Amazing value! $3.89
frederick's
1430 N. CAHUENGA BLVD
HOLLYWOOD 28, CALIF
Hollywood Honeymooners
#990 GOODIE
A strapless shortie gown in exquisite all-nylon lace. Stay-up top, keyhole midriff, and peek-a-boo slit skirt. Midnight Black, Gypsy Red. Sizes 32 to 38 $7.98
#705 GOOD GIRL?
Nylon sheer Baby Doll set that's very short and very sweet, with embroidered sentiment reading "I'm a good girl!" Sheerest Nylon lace trim. Bikini panty. Mad Pink, Turquoise, Charcoal. Sizes 32 to 38 $8.98
#776 FROTHY PIN-UP
Daring Frenchy rayon satin Chemise with lace trim and frilly garters. Boned bra. Elastic bands reveal you at sides. Detachable garters and shoulder straps. Black or Nude Pink. Sizes 32 to 38 $8.98
#705
#776
#990
"I'm a good girl"
frederick's
OF HOLLYWOOD
OUR NEW HOME
ORDER BY MAIL
1430 N. CAHUENGA BLVD DEPT. 3406
HOLLYWOOD 28, CALIF
Please send the following styles (order by numbers)
STYLE | QUAN | SIZE | 1ST COLOR | 2ND COLOR | PRICE
I enclose payment
send C.O.D. No C.O.D. without $1 deposit each item
NAME
ADDRESS
CITY
STATE
ZONE

Lovely Wanda's fingers were trigger-happy!

TIGER WOMAN'S SWEET REVENGE

by Henry Howard

IT ISN'T OFTEN that a male has two beautiful women battling over him, particularly when he is as paunchy and as middle-aged as Godfrey Barrington. It is even more remarkable when one of the two battling lovelies is as young and as brainy as Wanda Stopa. Whatever Godfrey Barrington may have had was invisible to the naked eye. No such libel could be leveled at Wanda Stopa.

At 21, Wanda was a member of the Illinois bar, the youngest woman lawyer ever admitted to practice; at 22, she was a deputy assistant United States Attorney General, ditto the youngest ever appointed; at 23 she was a murderess, and her life and her career were virtually finished.

Godfrey Barrington—"Just call me Barry," he told innumerable admiring females—was a fabulously successful commercial advertising artist with a studio on East Ohio Street, in Chicago. In his mid-fifties, he was of polished and urbane manner, full of glib phrases designed to turn the heads of far more experienced women than the brainy but naive Wanda.

The beautiful Pole's complete and instant adoration of him at first meeting, her generous, unstinted giving of herself, should have flattered his aging vanity, touched his heart with its great sincerity. Indeed, there is ample evidence that it did do just that—at first. But Wanda, like most beautiful women in love, was demanding. And when her demands began to include marriage, Barrington speedily lost interest. He jilted her with coldly grim and unsentimental detachment. Then Wanda thought upon murder.

It is likely that Barrington's role in Wanda's ruination was more or less coincidental. Actually, she was already married when she first met him, and no celibate. Secondly, her downfall appeared to be caused by inherent weakness within herself. It is certain that long before she met Godfrey Barrington, Wanda's downfall was well under way, for her husband, "Count" Theodore Glaskoff, introduced her to morphine.

Despite her undeniably great beauty—a gorgeous, voluptuous figure, milky white, baby-smooth skin, and classic features surmounted by a lovely halo of soft, shining brown hair—before Wanda met the Count she had been relatively innocent.

Raised in a strict, conservative Catholic family on Augusta Street, in the "Little Poland" section of Chicago, she had been closely supervised by her mother, her father and two older brothers. Her father was a sculptor, and she was constantly made aware of her aristocratic lineage through her grandfather, a Polish nobleman dispossessed of his lands near Warsaw and exiled for fomenting revolution against the ruling Czar of Russia.

Though it was not in the accepted Old Country tradition, her family, increasingly aware of her quicksilver mind, her brilliant intellectual perception, had encouraged her to study, and finally to embrace the law. At 21, she was graduated at the top of her class in law school; and less than a year later, confirmed a member of the staff of the United States Attorney in Chicago.

Meanwhile, her family had returned to Poland to visit. Wanda, for the first time in her life was freed of all shackles and old-fashioned, family guidance. She moved into a quite proper residence club for "professional women"—the term "bachelor girls" had not yet been coined—and began by being invited to quite proper parties. In an amazingly short time she was being invited to parties that were not quite so proper, and at one of these she first met the "Count."

Tall, not unhandsome, sensuous-lipped and oily-haired, he was variously known, for reasons of his own, as Vladimir Glaskov, Zdislaw Glasko, and Count Theodore Glaskoff.

Wanda learned from this son of the steppes a lot of things that are

(continued on page 46)

MAKE $15.00 A DAY AND MORE!

Learn practical nursing at home in 12 short weeks

Earn

A BIG STEADY INCOME IMMEDIATELY!

THIS IS THE HOME STUDY COURSE THAT *Will Change Your Whole Life!*

YES, YOU CAN BE A PROFESSIONAL NURSE. You can earn the respect of everyone you know by helping those who urgently need your help.

ALL THE REWARDS OF NURSING CAN BE YOURS. You can get out of your present rut and be completely independent. Select the very cases you want from the hundreds offered to you . . . work part or full time without interfering with your present home or social activities . . . work in hospitals, clinics, doctor's offices, convalescent homes, private duty. Specialize as you like . . . infant cases, hospital nursing, or travel with your patient all over the world.

IN JUST 12 SHORT WEEKS FROM NOW you can begin to earn as much as $20.00 a day and you need never worry about being "laid off." Never before was there such a crying need for nurses. Today 300,000 requests remain unfilled. Hospitals, convalescent homes, and doctors are begging for our graduates. No high school education is required for this complete nursing course. In fact many of our successful graduates, now earning top professional pay, have never even finished grammar school. If you are sincere and love people you have all the qualifications.

DO NOT LET AGE PREVENT YOU from realizing your fondest dreams. Students from 16 to 65 have successfully completed this doctors' approved course.

IN JUST 12 SHORT WEEKS FROM NOW you can be graduated and wear with pride your crisp white professional nurses uniform. Family and friends will respect your shining silver graduation pin and your highly prized diploma from the nation's outstanding professional training school.

STUDY AS SLOW OR AS FAST AS YOU WISH. Some of our students study on and off in their spare time. If you are anxious to begin your nursing career, you can complete the course in just 12 weeks. Or if you have had any previous training, you can graduate in 30 to 60 days.

BUT THE IMPORTANT THING IS to get free complete information right now. There is no cost or obligation. We will send you, as we have thousands of other ambitious women, a FREE sample lesson and a FREE nursing booklet. Clip the coupon at the right and mail right now. Your FREE material will reach you by return mail.

POST GRADUATE HOSPITAL SCHOOL OF NURSING
81L87 *Auditorium Bldg., Chicago 5, Ill.*

WHAT OUR GRADUATES SAY:

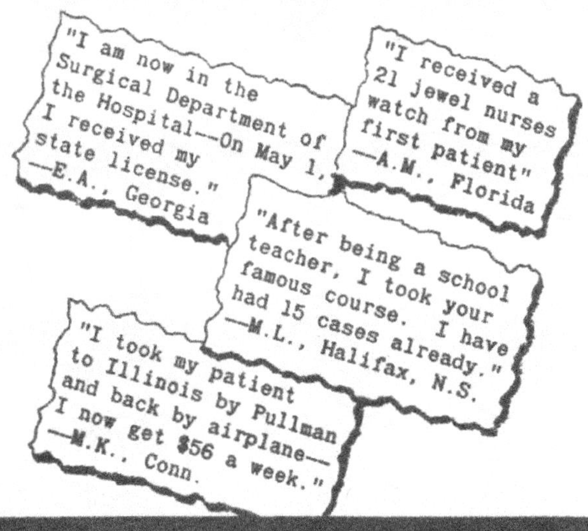

Mail Coupon Today for FREE Sample Lesson.

POST GRADUATE HOSPITAL SCHOOL OF NURSING,
81L87 Auditorium Bldg., Chicago 5, Ill.

Send me, without obligation, your FREE 16-page sample lesson and FREE booklet on High-Paying Opportunities in Nursing.

NAME ____________

ADDRESS ____________

CITY ____________ ZONE ______ STATE ______

THE PEOPLE of Rockland County were shocked by a vicious sex crime in quiet, peaceful Spring Valley, some 30 miles north of New York City. Two young, innocent girls, Esther Frances Nagy and Marjorie Boudreau, were assaulted and brutally murdered on a Sunday afternoon in March near their playground at the Lakeside Cottage School. Frightened mothers kept their children at home behind locked doors while the vast dragnet, searching for the killer, was spread over the snow-covered mountain area on the west shore of the Hudson River. A murderer was still at large.

AFTER ESTHER NAGY'S mother died four years ago when she was only two, her father sent her to the Lakeside Cottage School at Spring Valley because he was afraid she might be hurt playing in the street outside their apartment in the Bronx. The Lakeside School is not a place for delinquents, but a privately-endowed home for dependent children whose parents are unable to take care of them. It is a much sought-after home where intelligent children are given a new start in life.

Marjorie Boudreau, eight, had been at the school for two years. She was one of a family of 14 children whose parents had separated. There wasn't enough money coming in for her mother to buy the necessities of life for the large Boudreau family, and the Department of Welfare recommended that Marjorie be sent to Spring Valley.

The school consists of 10 main buildings and several smaller cottages, and two big brick dormitories—one for boys and one for girls. The thickly-wooded area a few hundred yards behind the school is known as the "Forbidden Forest," called that by the children because they are never supposed to enter it alone.

The school grounds cover 150 acres, all enclosed by a six-foot-high fence. There are 144 boys and girls at Lakeside, and one house mother for every 12 children. Their outdoor play is carefully supervised.

Even so, it was possible for two

SEX KILLER'S DEADLY DESIRES

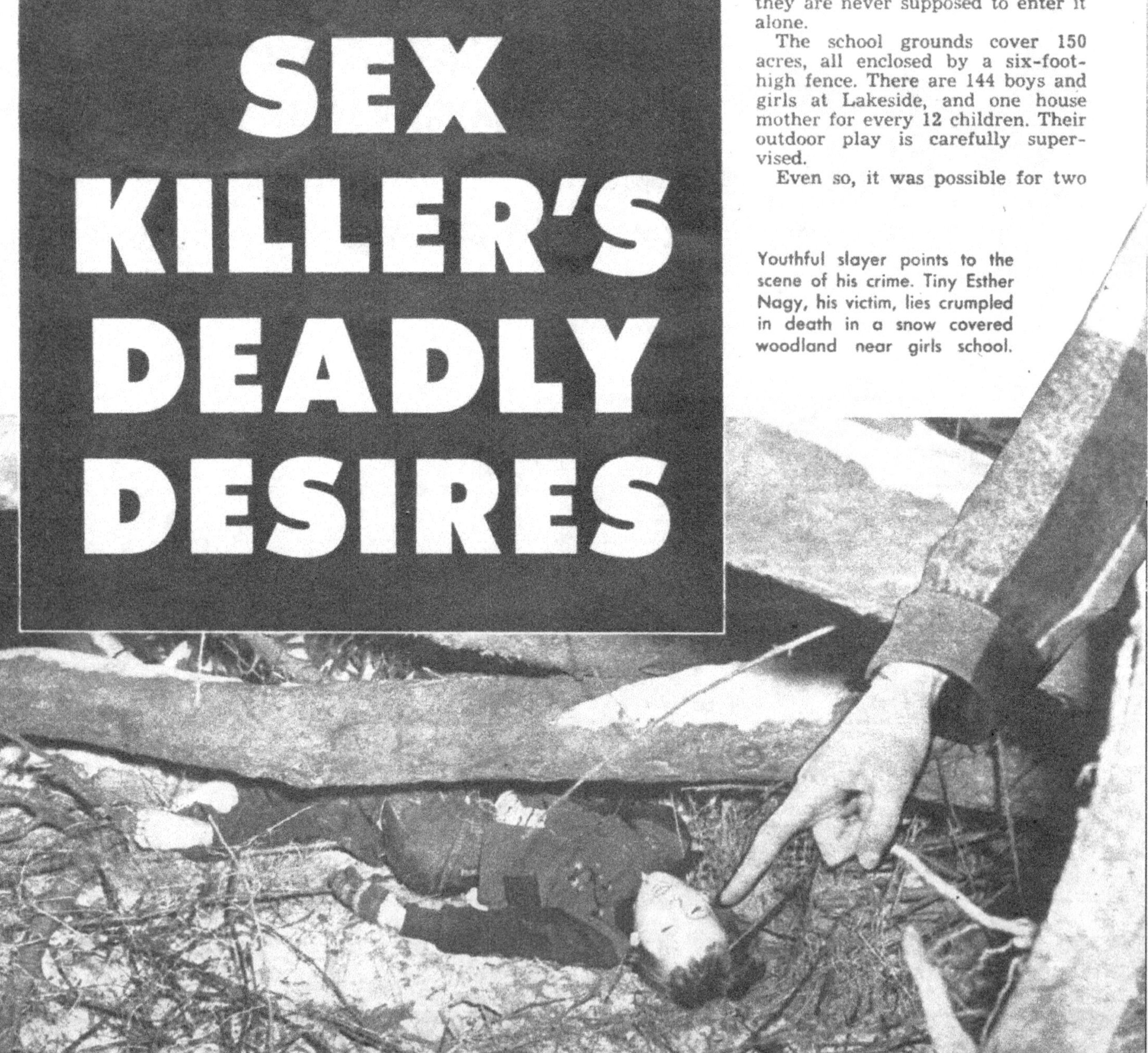

Youthful slayer points to the scene of his crime. Tiny Esther Nagy, his victim, lies crumpled in death in a snow covered woodland near girls school.

By Sam Carson

of them to slip away from the school's playground, unnoticed, late in the afternoon of Sunday, March 8th, 1953.

When Esther Nagy and Marjorie Boudreau failed to return to their dormitory at 5 P.M. to watch a television show, their house mother reported them missing. The two girls had last been seen by a playmate at four o'clock when they left the administration building on their way back to the playground.

Some of the older children immediately were sent out to look for the missing girls. Esther, not quite six years old, was a delicate little blue-eyed blonde. Dark-haired Marjorie, three years older, had a sweet smile and wide-set brown eyes. The two girls were dressed alike in dungarees and T-shirts, snowsuit pants, red overshoes, windbreakers and tasseled hats with bows under the chin.

For almost an hour, the search continued without success. Not a trace of either girl could be discovered anywhere on the grounds. Then, at 5:45, two of the older boys from the school suddenly came across Marjorie's battered body. She lay face down in a thicket of the Forbidden Forest, a half-mile from the school and about the same distance from Hungry Hollow Road. The back of her head had been crushed, and her snowsuit was ripped and torn.

The boys who made the gruesome discovery notified Russell Wright, the school's director. He immediately telephoned Chief Abe Stern of the Ramapo Township police and Dr. Max J. Moses of Spring Valley, the Rockland County coroner.

Within a few minutes Chief Stern and Dr. Moses reached the scene in two cars, accompanied by Sgt. Lloyd Goetschius and several township patrolmen. The coroner knelt beside the crumpled body of the little girl and made a brief examination. There were tears in his eyes when he arose. "This is a pitiful thing," Dr. Moses said, "and a horrible one. The child has been dead for only about an hour. Her skull was fractured by blows with a very heavy instrument."

Chief Stern gave the coroner a searching look. "Was she molested?" he asked.

Dr. Moses nodded. "That's putting it mildly. She was sexually assaulted viciously, probably by a pervert."

Although there had been no other recent sex crimes in the quiet community, the officers were well aware that a maniac could have escaped from one of the several institutions in the county. Rockland State Hospital for the Insane was only five miles away. Nearby also were Matteawan State Hospital for

Patrolman Lester Teicher holds leash of the bloodhounds as Officers Manuli and Goetschius search the Forbidden Forest for the slayer of two young school girls.

the Criminally Insane, and Letchworth Village for defectives.

This was not the only possibility. Less than six months before, on October 25th, two hunters had been slain in the same Ramapo Township area. Ramapo Town Clerk Robert Nugent, 46, and Charles E. Simpson, 38, of Saddle River, N. J., were found shot to death near the carcass of a deer just 11 miles from the Lakeside school.

This double murder was still unsolved. Had the same sniper who killed the hunters stalked the Forbidden Forest in search of a younger victim? Was it he who lured Marjorie Boudreau into the woods, ravished her and beat her to death?

Stern and his men were discussing these possibilities when a squad of state troopers arrived from the New York City barracks, led by Cpl. Clarence Sullivan. One trooper held a brace of baying bloodhounds on a taut leash, straining to be put on the killer's trail.

A search of the surrounding area meanwhile had failed to produce either the bloodstained rock with which the girl had been slain, or any other clue. The tramping of the searchers and school staff members on the snow-covered ground had obliterated any footprints which the killer might have left. Neither was there any sign of what had happened to the second missing girl, little Esther Nagy. Chief Stern and the other officers feared the worst.

"The killer either has kidnaped the Nagy girl and taken her away from this area," Stern reasoned, "or he has murdered her also and hidden her body. But if there's the barest chance that she's still alive, we've got to grab him before he kills her."

Joined now by Sheriff J. Henry Mock and his deputies, the officers moved swiftly to throw out a dragnet for the slayer, fully aware that it might turn up another victim before he was caught.

As the ambulance rolled away with the still-warm body of Marjorie Boudreau on its way to Rockland State Hospital morgue for an autopsy, the troopers unleashed their bloodhounds at the scene. After a few moments of frantic nuzzling and darting around the thicket, the dogs picked up a scent and dashed headlong into the woods with Corporal Sullivan close behind.

Other officers made a quick check with authorities at Rockland hospital and learned that none of its patients had escaped recently, and that all were accounted for at the time. Similar reports were obtained from officials of the other near-by mental institutions, including Matteawan and Letchworth.

No suspicious persons had been seen near the school, the officers were told, and no male visitors had been allowed there during the week-end.

Careful questioning of teachers and house mothers, including those who had charge of the Boudreau and Nagy girls, failed to cast any light on the mystery. They described the two children as sweet, good-natured and well-behaved. Marjorie and Esther had been constant companions during the past year, and got along well with all of the other children.

"We've never had any serious trouble here at Lakeside before," one of the staff members declared. "I just can't understand how such a thing could happen here."

Throughout the early evening, the investigators prowled over the school grounds and continued to question its staff, particularly the 10 men employed there. Searching parties of deputies and volunteers, armed with powerful electric torches, beat through the woods and up and down the hills and valleys of Ramapo Township in their hunt for the killer or some clue which would put them on his trail.

Shortly before midnight, six hours after the body of Marjorie Boudreau was discovered, the bloodhounds led the officers to the pathetic corpse of little Esther Nagy. The blonde child lay on her back under a fallen tree in another thicket, some 250 yards from where Marjorie had been found. The slayer had hidden her there in an apparent attempt to avoid discovery.

Unlike Marjorie, who had her skull crushed, Esther had been stabbed in the back with a large knife. Her shoes, stockings and red overshoes had been removed. Her snowsuit and underclothing had been ripped and torn, like Marjorie's, in a vicious sexual attack.

This was quickly established by Coroner Moses, summoned back to the scene by Chief Stern. Esther had been killed around the same time Marjorie had met her death, Dr. Moses reported. The coroner saw some significance in the fact that the Nagy girl's shoes were missing. Although her stockings lay near-by, her shoes could not be found, and apparently had been taken by the killer. A sex maniac, it was pointed out, often takes with him some item of clothing worn by his victim.

A thorough search of the terrain around the scene failed to produce either the lethal knife or any clues. But a few minutes later, Sergeant Goetschius and Patrolman Lester Teicher found the Nagy girl's red overshoes, still containing her tiny slippers. The overshoes lay some 25 yards deeper in the woods, where they had been dropped by the slayer. A trail of blood led from this point to the body, indicating that the girl had been stabbed near where the boots were found.

Bloodhounds were immediately brought to the spot and turned loose on this new trail after scenting the crimson spots on the snow-covered ground. But again the dogs began to circle around in confusion after following the trail for a few hundred yards. Either the killer had succeeded in covering his tracks, the officers decided, or he had doubled back over his original trail.

In the latter case, the murderer would have returned to the edge of the Lakeside school grounds. It seemed improbable that he would do so and run the risk of capture.

"That is," Chief Stern told Sheriff Mock, "unless our man knew he could hide somewhere around the school."

Mock nodded. "I have the same hunch," he declared. "We'll requestion the older students and the staff. Maybe the answer to this puzzle is right there under our noses."

The search for the slayer of the two little girls continued unabated throughout the night. Roadblocks were set up and the occupants of all cars leaving the area were questioned. The woods and the countryside were alive with searchers, combing the underbrush, checking at every occupied house and searching all the camp sites closed for the winter. A second check was begun of all the mental institutions in the area.

All day Monday, the officers questioned the personnel and pupils of the school, residents of the immediate area and even citizens of near-by villages in an effort to develop a tangible lead. The most important information they gleaned was the report of a house mother at the school who told the officers that on Sunday afternoon she saw a boy about 17 or 18 years old watching Marjorie and Esther as they played on the school grounds. That was only a few hours before they found Marjorie.

On the basis of the woman's story, Chief Stern and Sheriff Mock rounded up 15 boys for questioning, most of them near-by residents. Three of the boys, respecively 14, 15 and 17, were students at the Lakeside School. Through questioning the three, the officers learned that a fourth boy, a tall, gawky, 16-year-old named Carlton N. Mason, had possessed a large hunting knife of the type used to kill Esther Nagy. Ironically, Mason had been one of the two boys who found the Boudreau girl's body. It was he who had carried her limp figure from the scene to the school's infirmary, where it was examined by the coroner.

Asked to produce his knife, Mason said that he had lost it Sunday afternoon when he threw it at a tree in the woods.

Young Mason was unable to account for a half-hour of his time prior to the disappearance of the girls. He said merely that he was "walking around the grounds." Taken before the house mother who had seen a youth eyeing the girls suspiciously, Mason vigorously denied he was the one she had observed. The woman was unsure, but said he could have been the boy.

On Tuesday, Stern and Mock asked Mason to lead them to the spot where he had lost his long-bladed knife. The youth took the officers into the Forbidden Forest and up to a large tree only a few yards from where the body of Marjorie Boudreau was found. An intensive search was made around the base of the tree, but the knife was not discovered.

The state police sent for two electronic mine detectors and brought them into play, covering the entire area, inch by inch, in an effort to locate the missing weapon. A dozen troopers and nine detectives were engaged in the search, which also included dragging a near-by pond. But no trace of any knife had been found by Wednesday.

The officers meanwhile had centered their suspicions on Carlton Mason. He was unable to account for his activities just before the two victims vanished. He was known to possess a knife like the one used to kill Esther Nagy, and he could not produce it. His story that he had "lost" it sounded lame, indeed. Added to all these suspicious circumstances, it was learned that Mason had been accused of indecent sex acts by other children at the school.

By this time the officers were convinced that the killer was a student at the school since the two girls would not have entered the woods with a stranger. There was a second youth, also 16, who could not account for his activities during the hour before the victims had disappeared. His general appearance was the same as Mason's, tall and gawky, and the house mother who had seen the suspected slayer conceded that he might have been the one she had observed. He bitterly denied this.

The only course Stern and Mock could take, pending discovery of the knife which had killed Esther Nagy, was to subject both boys to lie-detector tests. Obviously, one of them was not telling the truth.

Late Wednesday, young Mason and the second youth were taken to the office of District Attorney John A. Shaken in New City. There they were separately questioned while their physical reactions were recorded by the polygraph, or lie detector, under the supervision of William Kirwin, director of the State Police Laboratory at Troy.

That evening, Kirwin returned to Troy with the graphs to study the results of the tests and evaluate

(continued on page 53)

Victims of brutal assault: Esther Nagy and (R.) Marjorie Boudreau. A vast police dragnet, tracking their killer, was spread over mountain area of Hudson River.

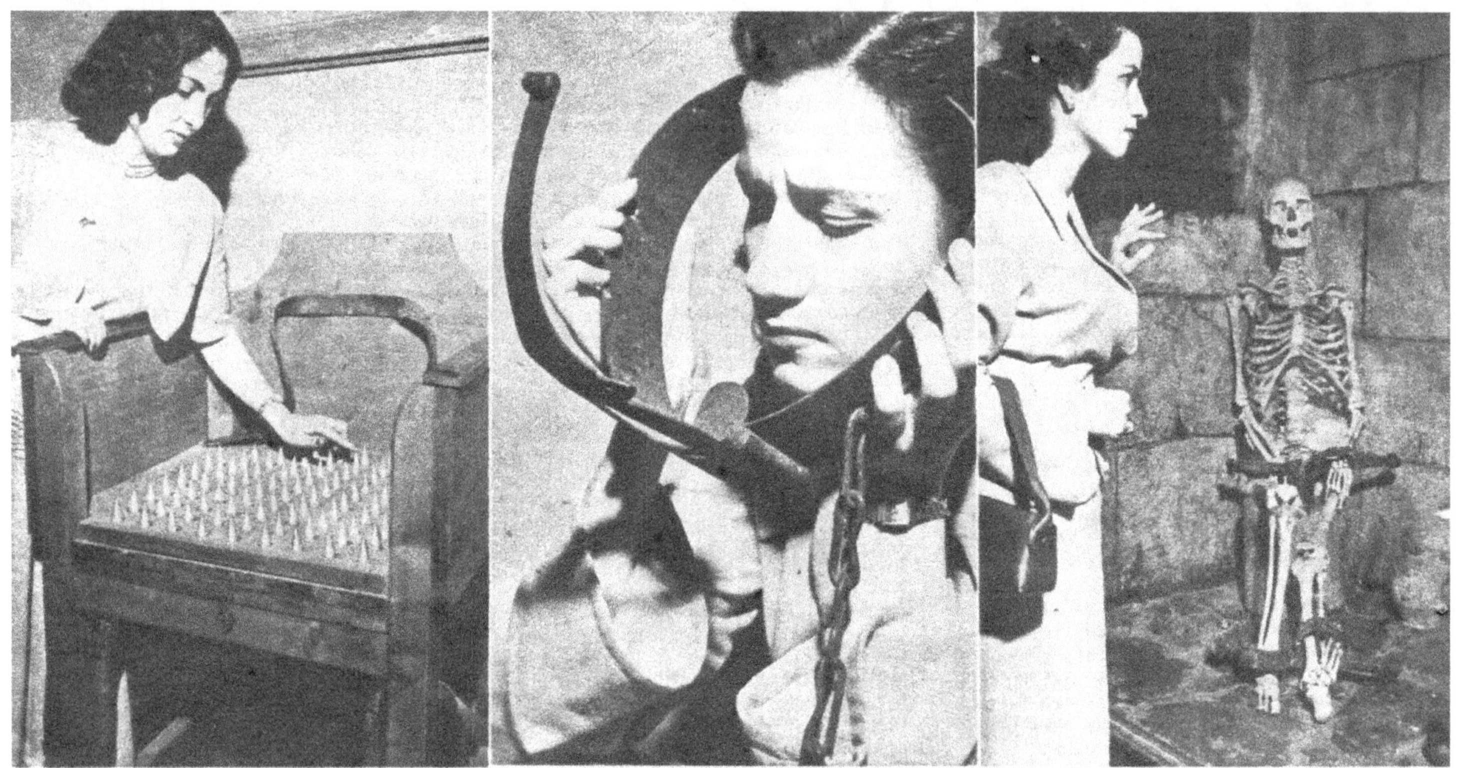

Original "hot seat" is gruesome punishment chair used to make criminals confess. (Center) "Womens Reins" punished talkative girls. It was put on like muzzle, and iron spike entered the mouth. (R.) Visitor looks at the remains of a victim of the cruel irons.

THIS IS TORTURE!

(Below) Ancient third degree consisted of tying victim by foot, dropping him several times into fire, and beating.

On the "ladder" culprit was tied to a cord, hung on a pulley, and banged successively on each rung of ladder.

Another type of torture with a cord: the culprit was made to fall on spikes until he was ready to confess crimes.

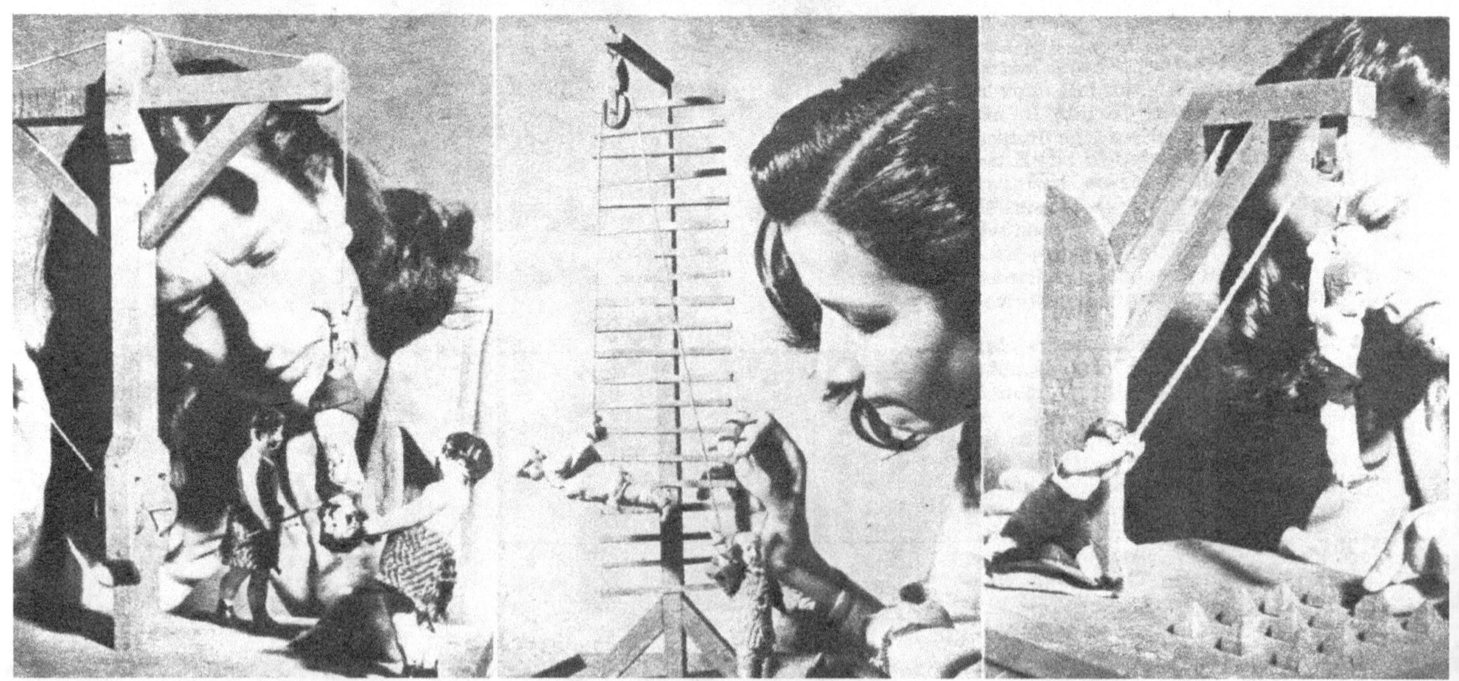

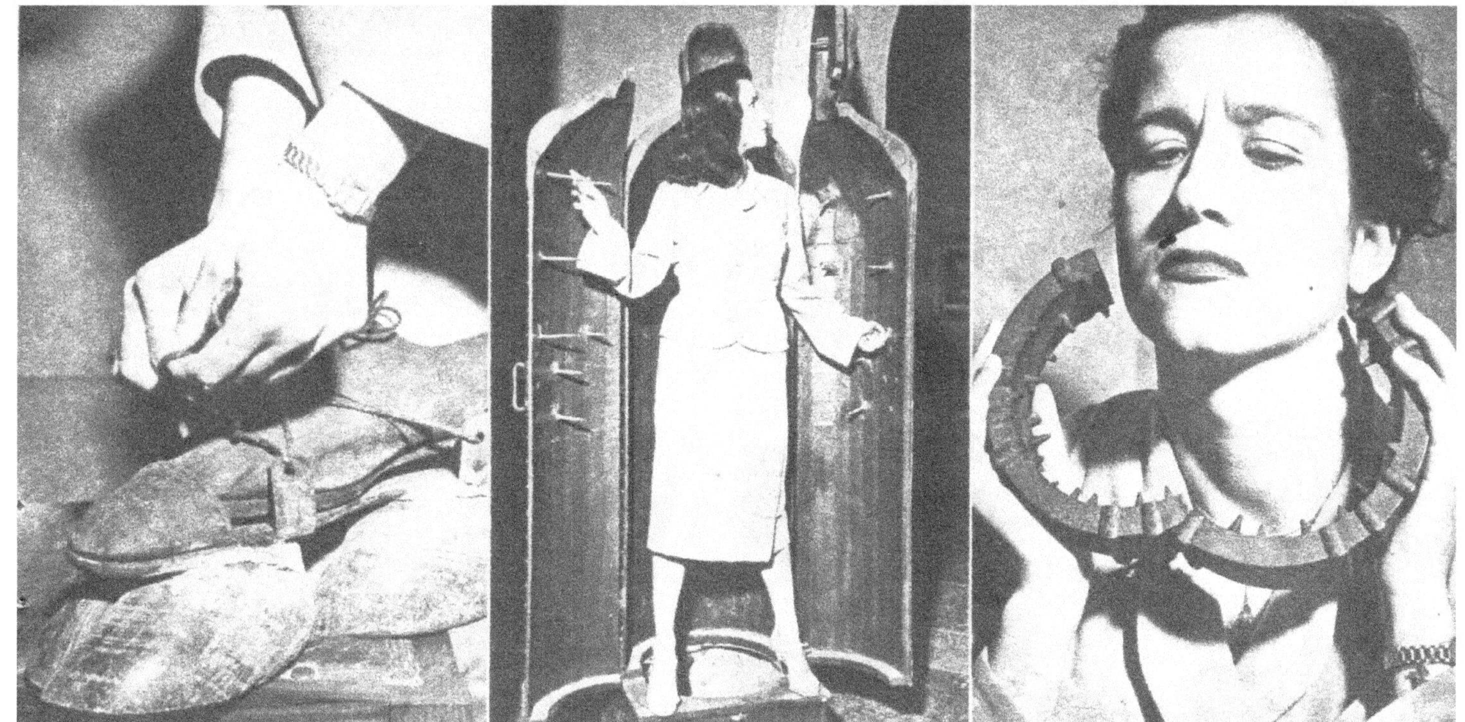

Hoofs of bull were attached to smugglers' boots to evade police. (Center) "The Virgin of Nuremburg" or Iron Maiden. Victim was placed inside and when the door closed, iron spikes penetrated the body. (R.) Prisoner's collar of nails, used in 1500.

The ancient Romans were probably the most scientific sadists of all time. Here is a photo look at some of their choicer techniques for torture . . .

TRUE MYSTERY PHOTO FEATURE

Scrounch! And the victim is squashed by the torture of the press. Screws were twisted until the pain reached the limits of human endurance (and often beyond).

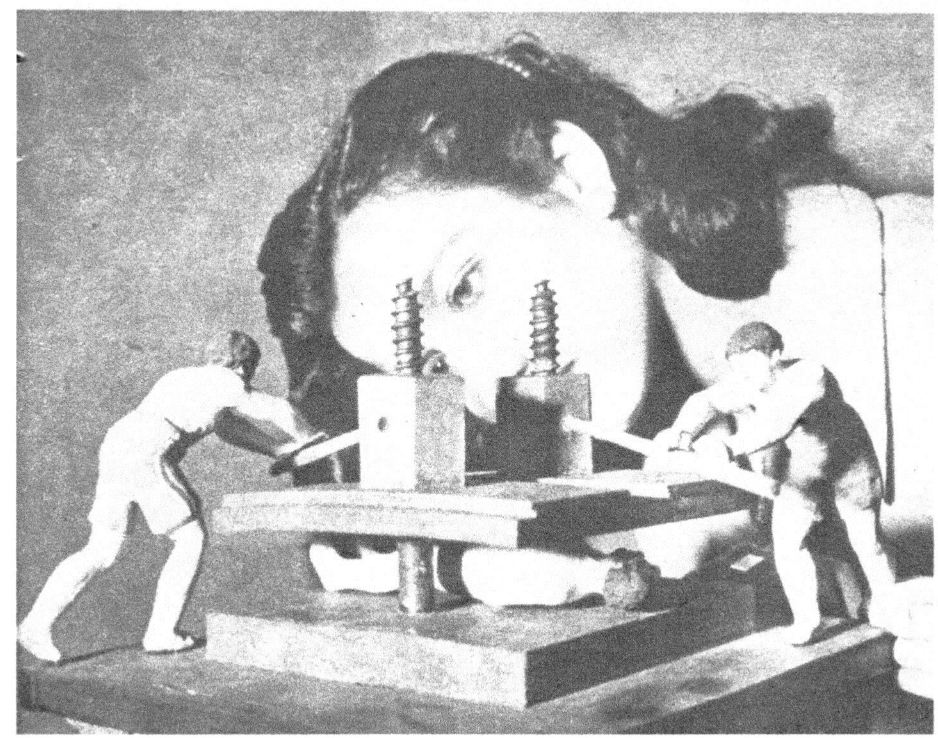

SCIENTIFIC SADISM has seldom had a more graphic exposé than in the blood-chilling exhibits now open to the public in the Criminal Museum of Rome. In order to give a more vivid idea of the instruments of torture and sadism, the organizers of the Museum have made some dummies which are submitted to torture.

Originally, torture was almost unknown to the Romans, at least until the days of the Empire, when it was adopted to punish crimes against the state. In the Middle Ages, it became popular and had its height in 1500 and 1600. It disappeared after the French Revolution.

The Criminal Museum of Rome, founded in 1932, is an ex-prison. The objects exhibited are divided according to a certain order, with the object of illustrating crime in its various forms and modes of carrying out the sentences.

One of the most unique machines designed by the scientific sadists was the famous "*Bull of Falardes.*" It is told that Falarides, Tyrant of Argento between 570 and 550 B.C., had

(continued on page 25)

The threstle was one of commonest tortures and consisted in the pulling apart of limbs by tying with cords, one around neck and feet, and pulling by winches.

On the spiked wheel, culprit passed over and over again on a series of

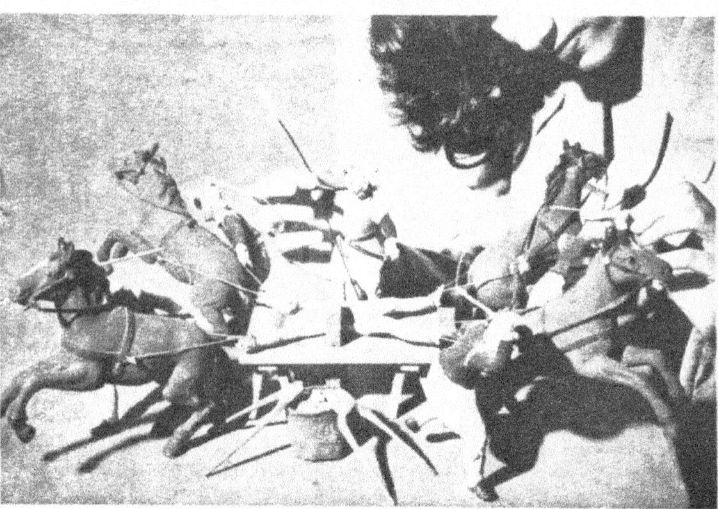

(Above) Treason was punished by "quartering." Horses were tied to each arm and leg and then made to gallop off in opposite directions. Assassin of Henry IV was killed this way.

Wooden winches on threstle, used to pull victims apart. (Below) Culprit was placed in belly of bronze bull and fire lighted underneath, screams sounded like bellowing of bull.

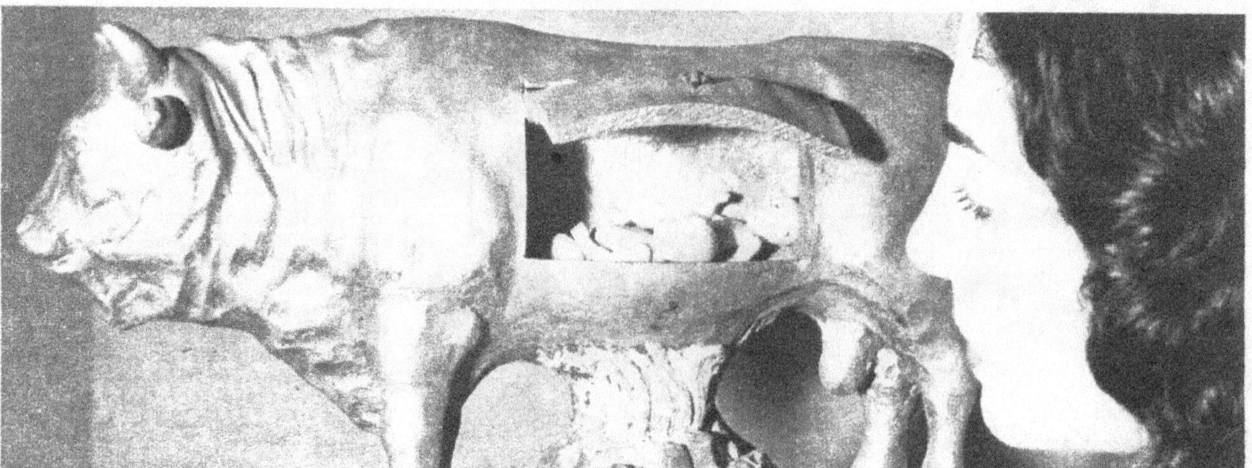

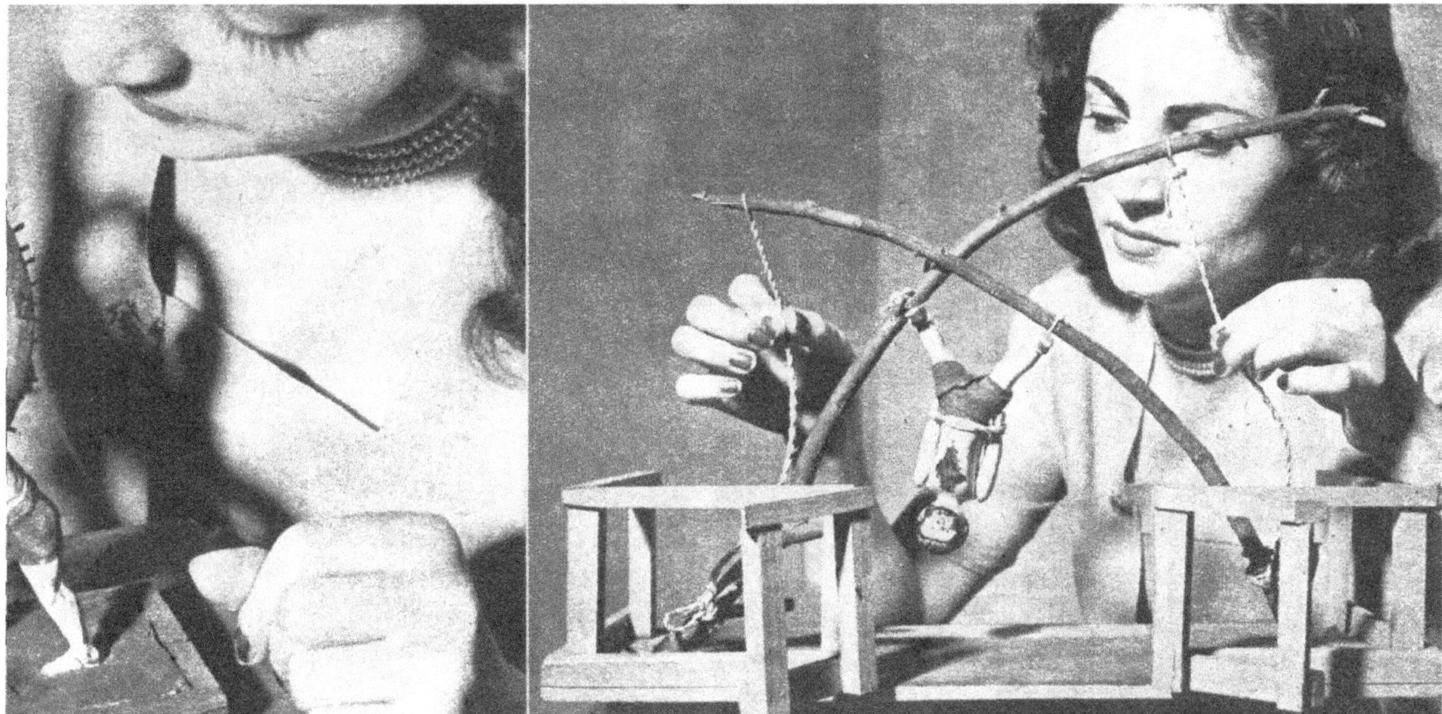

iron teeth placed on the ground. This was usually coupled with fire torture.

Quartering was accomplished by means of two trees drawn apart and then suddenly let go. This torture was particularly popular among the barbarian tribes.

(R.) Torture of keeping victim always awake. If about to fall asleep, he was pulled by pulley and jarred awake.

(continued from page 23)

this bronze bull constructed to be used against his enemies. The victim was placed inside the bull and underneath it a fire was lighted. The screams of the unfortunate victim in issuing from the throat of the bull sounded like the bellowing of the animal—much to the amusement and entertainment of the tyrant and his court. The original "bull" was never found, but the Romans discovered a similar one at Carthage.

One of the most popular, and particularly gruesome, methods of ancient torture was "quartering" by horses. To each leg and arm of the victim was tied a horse. Urged on by men with whips, the beasts would then gallop off in opposite directions, literally tearing the victim limb from limb.

Another type of quartering was accomplished by means of two trees drawn apart and then suddenly let go. This torture was used widely among the barbarian hordes. In Europe, it was used in isolated cases in the Middle Ages during the persecution of religious heretics. Against these inhuman practices scientists and men of law of all times protested; among others was Cesare Beccaria who in 1764 wrote his celebrated treatise "Of crimes and punishments" opening the way to newer and more humane ideas.

THE END

PICCADILLY: Where the V-girls of London make pickups among the funseeking tourists and Britain's lonely men.

case of the STRANGLED STREETWALKER

Her love had a price and when she tried to raise it there was only hell to pay!

TRUE MYSTERY FEATURE CASE

By STEPHEN R. HOYT

THE LOCALE happens to be London but the moral is universal. An ominous warning to all young and pretty farm girls who venture recklessly to the big city.

Agnes Walsh was one of these, a tall and straight-legged charmer fresh from her father's potato patch in County Galway, Ireland.

The smell of peat perfumed her dark, shining hair and the bloom of roses painted her petal-white cheeks. It was there even when Arthur Buxton opened her hotel door that ill-fated Saturday morning.

To Buxton, proprietor of the *Laura Hotel* hard by Paddington Station, Agnes Walsh was not Agnes Walsh. She was "Mrs. Davidson of County Durham, England"—or so she had registered at 1:30 A.M.

VICTIM of strangler (l), with her sister Margaret (r.) went to London to see the bright lights and fun of Piccadilly. She got life of shame and death, instead.

Actually, "Mr. Davidson" had done the registering; a slight, sandy-complexioned little man in his late 20's, with thinning red hair and an indeterminate accent. Though he carried no luggage, the couple were assigned to a secluded end room on the fifth-floor; "the bridal suite" it was called.

"Mrs. Davidson" had left orders for tea and crumpets at 10 A.M., but when Arthur Buxton knocked on the door, the couple failed to answer. Impatiently, he pushed open the door with his tray-free hand.

To the proprietor of the *Laura Hotel*, "Mrs. Davidson of County Durham,"—whoever she really was, whatever she actually had been—represented nothing so much now as a threat to his fair name of hotel keeper. For she lay very nude and very much murdered on his clean, new Turkish-style carpet. Buxton backed hastily from the room, spilling the tea and crumpets in the process.

In law-abiding, abundantly civilized England, a 999 call to Scotland Yard is seldom really necessary. When it is, the Murder Squad answers.

Arthur Buxton made such a call now, and Chief Superintendent Peter Beveridge and his aide, Inspector Evan Davies, trench-coat and briar-pipe men both of them, responded quickly. They reached the *Laura Hotel* in minutes.

The unknown nude was beautiful even in murder. Her arms and legs were sprawled open as if for embrace. She was pale but not too much so. Only by the handkerchief gag in her mouth, her nylon stocking wrapped tight around her neck, had the strangler spoiled the illusion of deep restful sleep.

The room itself was a shambles. Agnes, well-developed by years of farm work, had given "Mr. Davidson" a lusty fight for it. Clothes and bedding were strewn over the floor. The chairs and table were turned over, and even the large dresser bureau was tipped back on two legs against the wall.

Despite this, Arthur Buxton, the hotel staff and the lodgers denied hearing any untoward commotion during the night.

Beveridge surveyed them skeptically. "Oh, come off it now," he scoffed. "You mean to tell me that not a blooming one of you heard any racket? Even the deaf have ears for death, you know." But nobody would admit anything. The night had been as peaceful as an old maid's prayer, they said.

Davies pointed to the dead girl's scarlet handbag, gaping empty on the red-stained floor. "Robbery's not bloody likely the line of a husband, you know."

He looked sharply at Arthur Buxton. "You're certain that this couple was married?"

The little hotel proprietor drew himself to his full five-five. "Sir, I run a respectable house."

The detective grunted and asked details of the couple's arrival.

The night was soupy and the couple had come by taxi. Both were hatless and wore tan trench coats. The man was dressed in a gray tweed suit and spoke with an accent barely understandable to Buxton, the cockney.

"He might have been Polish—or even Welsh," he surmised. He admitted that "Davidson" had written his signature on the register unevenly, apparently undecided what name to use and how to spell it. The writing was barely decipherable.

"Not much of a clue," Beveridge said. He ordered the identification men to photograph it and make copies for distribution. Meanwhile, the cream-colored door of the murder room was unhinged and sent to the Home Office crime lab for study. It was smeared with blood.

The room itself was dusted for prints and the girl's body sent to Paddington Mortuary for examination by Dr. F. E. Camps, Home Office pathologist.

The dead girl's identity did not remain long in doubt. Among her few, pathetic possessions, police found an envelope addressed to Margaret Walsh, at Mornington Terrace, Camden Town, London, N. W. The Metropolitan Police quickly visited the addressee.

She, too, was tall and beautiful, almost a twin of the one lying in death. She told the police, "From your description, I'm afraid the murdered girl is my sister, Agnes." At Paddington Mortuary she confirmed the identity.

There were no tears in Margaret Walsh's eyes, just sorrowful reproach. "I'm afraid I've let Father down," she said, and explained: "When Agnes came to London, Father insisted that I accompany her. I was the quiet one. Agnes was more flighty and, while she was always Father's favorite, he recognized her weaknesses. He was afraid she'd get into trouble unless I watched over her.

"We got jobs as waitresses with a restaurant. But Agnes was headstrong and independent. She sassed the customers and dated them if it pleased her. Lately I'd lost all control over her. We still roomed together but sometimes she wouldn't come home for days. So I thought nothing of it when she didn't show up all Saturday. Besides, it's the beginning of the Whitsun Bank Holiday and I thought she'd gone away without telling me. That would be typical of the way she behaved."

"When did you see her last?" Beveridge asked.

"About one A.M. Saturday morning. We'd taken the train down to Piccadilly for a breath of fresh air and a look at the bright lights—Agnes loved them so. We were strolling along when a man approached and spoke to Agnes. I suppose I should have been mad but I'm used to it by now. I thought she knew him when they walked off together.

"They talked very earnestly a few minutes, then Agnes said she'd see me later and went off with him."

Margaret described the man as slender, sandy-haired and wearing a trench coat, the same description as "Mr. Davidson." Beveridge had no doubt he was Agnes Walsh's strangler.

The detective peered at Margaret quizzically. "And that is all you know about it?"

"That's all, so help me," the sister replied demurely. She could add only that the man had been very courteous and soft-spoken, with a strange accent that the Galway girl couldn't place.

"Did Agnes have many boy friends?" Beveridge wanted to know.

"Not any that came to our rooms," Margaret said. "But she had an address book of men's names and phone numbers."

Unfortunately the black book was missing from Agnes' rifled purse, along with two pound banknotes and a snake bracelet with gold-plated wrist watch.

Disappearance of the book led Beveridge to hope that it contained the strangler's name. He had Margaret Walsh draw up a list of Agnes' known men friends while a squad of bobbies canvassed the section's pubs and pawnshops for a clue to the watch and the killer.

Further confirmation of his description, if any was needed, came with the arrival at the Yard of two cab drivers. One had driven the pair to the *Laura Hotel* direct from Picadilly Circus. The other had taxied the strangler from the crime at 5:30 in the morning. He reported that he had picked up the man, his face now badly scratched, a block from the *Laura Hotel*. He had dropped him near Victoria Station, he said.

To Beveridge it sounded as if the quarry had fled London, even England, for Victoria Station is the railroad terminal for South Coast seashore resorts and Channel ports. Had the strangler, with the possible foreign accent, skipped to the Continent?

Checkpoints were set up at all terminals and railroad stations, and the floodtide of vacationists exiting from London was slowed to a thin trickle by the search.

Meanwhile, Dr. Camps and the identification experts had completed their reports. To nobody's surprise Agnes Walsh had engaged in sex just prior to her death—a multiplicity of sex in a variety of forms. That the killer was a sex maniac there could be little doubt. Certain fresh markings within and out indicated sadistic practices, which might have precipitated the quarrel.

She had battled back valiantly. Dug from beneath her fingernails were strips of raw, human flesh and the gray cloth of the tweed coat; apskipped out, obviously suspecting that he was sought by the police.

Now the manhunt began in earnest—but with a difference. This time the police knew who they were after. Photos of Davidson and a description of him were radioed throughout the United Kingdom and to the police at all seaports and roads crossing the Scottish border. But Davidson was not to be found.

Speeding away from home just a half hour before the police arrived, he was shrewd enough to realize that his car would be readily identified. Yet without it he couldn't get anywhere. Still he had no intention of surrendering, for he was fully aware of the swift, stern penalty that British justice metes out for the crime of murder.

He hadn't really meant to kill the girl. If only she didn't act such a bloody fool. They'd agreed to terms before going to the *Laura*. Yet when he dressed she insisted on more money.

STRANGLER of prostitute was the object of a manhunt that swept Britain.

He'd tried to laugh it off, but got mad when she started to scratch him. That's all there was to it.

Well it was too late now. But he didn't want to die. Two wrongs don't make a right. After all she had brought it on herself.

He wondered where to go, and thought of Finchale Priory. As a youngster he'd played under its crumbling medieval walls and in the thick, surrounding birches. And he remembered seeing the abandoned trailer there a few months ago.

He could only procure food by foraging in the fields of nearby farmers, but at least he would have time to think clearly, and to plan a course of action.

The following morning Farmer Franz Roesler thought he saw someone enter the trailer. Though not parked directly on his acreage, Roesler had been asked to keep it free of itinerants and squatters. His shotgun in the crook of his arm, he trudged across a field to investigate.

As he approached a face peered furtively from a dark window. Then Roesler heard a terrible blast. The trailer door tore off its hinges. The roof bulged like a blister of paint.

A man staggered out of the door, bleeding and his clothes burning. A revolver was clutched in his right hand.

He staggered a few yards and collapsed. Roesler ran to him, beat out the flames.

The man was unconscious. Powder burns blackened his temple where he had shot himself. He died in an ambulance on the way to Newcastle General Hospital.

He was quickly identified as Donald Davidson. Police examined the interior of the trailer, determined that Davidson had committed suicide, though in a much more horrible manner than he had anticipated.

He had sealed the windows and doors with cushions, opened the vent of the portable gas stove to asphyxiate himself. But the gas was non-toxic, would not induce death or even insensibility.

Then Davidson shot himself. A tiny spark from the revolver ignited the gas, caused the explosion. Thus Donald Davidson cheated the law, but not justice. For one brief moment at least he had suffered horrors comparable to those he had so callously inflicted on poor, misguided Agnes Walsh.

That he was her strangler the police took as much pains to prove as if they were readying his case for the Assizes. First. Davidson's fingerprints were compared with those on the bloodstained door of the murder room. They matched perfectly. Then Arthur Buxton was driven from London to the mortuary at Newcastle-on-Tyne, where he identified Davidson as the man who had registered with Agnes Walsh. At the inquest, Dr. H. Holden of the London Metropolitan Police laboratory testified that the hairs and pieces of gray tweed removed from Agnes Walsh's fingernails matched the hairs of Davidson's head and his gray tweed jacket.

With this corroborating evidence, Scotland Yard closed its file on the murder of Agnes Walsh, satisfied that she had been strangled by Donald Davidson. Davidson's fate, while not determined by a British court, had been referred to a Higher Jurisdiction, where even fallen angels like Agnes Walsh can exact justice from those who have wronged them.

EDITOR'S NOTE: *In order to protect persons innocently involved in this case, the names Arthur Buxton and Hubert Clarke are fictitious as used.*

THE END

KILL HER BY THE NEXT FULL MOON!

By Ken Arthur

A LITTLE after six o'clock on the Saturday evening of June 23rd, the call arrived at the Malone, New York barracks of the New York State Police. Picking up the phone, Lieutenant Harold Herrick listened intently for a moment, his face clouding.

"And you say she left the house at nine o'clock bound for this girl friend's home and hasn't returned or phoned back since?" he inquired.

After a brief reply from the other end, the lieutenant pulled over a pad and pencil and made a few quick notations. "Okay, Sir," he said finally. "We'll look into the matter right away. And we'll keep in touch."

Cradling the receiver, the lieutenant pressed the desk buzzer, and in a moment Sergeant Gerald Woolsey and Trooper Alden Rosbrook were striding into the office. Herrick made it brief.

"An 18-year-old Onchiota girl named Cleo Tellstone, a senior at Saranac Lake High, has just been reported missing by her father. At nine this morning she left the house for the home of a girl friend from whom she was going to borrow an envelope, and she hasn't returned yet. She's a quiet, home-loving type who's never done anything like this before, so naturally her family's worried. So supposing you two get busy and see what you can find out. Here's her description and her girl friend's name and address. Hop to it."

The troopers did not dally. Ten minutes later, they were pulling up in front of the girl friend's home. There, a brief interview with the girl in question disclosed that Cleo Tellstone had arrived there at about 9:30 and had left soon afterwards with the announcement that she was walking to the post office at Vermontville to mail a letter. She had been in the best of spirits, the friend said, and she had made no mention of any "date" or other plans for the day.

Further questioning in the vicinity soon unearthed a second young lady who told the same story. She had encountered Cleo on the road about halfway between Onchiota and Vermontville and, following the exchange of amenities, Cleo had continued on her way toward the latter village.

"At least we've stumbled onto her trail," Woolsey observed, back in the cruiser. "I guess our best bet now, is to call at the farmhouses along the route. There aren't many of them and they're widely separated. Could be somebody in one of the houses might have seen something."

Rosbrook nodded. "Yes, if she was okay when she left her friend at the halfway point, then whatever happened to her must have occurred between there and the village of

On her lovely exposed flesh was the unmistakable mark of the brutal slayer who had crushed her to death . . .

Vermontville, New York.

"Or between the village and home on the return trip," Woolsey said.

As it turned out, only eleven houses lined the road between the halfway point and Vermontville, but a questioning of the occupants failed to turn up a single soul who had seen anything of the girl. Accordingly, the officers decided to try another tack—a canvass of the Tellstone girl's closest friends.

The canvass netted them a valuable item of information via a girl named Betty Freen, a classmate of the missing girl. The latter revealed that she had encountered Cleo on a deserted section of the Onchiota-Vermontville road shortly after ten A.M., and that after "gabbing back and forth" for a short while, they had parted. Cleo headed in the direction of Vermontville.

A minute or two later, the Freen girl went on, a stake truck heading for Vermontville had appeared, the driver slowing down as he came abreast of her to shout an invitation to get in. Overcome with fear, Betty had immediately started running for home, whereupon the driver had let out a loud raucous laugh and stepped on the gas.

In her confusion and near panic, the girl had not thought to make a mental note of the license number of the truck. However, she remembered that the truck was painted a dark color and that the driver had been tall, dark and young-looking.

The disclosure had the inevitable result. Lieutenant Herrick, on being informed, immediately got in touch with Captain Charles A. Broadfield, the commandant, who lost no time getting into action. Within two hours of his arrival, a force of over 150 boy scouts, farmers, and other volunteers under Woolsey's direction were engaged in an all-out search for the missing young girl.

Throughout the night the dense woodland east and north of Saranac Lake, the famous resort area of New York State, echoed to the baying of bloodhounds, the shouts of sleepless men, and the sharp crackling of dried brush. But morning dawned without their having unearthed any trace of the girl, or a hint as to the cause of her disappearance.

When he conferred with the commandant at eight o'clork that morning, Woolsey said, "For my money, it looks like we've got a rape case on our hands."

The day passed without incident. However, the following morning when Woolsey and Private Rosbrook were inspecting a section of wood terrain south of Bloomingdale, a farmer pulled up in his car and motioned them over.

"I read in the papers as how you fellows have been lookin' for a stake truck," he volunteered. "I saw one of those things over near my farm the day that girl vanished. Only that ain't all. The fellow driving it was acting suspicious," he added.

Woolsey stiffened. The information, if authentic, was the first lead to such a vehicle, which was uncommon in that part of the county.

"How do you mean—suspicious?" he asked.

"I was about 100 yards away when I first saw him," the farmer replied. "Guess he spotted me too, because he jumped in the truck and set out for Bloomingdale like someone was after him."

At the place where the farmer had seen the truck, Woolsey and Rosbrook found diamond-shaped tire impressions and deep prints made by large-sized shoes. In a short time Broadfield and other troopers reached the scene and a search of an abutting patch of woods got under way.

Lieutenant Harold Herrick, leading the group, came across a freshly broken length of sapling stained with a gummy substance. He picked it up in his handkerchief.

"Blood," he told the others.

In another few minutes the troopers entered a clearing. Rosbrook, who was slightly in advance, gave a startled cry. When the others rushed up, he pointed to a clump of brush. Partly hidden from sight lay the body of Cleo Tellstone.

She had been tossed there like a bundle of rags, her limbs askew and her clothing disarrayed. One foot was bare, the shoe lying a short distance away from the gruesome body of the girl.

As the troopers gazed awestricken at the spectacle, the pattern of murder became only too clear. Innocently lured to her death, the girl had been unmercifully beaten by a vicious slayer.

A trooper picked up a recently discarded cigarette butt. It bore no marking but it had a distinct cinnamon smell.

"Cubebs!" the trooper exclaimed. "I haven't run across one of these in years. Only a few stores handle them now. This butt could be a clue!"

He extracted two envelopes from his tunic pocket. In one he placed the cigarette stub, in the second he carefully enclosed the few strands of hair removed from the girl's clenched fist by Herrick.

By this time Franklin County Coroner Edward Cargill, a State Police photographer, and two technical men had arrived on the scene. Everything was quickly photographed from all angles and casts made of the footprints and tire tracks. Then, after leaving Cargill to arrange for the removal of the corpse to the parlors of a local undertaker where an autopsy was to be performed, the officers were ready to depart.

Broadfield began assigning his men. Troopers under Lieutenant Herrick were ordered to make an all-out search for the truck and its driver. Woolsey and Rosbrook were directed to check on all Cubeb smokers in the vicinity—if any could be found.

Broadfield had but one fear—that the Tellstone girl's killer was a transient who had escaped notice by using backroads, and who, by now, had put miles between himself and the authorities. However, the anger of the residents of the county, as the news spread like wildfire from town to town, fanned the flame of the commandant's determination to leave no stone unturned in the manhunt.

By noon a deluge of tips began

(continued on page 58)

(R.) Battered body of Cleo Tellstone was discovered in a clump of brush where she had been assaulted by killer.

TRUE MYSTERY FEATURE CASE

By LAUNCELOT WHIG

LEONARD TARRANCE and his father, Roy, were inseparable. They went everywhere together. Leonard was often seen with his arm about his father's shoulders as they walked along the quiet streets of Jeffersontown, Kentucky, which was their home, or started out on a hunting or fishing expedition.

The bond of affection between father and son went even deeper.

For example, when Leonard, still in his teens, fathered two children out of wedlock his Dad was very philosophical about the matter, if not a little proud of his son's prowess. His attitude was one of "boys-will-be-boys" and "those things are bound to happen, you know."

As Roy Tarrance was to say, Leonard could no no wrong.

"I could never feel angry or anything but good toward Leonard," he said. "He'd do anything in the world for me. He'd die for me and I'd do the same for him."

On one occasion, when Leonard tried to pistol-whip another youth, and his victim struck back, his father grabbed the gun and shouted:

"Don't you hit my boy. If you do it again, I'll shoot you."

So, it was like that with Leonard Tarrance and his father Roy.

And it would be like that all of their lives . . . .

BUT THIS CHRONICLE of sordidness, of savage senseless violence perhaps properly begins on the afternoon of February 28th, 1952, in Louisville, Kentucky, 15 miles distant from Jeffersontown, where the Tarrances made their home.

It begins with Francis J. McCormack, Louisville attorney, leaving a supermarket laden with purchases.

The market was situated at Oak and Fourth Streets, only a block from the 54-year-old lawyer's home where his wife, Mary, waited for him. Half an hour before, Mrs. McCormack had talked to her husband on the phone and had given him her grocery list.

McCormack stepped out into an alley behind the market and had walked only a few paces when he was set upon by two men. Five witnesses watched from a distance, in windows, as the pair slugged and pummeled McCormack unmercifully—and dragged him into a gray car and sped away.

It all happened so quickly that none of the witnesses had time to

HARRODS Creek gives up victim's body to police. Father and son killers (r.) paid the supreme penalty for murder.

"Boys will be boys", said the wild youth's father, when told of his lad's wrongdoing . . .

Prodigal Son

come to the lawyer's assistance. But they did have time to get the license number of the kidnap car, a gray Chevrolet.

But none of the witnesses had recognized either the victim of the savage attack, or his assailants.

Tracing the car, however, was a simple matter. The trail led straight to Roy Tarrance, 46-year-old fireman in a Jeffersontown distillery.

The gray Chevrolet was standing in front of a neat, if small, frame house in Jeffersontown when police arrived. Heavy-set Roy Tarrance, the owner, came to the door when the officers knocked.

Certainly, said Tarrance, the car in front of the house was his. And, of course, nobody ever drove it but himself. Had he been anywhere that day?

"About three o'clock this afternoon," he said, "I drove around looking for a friend. I looked for him for five hours. When I couldn't find him, I came home."

Nobody believed Tarrance's story. Indeed, Sergeant James W. Bibb of the Louisville Crime Prevention Bureau doubted it so profoundly that Tarrance was brought into Louisville and paraded before the five witnesses.

Not one could identify him. To the chagrin of police, and the arrogant contempt of Tarrance, he was released.

ALL THAT NIGHT, Mary McCormack wondered and worried at the failure of her husband to come home. She telephoned Wilson Beatty, his law partner, who did his best to reassure her.

But when the night passed and morning came and still McCormack had not appeared, Beatty himself became alarmed and notified police.

No master mind was needed then to solve the mystery of the identity of the kidnap victim. It was done in short order when Mrs. McCormack recognized her husband's spectacles, picked up at the scene of the attack, and saw that the groceries strewn in the alley were the very same which were on her list.

Beatty gave police all the information they needed to connect Tarrance with McCormack's kidnaping—although it was not readily apparent just what this connection might be.

McCormack, revealed Beatty, had for two years acted as attorney for Leonard Tarrance's 21-year-old wife, Gwendolyn, in a series of court actions which ranged from seduction to non-support.

Police set out to find Leonard Tarrance. It would certainly be worthwhile asking him a few questions.

They found that Leonard was an Army private at Fort Knox. But they did not find Leonard—for he had been AWOL for three weeks.

At the Fort, however, investigators obtained a picture of Leonard. When it was shown to the witnesses of the attack all were positive in their assertions—"That's one of them, for sure."

As an alarm went out for Leonard (who was already being sought by Military Police) investigators called again at the Tarrance home. They found his mother there. They also found a blonde girl who identified herself as Myrtle Blevins, "Leonard's girl friend."

Both Mrs. Tarrance and Myrtle admitted that Leonard had been in the home Wednesday and Thursday —and Thursday was the day of the unfortunate Francis McCormack's kidnaping.

"He was home sick," Mrs. Tarrance said. "But he left Thursday night."

"He got food poisoning at Fort Knox," added Myrtle, "and they weren't giving him good treatment. So he came home."

Myrtle also explained that Leonard's wife, Gwendolyn, was making it tough on him, which was another reason for his taking off AWOL.

She could have been right in the second case, at least.

Gwendolyn Abbot and Leonard met in the fall of 1949 and soon she was spending weekends with him and his family. Also soon enough, Gwendolyn informed Leonard that she was going to have a child and that he was the father.

Leonard's reaction to this announcement was something less than joyous. In fact, he was so annoyed and determined not to assume any responsibility in the affair that Gwendolyn took him to court on a charge of seduction.

McCormack represented Gwendolyn in this action and the charge was dropped when Leonard married the girl. But the reluctant husband had already abandoned Gwendolyn when a baby girl was born to her in August, 1950.

So Gwendolyn had Leonard in court again and he was ordered to pay $7.50 a week for support of the child.

Then Leonard was drafted. In the Army now, he resisted all his wife's efforts to obtain an allotment from his pay. Once again Gwendolyn put the law on him and he was indicted for child desertion in January, 1952. Military authorities took over the case with a briskness that no doubt dismayed and angered the spoiled youth.

All the way through, of course, Leonard was only too aware that Francis McCormack was his pursuing wife's lawyer.

As can be seen, Gwendolyn, just as Myrtle had said, was making it hot for him.

Roy Tarrance was present at this session with the police and insisted, "my boy is completely innocent."

SLAYER (back to camera) tells Kentucky officials how he and his ne'er-do-well father killed Louisville attorney in fit of anger over outcome of court case.

He also protested his own innocence. As for the license plate on his Chevvy tallying with the tag on the kidnap car, he said that was beyond his comprehension.

"I simply can't understand that," he said. "Maybe somebody painted their plate with the same numbers as mine. I just don't know."

On the Monday following the attack and kidnaping, and still without the slightest trace of the victim, Leonard, accompanied by his doting father and distressed mother, walked into the Louisville Police Station and gave himself up.

Leonard, a good-looking youth, was sullen and uncooperative when questioned. About all investigators got out of him was his repeated statement that he had had no part in the abduction of lawyer McCormack. He even went so far as to express the hope that McCormack would "come back soon" because he (Leonard) wanted to be relieved of the shadow of suspicion which had been cast so unfairly upon him.

The following day, Leonard's mother and Myrtle Blevins, escorted by a covey of newspaper reporters, visited him in jail. The newsmen asked Leonard who Myrtle was.

"She's my girl," he said.

The reporters reminded him that he already had a wife and child.

"Sure, I know," he responded, adding boastfully. "I've got two kids. Me and Myrtle have got an 11-month-old daughter. I'd been going with her a long time before I married Gwendolyn."

A short while later that day, Leonard was arraigned on charges of malicious striking and kidnaping and was held with bail. Soon after, father and son, who had been rarely separated, were together again. Roy Tarrance was arrested on similar charges.

Prisoners in the Louisville jail where Leonard Tarrance and his Dad were held are permitted to listen to the radio. It was this circumstance which unexpectedly broke the case and brought from both father and son full confessions.

It was one week after McCormack's disappearance that Leonard heard a news broadcast saying the FBI had entered the case and, moreover, it was *not* essential to find a body to obtain a conviction and put into effect the death penalty for kidnapers.

Frightened, and hoping to save his skin, Leonard said he would talk. Although authorities would not bargain, and promised him nothing, he took the gamble.

Leonard began his story with a bitter condemnation of McCormack.

"That lawyer," he said, "promised to get me a divorce if I married Gwendolyn. But he lied to me. And I hate a damned liar.

"Pop and me were riding on Fourth Street that afternoon and we saw him go in the market," Leonard said. "So we pulled up in the alley and waited.

"When he came out we hit him with our fists and shoved him into the car and drove to Harrods Creek. We stopped and took him out and walked him across the field to the fishing cabin. It was just about getting dark out . . .

"He didn't say anything, except to ask what it was all about. So I told him and we hit him again and he fell down.

"Then he said, 'Do whatever you're going to do to me, but get it over with.'

"We walked him some more, about 100 yards, down to the bank of the creek. We made him walk down the steps to the boat landing.

"I hit him with my fists and my dad picked up something to hit him with . . . Then we found a concrete slab and some barbed wire.

"We put the slab on his stomach and tied it with the wire. Then we shoved him off the boat landing into the creek. I don't know whether he was dead then or not . . .

"When he didn't go out far enough . . . I got part of an iron hand rail and we shoved him out farther with that.

"Then we went home . . ."

County Coroner Dr. George Dwyer examined Francis McCormack's body after it had been dredged from the creek. A hole had been knocked in the back of his head; there was a three-inch gash over the left eye; the skull was fractured in a dozen different places and three ribs were broken.

Dr. Dwyer said death was caused by the fractures and a brain hemorhage. It was doubtful, in his opinion, that McCormack was alive when he was dumped into the creek, for there was very little moisture in the lungs when he was examined.

The elder Tarrance went to trial first, on April 1st. He swore that his only part in the murder was to help his son dispose of the body.

When Leonard took the stand, he corroborated his father's story.

The case went to the jury on the second day of trial. After deliberating five hours and 45 minutes, the 12 men returned to the tense, packed courtroom at 4:32 A.M. with their verdict—

They found the defendant guilty, with no recommendation for mercy, which meant death in the electric chair.

Roy Tarrance's wife, from whom he had never been separated before his arrest in 26 years, screamed hysterically while her sobbing husband tried to comfort her.

Three weeks later, Leonard went to trial. On the first day, he displayed an air of indifference, and read a Bible most of the time. But his attitude changed when Assistant Commonwealth Attorney Carl Ousley picked up the 122-pound concrete block with which Francis McCormack's body had been weighted, and dropped it.

This was something Leonard couldn't take . . .

Then toward the last hours of the trial, during the closing arguments, he went to pieces altogether.

Sobbing uncontrollably he slumped against his mother, who sat be-

(continued on page 45)

ACCORDING to youth's confession, he and his dad parked their car off this highway, marched victim across field, past cottage (arrow), down steps and beat him unconscious. They tied concrete slab to body (r.) and dropped victim into creek.

By LARRY WARREN

AT EXACTLY 1:25 in the morning—Friday, November 13th, 1953—the call came in at Police Headquarters in Seattle, Washington. The desk sergeant talked with the woman and made a few notes on his pad. Hanging up, he contacted the radio dispatcher on the inter-com.

"Suicide reported at 1132½B on 15th Avenue," the sergeant said. "Mrs. William Johnson says a young woman, Miss Opal Montgomery, who rents a small cottage behind Johnson home, stabbed herself to death. Have cruiser squad check."

Arriving at the Johnson house in three minutes, Patrolmen C. F. Watson and "Dockie" Dorris were met by a woman and two men.

"I'm Mrs. Johnson," the woman announced breathlessly, "and this is my husband." Turning to the second man, she explained: "This is Marvin Sugg, our other tenant. He found Opal dead and woke us up."

The Johnsons and Sugg led the officers to Opal Montgomery's tiny cottage, one of two identical units behind the large Johnson house. Only two or three feet separated them, the dead woman's place being on an alley.

Music from a radio drifted from the cottage. Entering, the patrolmen encountered a bizarre sight. On the bed in one corner of the neatly furnished one-room residence was the nude body of a dark-haired young woman. A paring knife was held loosely in her right hand, which was raised over her head. But what startled the officers was a nylon stocking tightly twisted around her neck. It obviously had strangled her to death.

The patrolmen were further startled to discover, on closer examination, that not only had she been stabbed in the abdomen and breasts, but her body bore countless dabs of what looked like face powder and fingernail polish.

"This is one for the book," Watson remarked, shaking his head. "Why would anybody do a job like that?"

"I don't know," answered Dorris, "but I do know she didn't strangle herself with that stocking. Whoever killed her must've done the decorating, too."

They hurried outside where the Johnsons and Sugg waited. Dorris asked the tenant, Sugg, "Why did you think Miss Montgomery killed herself? Didn't you see she'd been strangled by one of her nylons? And how about the nail polish and face powder on her body? Think she did that herself?"

Sugg explained that he hadn't taken a close look at the victim after seeing the knife in her hand and the stab wounds on her body. He had simply assumed she had taken her own life.

"Well, it's definitely murder," Watson informed the threesome. "We'll appreciate it if you'll wait in the house until the detectives can talk to you."

Headquarters, notified over the cruiser radio, immediately dispatched Sergeant Vic Berg and Detective Steve Brozovich of the night Homicide Detail. After getting the rundown, they dismissed the uniformed men, then entered the slain brunette's cottage.

Quickly confirming the patrolmen's murder theory, they radioed a request to the dispatcher to summon Captain Charles Rouse, Homicide Detail commander, from home.

While awaiting his arrival, Berg and Brozovich inspected the cottage. On a nightstand by the bed they discovered a half-filled box of face powder and an empty nail polish bottle. Scattered about the floor were feminine garments, some of them torn.

"No question that whoever killed the girl ripped her clothing off," the sergeant declared. "Probably strangled her with the stocking when she yelled. But that nail polish and powder on her body beats me. I can't dope it out."

Brozovich shrugged. "It doesn't make any more sense," he remarked, "than trying to make this look like she killed herself."

Adding to the futility of the crudely-faked suicide was the finding of an almost-empty bottle of Canadian Club whisky and two empty drinking glasses on the sink of the tiny kitchen at the other end of the room.

"If whoever killed her had taken one of the glasses away," the sergeant observed, "they'd have had some chance of making it look like the woman committed suicide while drunk. But that glass definitely puts another person in the room. If our luck is good, we'll find fingerprints."

Captain Rouse and the coroner's deputies arrived almost simultaneously. The medical examiners verified the belief that the victim had been strangled to death by the nylon stocking. They estimated she had been dead for 24 hours.

The weapon in her hand, an ordinary paring knife, was turned over to the detectives.

"Lack of blood on her hand or arm removes the slightest possibility of suicide," Captain Rouse said.

After the body was removed, Captain Rouse and his men went to the other cottage to question Marvin Sugg.

"Opal and I not only were neighbors," he told them, "but we worked together at a tavern on Pike Street where I tend bar. Opal was a barmaid. Everybody liked her."

'I told her she had no business inviting me in

Sugg said that she hadn't worked for the past week or so because of the flu. But Wednesday afternoon she came to the tavern and announced she was feeling fine again. She said she would be back Thursday to talk to the tavern owner about resuming her job.

"She didn't come in, though," the bartender continued, "and I figured she had a relapse. I phoned her place last night, but she didn't answer. When I got home around 1 o'clock this morning and heard her radio, I knocked on the door. I got no response, so I assumed she'd gone to sleep with the radio on."

Sugg said that after going to his cottage and starting to undress, he remembered that Opal's radio was playing when he got home from work the previous night. Alarmed, he had put on his bathrobe and returned to her place. The door was unlocked, so he entered, switched on the light, and found her dead on the bed. He immediately notified the Johnsons.

"Just how friendly were you and the girl?" asked Captain Rouse.

"Well, I thought a lot of Opal," Sugg replied. "She was pretty and friendly—good company. But that's as far as it went with me."

"Did it go any farther with anybody else?"

The bartender said he didn't know. Opal had never mentioned her personal affairs to him.

"Did she leave the tavern with anybody on Wednesday?" the captain inquired.

"I didn't see her leave the second time. In the afternoon she played shuffleboard with several young fellows. Later on she went out alone and came back with the Zimmermans. That's Mr. and Mrs. Leonard Zimmerman, Opal's closest friends."

The trio had sat in a booth with one of the young men Opal had played shuffleboard with, and the

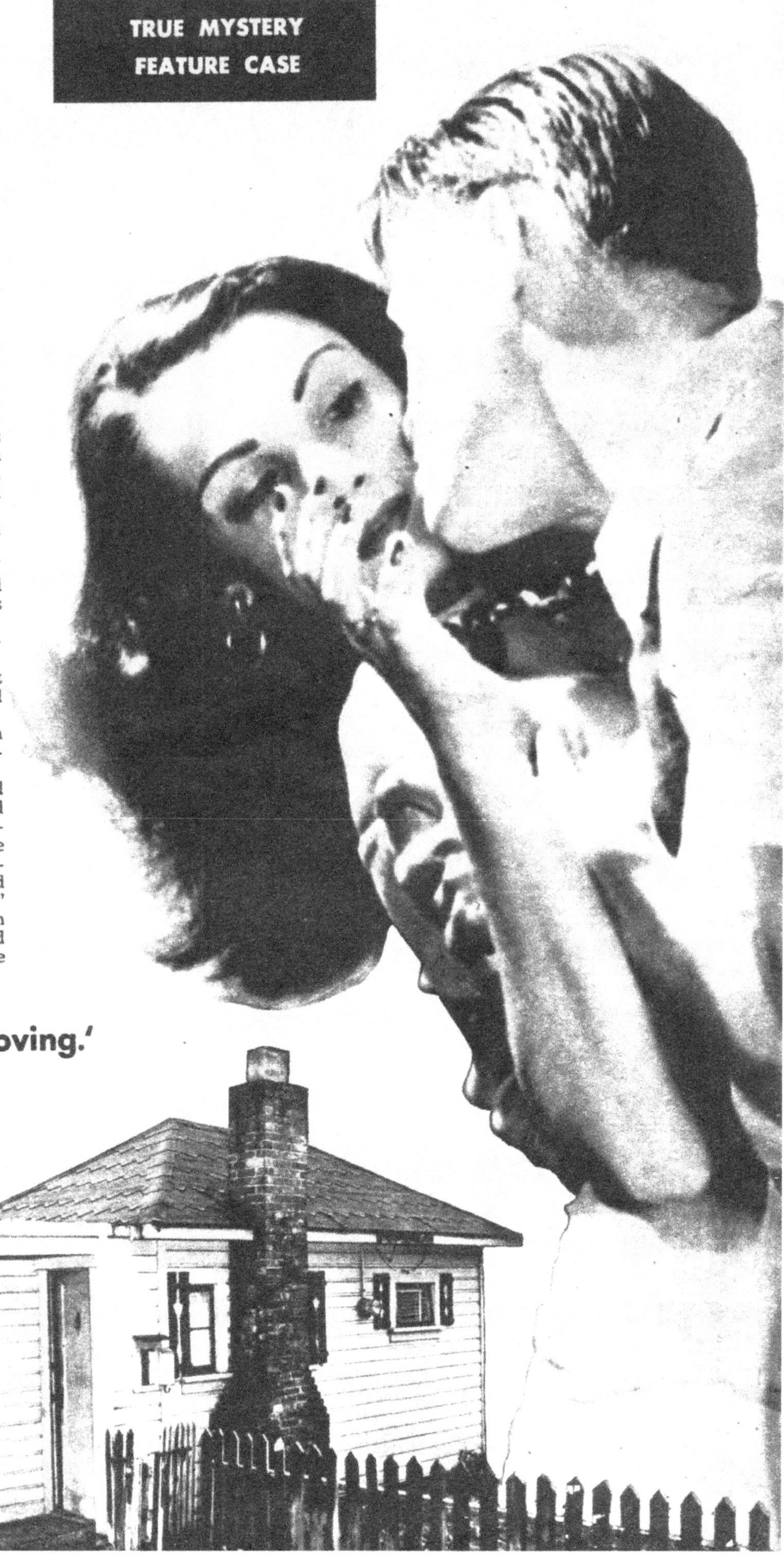

unless she wanted loving.'

"How to Make Money with Simple Cartoons"

A book everyone who likes to draw should have. It is free; no obligation. Simply address FREE BOOK

CARTOONISTS' EXCHANGE
Dept. DEPT. 698 Pleasant Hill, Ohio

BIKINI STYLE PANTIES
Personalized With Your Name or Hers
The Ideal Novelty Gift — Sheer Nylon Panties Trimmed with PEEK-A-BOO Nylon Lace
Colors: Bewitching Black, Bridal White. Sizes: Small, Med., Large
Gift Card Enclosed If Requested.
$2.25 P.P. — Two Pairs $4.00
R. & M. SALES CO.
Box 5022 • St. Paul 4, Minn.

WIN with MAGIC CARDS

This special deck of playing cards with secret code on back of each card tells YOU what each card is when lying face down. Easy directions explain code and how to do many kinds of "Magic" tricks. Use same deck for usual card games, such as poker, bridge, etc. Only $2.98. Get a deck today. SEND NO MONEY. Send Name and Address. Pay postman on arrival only $2.98 plus postage. Address HOLLISTER-WHITE CO., DEPT. 598-M
3016 W. VAN BUREN ST. • CHICAGO 12, ILL.

Party Records
FOR ADULTS ONLY

THEY'RE TERRIFIC! Brand new series of exclusive records. Racy ditties and gay parodies about those spicy, intimate moments. Really shocking, but so much fun for you and your guests. Complete set of EIGHT DIFFERENT SELECTIONS on finest quality 78 or 45 r.p.m. records (state choice), sent prepaid in plain, sealed package for $4.95 (no c.o.d.'s). SPECIAL OFFER: Two Different Sets of 16 Recordings for only $8.95. For a thrilling adventure in adult entertainment, order yours Today!
NATIONAL, Dept. 26-F, Box 5, Sta. E, TOLEDO 9, OHIO

BRAND NEW BLUE-STEEL
.22 cal. Blank Cartridge
German AUTOMATIC Clipload
6 shot Repeater
NO PERMIT REQUIRED

Latest model, not a clearance item. Gun is fully automatic, has positive safety catch, self ejecting clip. Adjustable firing spring. Machined with all the care and precision of West Germany's finest gunsmiths. Ideal for sporting events, theatrical performances, etc., 4" long, perfectly balanced. Satisfaction guaranteed. Send check or money order and save C.O.D. charges.

$7.95 postpaid

BIG THREE, Ent. DEPT. GM8, 1109 Sixth Ave., New York 36, N. Y.

Amazing New Creme Color Shampoo
RE-COLORS HAIR IN 17 MINUTES

Change streaked, gray, graying, off-color or drab hair to new lustrous youthful-looking color. TINTZ Creme Color Shampoo recolors hair at home as it shampoos. No artificial look . . . no hairline difference. Easy. Won't wash or rub off. Won't affect permanents. Choice of 14 shades each so natural-looking no one will suspect your secret. Color chart on package. Ask for TINTZ Creme Color Shampoo. Only $1.50 plus tax at druggists.

2½"x3½" photos for classmates, loved ones—for job and college applications. Send pictures or neg. 25 for $1.25 plus Free 5"x7" (60 for $2.25). Satisfaction guaranteed.
ROY PHOTO SERVICE • DEPT. 41, GPO Box 644, N.Y. 1, N.Y.

Write today for a FREE copy of illustrated law book, "THE LAW-TRAINED MAN," which shows how to earn the professional Bachelor of Laws (LL.B.) degree through home study of the famous Blackstone Law Course. All necessary books and lessons provided. Moderate cost; convenient terms. Write for FREE law training book today.
Blackstone School of Law, 225 N. Michigan Ave.
Founded 1890 DEPT. 260C . Chicago 1, Ill.

KILLER (seated at left) tells his version of weird murder to Sergeant Austin Seth (standing) and Detective Don Sprinkle of homicide detail (seated, taking statement).

group had consumed a few beers. The bartender hadn't seen them leave, so he didn't know whether they all had gone together or if Opal went with the Zimmermans or the youth. He said it was about 10:30 when he noticed that all of them were gone.

Sugg gave them the approximate location of the Zimmerman residence on 15th Avenue, only a few blocks away. But before checking there, the detectives went to the Johnson house to see whether they could give any important information.

Neither had any idea who had killed their tenant or why. Although very friendly, she had told them little about herself. They said she was about 27 and quite attractive and well-behaved. They hadn't heard or seen anything Wednesday night or early Thursday morning that could be connected with her fantastic murder.

Next, the investigators hunted up the Zimmerman home. The middle-aged couple, summoned from bed, were shocked by the news.

The Zimmermans stated that they had known the attractive brunette for six years and thought highly of her. Asked why such an apparently desirable woman wasn't married, they explained that she had been at one time, but the marriage hadn't worked out.

"It was before we met Opal," Zimmerman said. "She told us it was one of those 'kid things' that didn't last. She got a divorce and took her maiden name again. That's all we know about it. Don't even know her ex-husband's name or anything about him."

Opal, they related, had enjoyed the company of men but wouldn't be serious with them because of her unhappy marriage. "Once was enough," was the way she put it.

Regarding Wednesday night, the Zimmermans said she had come to their place around 6 o'clock and asked them to go back to the tavern with her. She told them she had been playing shuffleboard with a "nice young man," and he had invited her to have a beer or two.

At Opal's suggestion that they get the Zimmermans to join them, he had said that would be fine and had given her the keys to his Chevrolet, a fairly new two-tone sedan.

"We went with her and met the young man," related the wife. "I don't remember his name, but he was around 25, quite handsome, well-dressed, and very polite. Although he didn't talk much, he seemed to have a good time."

After the group had had a few rounds of beer, the youth had offered to buy a bottle of whisky. So Zimmerman went with him to a liquor store, and the lad bought a fifth of Canadian Club. Back at the tavern, the foursome had one round of whisky and then Opal said she should be getting home, as she wanted to get up early and see the tavern proprietor about getting back her job as barmaid.

Opal and her companion drove the Zimmermans home, then departed with the bottle of whisk·

FROM FAMOUS HOLLYWOOD FILM STUDIOS
Just to get acquainted, we will make you a beautiful studio quality 5 x 7 enlargement of any snapshot, photo or negative. Be sure to include color of hair, eyes and clothing, and get our Bargain Offer for having your enlargement beautifully hand-colored in oil and mounted in a handsome frame. Limit 2 to a customer. Please enclose 10¢ to cover cost of handling and mailing each enlargement. Original returned. *We will pay $100.00 for children's or adults pictures used in our advertising.* Act NOW!
HOLLYWOOD FILM STUDIOS, Dept F-325
7021 Santa Monica Blvd., Hollywood 38, Calif.

Write Stories that SELL

Mrs. Grace Blanchard had an IDEA for a story. We criticized her story, gave it a new title and told her WHERE TO SEND IT. She got a substantial check. THE FIRST TIME OUT. That is a THRILL many of our graduates have each month. Let 22 years of experience guide YOU. Endorsed by Jack London.
FREE BOOKLET "THE ART OF STORY WRITING" with explanation of our personal criticism and manuscript sales service. No obligation. Write!
HOOSIER INSTITUTE, DESK 53, PICKWICK BLDG., KANSAS CITY, MO.

LOWEST-PRICED REAL
ADDING MACHINE
Adds up to One Billion.. Subtracts Multiplies.. Divides.. Guaranteed only $2.95 postpaid

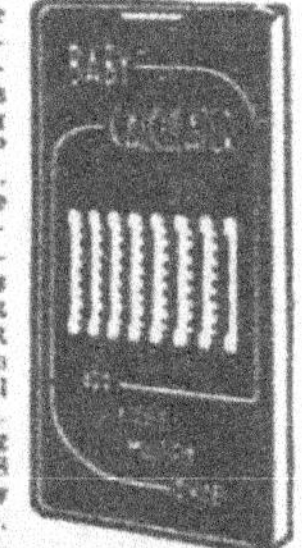

Stop making costly mistakes! Become a "wiz" at figures. BABY CALCULATOR is not a toy, but a real calculator that works as accurately as expensive machines. With just a flick of your finger, YOU CAN ADD UP TO ONE BILLION, OR SUBTRACT, MULTIPLY, DIVIDE. Precision made—palm size—compact as a watch. Thousands in satisfactory use by Bookkeepers, Cashiers, Students, Business Men, Housewives and others who can't afford making mistakes. Supermarket shoppers carry in pocket or purse to keep purchases within budget and total them before reaching checkout counter. Comes in handsome suede-like carrying case. ORDER NOW FOR 10 DAYS FREE TRIAL. Send $2.95 and we pay postage. Postage added on C. O. D. orders. MONEY BACK GUARANTEE.
MERIDIAN CO., 366 Madison Ave., DEPT. C-26 New York 17

SKINNY?

New Way Quickly PUTS POUNDS and INCHES FIRM FLESH on Scrawny Skinny Figures When Underweight is Caused by Poor Appetite or Poor Eating Habits

NOT A SUGARY MIXTURE, NO FISHY OILS, NO DRUGS, NO OVEREATING

If you are skinny, thin and underweight because of poor appetite or poor eating habits, try WATE-ON. Fast weight gains of 5 pounds .... 10 pounds .... 20 pounds and more reported. New WATE-ON is the body building all in one meal of easily digested calories you've long heard was coming HOMOGENIZED. Fortified with Vitamin D, blood building vitamin B-12 and quick energy elements. Cheeks fill out, neck and bustline gains, skinny underweight figures that need these extra calories fill out all over the body. Fights fatigue, low resistance, loss of sleep, poor endurance.

STARTS PUTTING ON FLESH FIRST DAY

Maximum daily dosage of WATE-ON is as rich in calories as in many a skinny person's regular meal. Wonderful for folks with small stomachs who fill up and lose appetite fast. War prisoner gained, children gained, men and women gained. Take WATE-ON with weight maintaining meals as directed. Starts putting on firm flesh first day. Put on weight to your delight or money back. When underweight is caused by disease take WATE-ON under direction of your doctor. Get WATE-ON today.

WATE-ON (Also in TABLET Form) HOMOGENIZED LIQUID EMULSION
AT ALL DRUG STORES

The couple said the youth was of medium height, athletic of build and had dark hair and a small, well-trimmed mustache. He had worn a gray hat, brown topcoat, tan sport shirt, and tan slacks.

On the possibility that the mutilation murderer had a record, the investigators took the couple to Headquarters to look through the photos of sex offenders.

After two hours of scanning "muggs," the Zimmermans came across one they said strongly resembled Opal's companion, though the man in the photo was younger.

Captain Rouse looked at the picture and said, "That's John Alfred Monner. He strangled a girl to death and mutilated her six or seven years ago. We sent him to the penitentiary. Naturally, he'd look a lot older now. But I haven't heard about him being turned loose."

Since it wasn't possible to check on the suspect until the office at the state prison in Walla Walla opened some hours later, the captain sent the Zimmermans home in a police car, then he and his men took care of routine procedure. This included an all-state alert for Opal's tavern companion and his two-tone Chevrolet sedan.

At 8 A.M. Sergeant Berg and Brozovich were relieved by Sergeant Austin Seth and Detective Don Sprinkle of the day Homicide Detail. After a briefing, the newcomers and Sergeant Max Allison, crime lab director, and an assistant, Gerald Presba, left to search the murder scene for fingerprints and other evidence.

When Captain Rouse phoned the penitentiary, he learned that Monner had been paroled two weeks previously after serving the minimum of his sentence for the mutilation slaying of the girl in 1946. He now was under jurisdiction of the state parole office in Seattle.

From that office Rouse quickly obtained the name of the large industrial plant where Monner was working, as well as his home address. The captain noted that the latter was in the same district where Opal Montgomery had been killed.

Phoning the Montgomery cottage, Rouse instructed Seth and Sprinkle to locate Monner. They found him at the plant, and he fitted the description of Opal's youthful companion down to the neatly-trimmed mustache.

But he insisted he had gone to the downtown *Paramount Theatre* after supper Wednesday, returning to his rooming house about 11 P.M. He denied being in a tavern, or becoming acquainted with a girl since his release from prison.

Although he described in some detail the movie he claimed to have seen, the detectives realized he could have viewed it prior to the murder night, as it had been playing for several weeks.

SELL TO UNCLE SAM!

That's how I made $20,000 a year—selling junk jewelry to the U. S. Government. Send me your name and I'll show you how I did it.

LEARN AT HOME IN ONE EVENING
This is the most fantastic way of making money you ever heard of. That's because you do all your "selling" BY MAIL *to one customer*—the U. S. Government! Uncle Sam will buy all the old junk jewelry you send in at $35.00 AN OUNCE for the gold it contains. Just follow my Plan and you can pick up gold on any street in your town. I show you where to find it, what to pay, how to test and how to mail to Uncle Sam for cash. I'll teach you the secrets by which I made $20,000 a year. No charge for facts. No salesman will call. Send no money—just your name, address on postcard. Leslie Patton, 335 W. Madison St., DEPT. P-268, Chicago 6, Ill.

"PSYCHIC DOMINANCE
How to RULE OTHERS WITH your THOUGHTS." (Full course). No promises. Telepathy controversial. But USED by unusual persons, mystics, Yogis. (For adults). $2. Satis., or ref. WISDOM, 846-D2 Sunnyside, Chicago 40.

RUPTURED
BE *FREE* FROM TRUSS SLAVERY
Surely you want to THROW AWAY TRUSSES FOREVER, be rid of Rupture Worries. Then Why put up with wearing a griping, chafing and unsanitary truss. For there is now a new modern Non-Surgical treatment that is designed to permanently correct rupture. These Non-Surgical treatments are so certain, that a Lifetime Certificate of Assurance is given.
Write today for our New FREE Book that gives facts that may save you painful, expensive surgery. Tells how non-surgically you may again work, live, play, love and enjoy life in the manner you desire. There is no obligation.
Excelsior Hernia Clinic, Dept. 8805, Excelsior Spgs., Mo.

help your heart fund

DIRECT TO YOU...EASY TERMS
Genuine Rockdale Monuments and Markers. Full Price $14.95 and up. Satisfaction or MONEY BACK. We pay freight. Compare our low prices. WRITE FOR FREE CATALOG.

ROCKDALE MONUMENT CO. • DEPT. 408 • JOLIET, ILL.

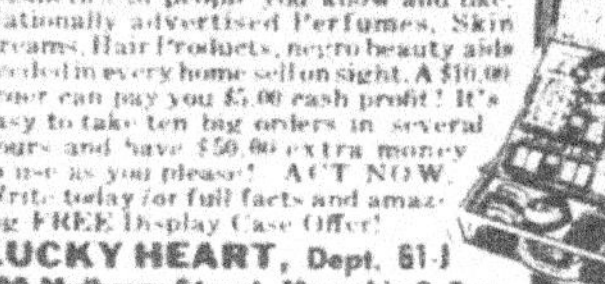

Mr. Greenwood, Calif.

You, Too, Can Earn This Easy Way!
Need extra money? Mr. Greenwood made $45.00 cash in his first spare hours. A busy mother in California made $715 in just spare time. Now it's *your* turn to cash in!

NO EXPERIENCE NEEDED!
Just show exclusive quality Lucky Heart Cosmetics to people you know and like. Nationally advertised Perfumes, Skin Creams, Hair Products, negro beauty aids needed in every home sell on sight. A $10.00 order can pay you $5.00 cash profit! It's easy to take ten big orders in several hours and have $50.00 extra money to use as you please! ACT NOW. Write today for full facts and amazing FREE Display Case Offer!
LUCKY HEART, Dept. 61-J
400 Mulberry Street, Memphis 2, Tenn.

"MY GREY HAIR IS A NATURAL LOOKING COLOR AGAIN" says JAN GARBER, Idol of the Airlanes

"TOP SECRET gives my grey hair a natural looking color!" says famous dance band leader Jan Garber. "I noticed results after just a few applications. And TOP SECRET is easy to use—doesn't stain hands or scalp. TOP SECRET is the only hair dressing I use."

A FAVORITE OF THE STARS

TOP SECRET has been a favorite with famous personalities for years. Exclusive formula imparts a natural looking color to grey or faded hair. Does not streak or injure hair; does not wash out. Send $5.00 for 6 oz. plastic container. (Convenient for traveling, too.) Ppd. No COD's. Money back if not delighted with results of first bottle. Albin of California, **Room 84, 1401—31 W. 8th St.**, Los Angeles 17, California.

AMAZING NEW AIR-CUSHION SUPPORT FOR **RUPTURE**

Comfortaire Truss

with adjustable pressure inflated pad shaped for securest most comfortable rupture support. 30-day free trial. Money-back satisfaction guarantee. Write now for free literature.

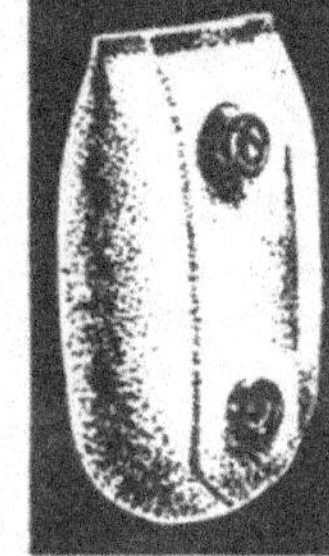

COMFORT APPLIANCE CO.
403-409 University Street
Healdsburg 11, California

Cabinet Making

LOW COST HOME TRAINING COURSE for Beginners & Advanced Craftsmen

Make money. Learn skills and secrets of fine woodworking and tool use. Professionally prepared shop method training tells and shows how. Covers everything. Easy to master.

Write for Free Booklet **INTERSTATE TRAINING SERVICE**
DEPT. F-39 PORTLAND 13, OREGON

BUILD MUSCLES & HEALTH with BODY BUILDER $1 post paid

This new Chest Pull Body Builder develops powerful he-man muscles F-A-S-T. Ideal for the beginner to give him a real start in championship muscularity and perfect for the more advanced bodybuilder to combine with his regular training for faster, all around muscle growth. Body Builder is wonderful for developing massive arms, shoulders, chest and back. Mail your order today. Only $1.00 postpaid. No C.O.D.
MEDFORD PRODUCTS, INC., DEPT. SK-7
Box 39 Bethpage, N. Y.

JOBS ON SHIPS & YACHTS

MEN (16 to 50) Go to Sea. Travel foreign countries. Experience unnecessary. Civilian occupation. Excellent pay. Ship and yachting jobs adventurous-exciting.
Write for FREE information.
DAVENPORT SEAMEN'S SERVICE, DEPT. 24
BOX 1354, G. P. O. NEW YORK 1, N. Y.

TROUBLED WITH UNWANTED HAIR?

You needn't be! Now you can remove unwanted hair forever — in the privacy of your home — with the famous Mahler Hair Removal Epilator! Acclaimed by thousands of women who have discovered how Mahler destroys the hair root permanently! By following our instructions you, too, can learn to use the Mahler safely and efficiently! Positive money-back guarantee! Act today!

MAHLER'S INC.
DEPT. 677-K
PROVIDENCE 15, R. I.

Send 5¢ for illustrated 16-page booklet "New Radiant Beauty"!

Learn **BAKING** *at home*

Baking is one of America's high industries in wages. Not seasonable, but year 'round good field for trained and experienced men. Thorough basic spare time home study course lays solid foundation. If you have the aptitude for this type of work, send for FREE Booklet, "Opportunities in Commercial Baking."

NATIONAL BAKING SCHOOL
835 Diversey Pkwy., Dept. 150C, Chicago 14, Ill.

DETECTIVE CAPTAIN Charles A. Rouse, head of Seattle, Washington's homicide detail, reads killer's confession. Rouse was in charge of solving mysterious killing.

Because he allegedly had gone to the show alone, his alibi was uncheckable, so Seth and Sprinkle took him to the place where Leonard Zimmerman worked.

Zimmerman immediately blasted hopes of a quick solution to the murder. "No, he isn't the one Opal was with," he declared emphatically. "They do look somewhat alike, though."

That cleared the ex-convict. After returning him to the plant, the investigators went back to the Montgomery cottage, where they phoned the news to Captain Rouse.

Another disappointment quickly followed. Sergeant Max Allison and Technician Gerald Presba finished processing every likely object in the murdered girl's cottage without finding a usable fingerprint specimen. Even the nearly-empty whisky bottle and drinking glasses yielded only worthless smudges.

"Only thing left is the paring knife that was in the girl's hand," Allison said. "Chances are that the killer wiped it off before putting it there, but I'll process it anyway."

After the technicians had gone, Seth and Sprinkle began searching the neighborhood for clues to the killer's identity. Finally they came across a man who had passed the residence of Opal's landlord about 1 o'clock Thursday morning on his way home from work. He reported that a youth had appeared from behind the Johnson house and hurried in the opposite direction.

The witness hadn't seen his face clearly, but described him as tall, slender, and having a slight limp. He wore a dark topcoat and was bareheaded. His hair was light.

As this didn't jibe at all with the description of Opal's tavern friend, the detectives wondered whether someone else had visited her the night she was murdered.

"Since she supposedly didn't invite men into her cottage," remarked Sergeant Seth, "this fellow might have forced his way in. Let's see if anybody at the tavern where she worked knows who he is."

The proprietor didn't. Nor did he have any idea why his barmaid had been murdered. Adding to the puzzle, he declared that he had never heard of Opal's having a date unless another couple went along, usually the Zimmermans.

But one of the other barmaids, a pert blonde, revealed that a man had been after Opal for several weeks. He had come into the tavern frequently in an effort to date her, and when this failed, he persistently phoned her at home. Opal hadn't seemed worried or frightened —only annoyed.

The blonde hadn't seen the man and the only thing she recalled Opal's saying about him was that he was a sailor on an Alaska line.

The detectives went to the Seamen s Union headquarters. They learned that the suspect's description fitted that of "Slim" Ferguson, age 24, who had a slightly crippled leg. They heard from several sailors that he was known as the "Waterfront Wolf."

Soon the investigators confronted Ferguson in his room in a cheap hotel on Second Avenue. Asked if he had been in the 1100 block on 15th Avenue Wednesday night or early Thursday morning, he looked startled. After a moment's hesita-

AIR CONDITIONING
REFRIGERATION
OFFERS TOP-PAY JOBS
More jobs and less competition in this field! Earn more money in a better job, or open a shop. Learn Refrigeration Mechanics at home by practicing with 23 kits we send. Build and keep an air conditioner, freezer, refrigerator or milk cooler. See photo. *Write for 2 free books.* Get facts now—Decide later.
COMMERCIAL TRADES INSTITUTE DEPT. R-357
1400 Greenleaf Avenue • Chicago 26, Ill.

CHARM DROPS

An enchanting perfume of irresistible charm, clinging for hours like lovers loath to part. Just a tiny drop is enough. Full size bottle 98c prepaid or $1.32 C. O. D. Directions free. One bottle FREE if two ordered.
Rolldex ROLLDEX, P. O. Box 516, Dept. 87
Safety Harbor, Florida

BE A DETECTIVE
WORK HOME or TRAVEL. Experience unnecessary. DETECTIVE Particulars FREE. Write to
GEO. B. K. WAGNER, 125 W. 86 St., N. Y.

PORTABLE GARAGE
$6.75
Plastic Vinyl
USE IT ANYWHERE

• Folds compactly • Keeps rain, snow, dust, salt air, sun or sleet away • Protects your car's finish • Durably constructed of vinyl plastic • Springtite elasticized bottom, holds securely in all kinds of weather • Fits all makes • Direct from manufacturer • Enclose check or money order for $6.75, or sent C.O.D. 10-Day Money Back Guarantee.
MARDO SALES CORP.
480 Lexington Ave., Dept. G-35 . New York 17, N. Y.

DEVELOP A STRONG HE-MAN VOICE

STRENGTHEN *your* voice this tested *scientific* way. Yes—you may now be able to improve the **POWER** of your speaking and singing voice—and in the privacy of your own room! Self-training lessons, mostly silent. No music required.
WRITE TODAY FOR FREE BOOK
Eugene Feuchtinger's great booklet "How to Develop a Successful Voice." It's absolutely FREE! You must state your age. Booklet mailed postpaid in plain wrapper. No salesman will call. Send your name, age now!
PREFECT VOICE INSTITUTE
210 S. Clinton St., Studio GT-87, Chicago 6, Ill.

"LOVE ME ALWAYS"

"**LOVE TIME**," the alluring perfume, delicately blended to linger for **HOURS** . . . an irresistible scent, suggesting **LASTING LOVE** and **ROMANCE**. Men never tire of delicate perfume, as it conjures in them all the **ENJOYMENT** of **LIFE** and **LOVE**. "**LOVE TIME**" hints of a great many delights in store for you. **A FEW DROPS AT A TIME IS ALL YOU NEED! MONEY BACK GUARANTEE!** "**LOVE TIME**" must satisfy you in every way or your money returned at any time! **FULL** directions with every order. Only $2.00 with order. ($2.50 COD.) **FREE GIFT IF YOU SEND MONEY WITH ORDER!**
MADAME BEATRICE. DEPT. 534-A
604 Hicksville Rd., Massapequa, N. Y.

REAL ESTATE
BE A BROKER
PAYS BIG! SEND FOR FREE, BIG, ILLUSTRATED CATALOG NOW! Graduates report making substantial incomes. Start and run your own business quickly. Men, women of all ages, learn easily. Course covers Sales, Property Management, Appraising, Loans, Mortgages, and related subjects. **STUDY AT HOME** or in classrooms in leading cities. Diploma awarded. Write TODAY for free book! No obligation. Approved for World War II and Korean Veterans
FREE BOOK TELLS HOW
WEAVER SCHOOL OF REAL ESTATE Est. 1936
2022J Grand Ave. Kansas City, Mo.

Learn PHOTOGRAPHY at Home
Splendid Hobby or Vocation
Prepare in spare time. Practical basic training. Long-established school. Send for free booklet, "Opportunities in Modern Photography" and particulars. Sent postage prepaid. No obligation.
AMERICAN SCHOOL OF PHOTOGRAPHY
835 Diversey Pkwy., Dept. 150C . Chicago 14, Ill.

tion, he replied, "Yeah, I was around there about 1 A.M. looking for a friend of mine. How come you're interested?"

"Routine checkup, Ferguson," the sergeant said. "Who is the friend and what did you do there?"

"Her name's Opal Montgomery. But I didn't even see her. She had company, so I beat it."

Ferguson claimed he had gone to the tavern about 12:30, hoping to walk Opal home from work. However, he failed to see her when he looked inside. Assuming she had left, he went to her place, the address of which he had obtained from the telephone book.

"I heard her radio playing," he related, "and just as I was going to knock, I heard a man's voice. Then I noticed a car parked in the alley. So I took off."

When he described the auto as a late model two-tone sedan, the detectives felt certain he was telling the truth. That was the type of car owned by the mustached youth with the soft voice who had taken Opal home from the tavern.

Obviously, he had stayed at her place for at least two hours, making it fairly certain he had executed the mutilation murder.

Seeking some information that might lead to his identification, Seth and Sprinkle went back to Leonard Zimmerman's office. Although still eager to aid the investigation, he couldn't recall anything else about Opal's companion.

Sergeant Seth then asked him where the youth had purchased the whisky. Zimmerman said he didn't know exactly, but the liquor store was in the Broadway district.

He was unable to give the exact address, however.

Hoping Zimmerman could retrace the route he and the suspect had taken, the detectives took the witness to the tavern neighborhood, then set out for the Broadway area. A short time later, Zimmerman exclaimed, "Now we're on the right street. There's the drug store where he stopped just before we got to the liquor store."

"Drug store?" Sprinkle echoed. "You didn't say anything about a drug store before."

Zimmerman explained that it had slipped his mind, as it seemed unimportant. The young man had said he wanted to get something and had dashed in alone. Soon he was back, then they went on to the liquor store.

Overlooking no leads, the detectives parked and entered the pharmacy. The proprietor, C. A. Smith, informed them that a clerk named Logan had been on duty Wednesday night. Hastening to his home in the University District, the detectives and Zimmerman described the suspect to Logan.

Logan remembered him instantly, saying he shopped there frequently.

They seek you out, they come tearing down your doors, they won't let you go! They are yours. YOURS ALONE. In these confidential books you'll find ancient love magic and modern techniques . . . Don Juan and the Man-About-Town . . . And ways to make the male personality more potent and irresistible!

It's a double secret – Intimate Romance and social strategy. That's why YOURS ALONE offers in 2 complete books an *Art of Love* and a *Way of the World*. Single, engaged or married, you'll be thrilled with your new power. It's so easy when you know how! Only $2. Money-back guarantee.

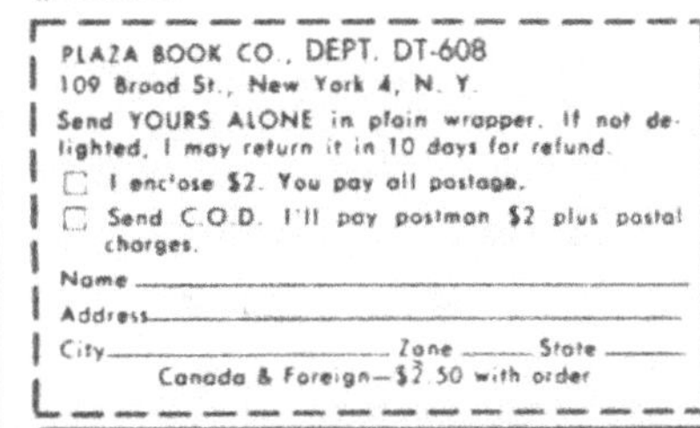
PLAZA BOOK CO., DEPT. DT-608
109 Broad St., New York 4, N. Y.
Send YOURS ALONE in plain wrapper. If not delighted, I may return it in 10 days for refund.
☐ I enclose $2. You pay all postage.
☐ Send C.O.D. I'll pay postman $2 plus postal charges.
Name
Address
City Zone State
Canada & Foreign—$2.50 with order

Earn more from the start! Set up your own profitable business in your own home, enjoy steady income, independence for life—in the booming field of CUSTOM UPHOLSTERY.

Right off you start learning with tools, complete frames, fabrics and materials, included FREE with your UTS course. You learn skilled professional custom upholstery, reupholstery, furniture finishing, repair, how to make beautiful slip covers, window cornices, cushions and draperies. EARN WHILE YOU LEARN, in your spare time . . . the UTS easy way.

Send for FREE Illustrated Book, With Sample Lesson.

Get ready for well-paid job, big profits from steady work, as your own boss, running your own business. Training in N. Y. School also available. Mail coupon NOW!

APPROVED FOR VETERAN TRAINING

UPHOLSTERY TRADES SCHOOL
Dept. FM-2410 , 721 B'way, N. Y. 3, N. Y.
Send me free book "Your New Way to a Successful Career." No obligation—no salesman will call.
☐ Home Study ☐ N. Y. School
Name
Address
City Zone State
☐ Check if Korean Veteran

On Wednesday night he had asked to cash a $10 check. The clerk requested his driver's license, and after seeing that he lived in the neighborhood, cashed the check.

"I can't remember the name exactly," Logan added. "But it was rather uncommon. Barringer, or Ballinger, or something like that."

Learning where the pharmacy banked, the detectives and Zimmerman hurried there, only to discover that the check had already gone to the clearing house. Seth and Sprinkle went there after returning Zimmerman to his office.

After hours of searching, a check for $10 was found, made out to the drug store, and signed by Virgel J. Bussenger, Jr.

"That must be it!" exclaimed the sergeant. "That's close to Ballinger or Barringer."

The check was drawn on the West Seattle branch of the Peoples Bank of Washington. There the detectives learned that Bussenger lived at 1608 East Republican Street.

Captain Rouse was immediately notified of the development. Within minutes he met his homicide aides at the address, an apartment building. After ringing Bussenger's number without a response, they summoned the manager, who told them he had seen the suspect and his wife drive away an hour before, apparently to shop.

He said Bussenger was a soldier stationed at Fort Lewis, 50 miles south and commuted in his car, a late model two-tone Chevrolet sedan. His current assignment was delivering milk to camp messhalls from 4 A.M. until 2 P.M. each day.

"Does he have a mustache?"

"He did. But when he came home yesterday afternoon, it was gone. When I asked him about it, he said he did a bad job of trimming it that morning and so he shaved it off."

As the officers were talking to the manager, the Bussengers drove up. The detectives approached, and Rouse asked the suspect if he were Bussenger.

"Yes," the man replied softly.

"We're police. We want you to come to Headquarters with us."

"I haven't had any tickets."

"It's not about traffic violations," declared Sprinkle.

When Mrs. Bussenger asked what the trouble was, the captain told her they would discuss it with her husband downtown.

In Rouse's office, the handsome and husky soldier, who appeared perfectly at ease, readily admitted becoming acquainted with Opal Montgomery in the tavern Wednesday afternoon. He explained that he had stopped there for some beer on his way home from camp.

His account of the happenings from then until he reached the pretty brunette's cottage checked with what the officers already knew.

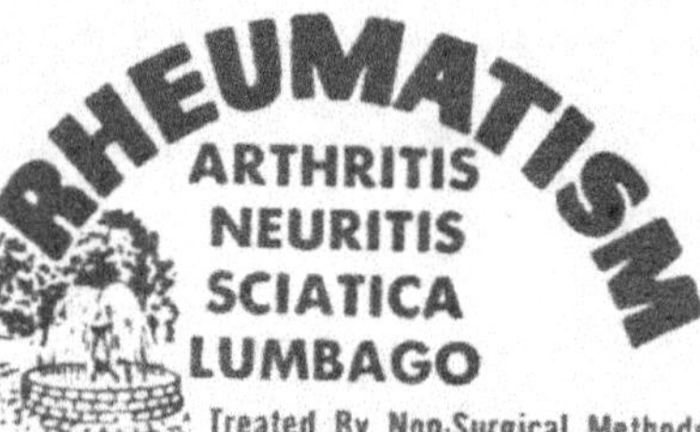

Treated By Non-Surgical Methods At Famous Health Resort

A greater variety of mineral waters here than any other place in the world

Rheumatism and its kindred diseases attack bodily functions and organs. When you take medicines for temporary relief of pain only you are ignoring nature's warning and permitting the cause of your condition to grow worse.

Resultful Treatments Available Now

The Excelsior Institute trustworthy and scientific treating methods are designed to correct the real underlying causes of your ailments and start the removal of those poisons in your system which are causing your suffering.

Revealing Free Illustrated Book

Our New FREE Book tells how thousands have been successfully treated in recent years. Write today. It may save you years of suffering. No obligation.

Non-Surgical Treatment of CHRONIC HEALTH DISORDERS

EXCELSIOR INSTITUTE, Dept. C7850, Excelsior Spgs., Mo.

PRAYER

is a Tremendous Mighty Power! Are you facing difficult Problems? Poor Health? Money or Job Troubles? Love or Family Troubles? Are you Worried about someone dear to you? Is someone dear to you Drinking too Much? Do you ever get Lonely—Unhappy—Discouraged? Would you like to have more Happiness, Success and "Good Fortune" in Life?

If you have any of these Problems, or others like them, dear friend, then here is wonderful NEWS—NEWS of a remarkable NEW WAY of PRAYER that is helping thousands to glorious NEW happiness and joy! Whether you believe in PRAYER or not, this remarkable NEW WAY may bring a whole NEW world of happiness and joy to you—and very, very quickly, too!

So don't wait, dear friend. You will surely bless this day—so please don't delay! Just clip this Message now and mail with your name, address & 3¢ stamp to LIFE-STUDY FELLOWSHIP, Box 6308, Noroton, Conn. We will rush this wonderful NEW Message of PRAYER and FAITH to you by AIR MAIL absolutely FREE!

Safe as America – U.S. Savings Bonds

EARN EXTRA CASH

MAKE 72% PROFIT

It's E-A-S-Y to sell our Copyrighted Employment Opportunities book. COMPLETE INFORMATION given on U. S. and Canadian Civil Service, Postal Service, U. S. Oil, Steamship, Mining and Construction companies, Airlines, Importers and Exporters, etc. Big Manufacturers Directory also. COMPLETE NAMES AND ADDRESSES of ALL FIRMS mentioned above included FREE!

Sells nationally at $3.50. Send $2.00 for sample copy, $9.00 for ½ dozen, or rush ONLY $12.50 FOR FULL DOZEN! WE PAY ALL SHIPPING CHARGES. If you act promptly, we'll include ONE FREE COPY with your first dozen order, so you'll make OVER 72% PROFIT on your first dozen! See our guarantee below. Write today to: Dept. 210, North-West Research Institute, South 11 Altamont Street, Spokane, Washington. Airmail reaches us in 24 hours.

YOU MUST BE COMPLETELY SATISFIED OR YOUR MONEY REFUNDED IN FULL.

Shrinks Hemorrhoids New Way Without Surgery

Science Finds Healing Substance That Relieves Pain—Shrinks Hemorrhoids

For the first time science has found a new healing substance with the astonishing ability to shrink hemorrhoids and to relieve pain – without surgery.

In case after case, while gently relieving pain, actual reduction (shrinkage) took place.

Most amazing of all – results were so thorough that sufferers made astonishing statements like "Piles have ceased to be a problem!"

The secret is a new healing substance (Bio-Dyne*)—discovery of a world-famous research institute.

This substance is now available in *suppository* or *ointment form* under the name *Preparation H.** Ask for it at all drug counters—money back guarantee. *Reg. U. S. Pat. Off

Fires 8 Rounds

An automatic full size model of a high powered "45" caliber automatic pistol that looks and feels just like the real thing and contains over 15 moving parts. Loads 8 complete rounds in the magazine clip which snaps into the hard butt just like an army "45". Then fires 8 bullet-like pellets as fast as you can pull the trigger. You've got to see the automatic slide action and feel the power to believe it! Great for shooting fun. This is the most authentic model gun we've ever seen.

Learn the Working Mechanism of a "45"

This accurate model of a high-powered, "45" comes to you disassembled with all the working parts of a "45". It assembles in a jiffy and full instructions are included so that in no time at all, you'll learn working parts of an automatic. Comes with instructions, full supply of pellets and man-sized silhouette target.

10 Day Free Trial

Try it for 10 days free. If you are not 100% delighted simply return after 10 days for prompt refund of full purchase price. Don't delay! Order now! Simply send $1 plus 25c shipping charge to:

HONOR HOUSE PRODUCTS DEPT. PP-6
Lynbrook, N. Y.

But the suspect insisted he hadn't entered her home, claiming he had left immediately after giving her the bottle of whisky.

He said he had driven back to camp for a few hours of sleep before doing his work, rather than going home so late and waking up his wife. When he got home Thursday afternoon, he explained he had been kept at the camp overnight.

The G.I. denied shaving off his mustache for fear it might lead to his apprehension.

No amount of questioning could change his story of complete innocence. Hoping to get definite proof that he had been inside the murdered girl's cottage, Sergeant Seth went to the crime lab to learn whether Sergeant Allison had found fingerprints on the paring knife taken from the victim's hand.

"Nothing but smudges," Allison reported. "The killer either was careful enough not to leave any good prints—or just plain lucky. If it was luck, he wouldn't know whether he left his prints or not. Why not make him think he did?"

"It's an idea," the sergeant said. "Let me have that knife."

Seth then burst back into the captain's office, an expression of victory on his face. Showing the knife to Rouse, he winked and said:

"Here's a real break, Skipper! There are two good prints on this. We can soon find out whether or not Bussenger handled it."

The captain went right along with it. "Good news, sergeant!" he asserted. "Get a technician in here and take Bussenger's prints."

When Seth returned with the aide, the soldier changed his tune. "You're right—I was in Opal's house,' he admitted. "But I didn't kill her. It was an accident."

With his words being wire-recorded, Bussenger gave this account of what had happened in the slain girl's cottage:

"We sipped two or three highballs and listened to the radio for a couple of hours. Opal was very friendly, so I started making love. She got mad and ordered me out. I told her she had no business inviting me in unless she wanted loving.

"She said she thought I was above that or she wouldn't have had anything to do with me. I figured she was playing hard to get, so I kept after her. She ran to the sink and grabbed up a knife. She came after me, and I tried to take it away from her. We wrestled around and fell on the bed.

"She quit fighting, so I pulled off her clothes. Then I saw she had been cut in several places and was bleeding. I rushed into the bathroom to get something to treat the wounds with. I grabbed a couple of medicine bottles and tried to stop the blood.

"She started groaning, so I took

one of her stockings and twisted it around her neck until she was quiet. Then I cleaned up and left. I thought she'd be OK by morning."

The detectives refused to accept Bussengers' story in view of the evidence, but they had to wait until the post mortem report before attempting to disprove it.

Late Saturday, Coroner John P. Brill, Jr. and his autopsy surgeon, Dr. Gale E. Wilson, revealed that the stab wound in Opal Montgomery's abdomen and the cuts on her breasts had been made *after* death.

Confronted with this damning evidence, the handsome soldier admitted he hadn't told the truth. He then made another official statement, in which he said that when the pretty brunette resisted his advances, he went wild and began tearing off her clothes.

When she screamed, he twisted one of her stockings around her neck until she was silent. Then, realizing she was dead, he got the paring knife from the sink, stabbed her several times and placed the weapon in her hand to make her death look like a suicide. He couldn't explain why he had dabbed her body with face powder and fingernail polish.

"That's closer to the truth," Captain Rouse told Bussenger, "but I don't think you've given us the entire story. The evidence convinces me that you mutilated the victim through sheer sadism. I'm also convinced that you strangled her to death for the same reason."

Although Bussenger heatedly denied any sadistic urges or premeditation of the murder, he was unable to explain his bestial acts. But the prosecuting attorney's staff realized it would be virtually impossible to prove premeditation, so the soldier was charged with second-degree murder. When being booked, he gave his age as 36, though he looked ten years younger.

So convinced was Captain Rouse that the suspect had slain pretty Opal Montgomery out of a sadistic drive, that the homicide chief conducted a thorough search into Bussenger's background. Eventually Rouse's opinion was substantiated by the revelation that some years previously Bussenger had choked a girl in Detroit, Michigan, until she was unconscious, then had covered her nude body with hair oil, just as he had used nail polish and face powder on Opal.

However, in the Detroit case, the victim recovered, and Bussenger somehow escaped prosecution. He joined the Army shortly thereafter and left that part of the country. Later he married.

In his trial in King County Superior Court in Seattle, his defense was "mental irresponsibility." But after hearing all the evidence, the jurors took only 90 minutes to find him guilty as charged.

On March 12, 1954, Judge Malcolm Douglas sentenced Bussenger to 30 years in the state penitentiary. The convicted murderer waived his right to appeal and requested immediate committment to prison.

EDITOR'S NOTE: *To protect persons innocently involved in this case, the names Marvin Sugg, Mr. and Mrs. Leonard Zimmerman, John Alfred Monner, and "Slim" Ferguson, are fictitious as used here.*

THE END

PRODIGAL SON

(continued from page 35)

side him, and began sliding from his chair. Courtroom attaches rushed to his aid, whereupon he began struggling and kicking violently until he was borne bodily from the courtroom by bailiffs and deputies assigned to the Tarrance trial.

Ten minutes later he was brought back, subdued and composed enough to apologize to the judge. "I'm sorry for all the disturbance I've caused the court," he said contritely.

Promptly, Leonard's attorney, Sandy Paniello, informed the jury that the accused's behavior was "the result of a human body under strain."

But the prosecutor scoffed. He called it "a shameful show."

The jury needed only two-and-a-half hours to find Leonard guilty as charged and he, like his dad, was sentenced to death.

And so father and son were together again. When they were taken to the Kentucky State Penitentiary at Eddyville, at their urgent request they were permitted to occupy the same cell. They were separated, however, in February, 1954.

During the ensuing two years after conviction and sentence, Attorney Paniello won repeated stays for the slayers of Francis McCormack, while Leonard taught his theretofore–illiterate father to read.

At last, when Paniello had exhausted every legal means and technicality to save his clients, father and son came to the brink on March 18th, 1955.

Roy Tarrance was the first to go. He went to the chair mumbling the Lord's Prayer.

A few minutes later, the son followed.

So today, the inseparable Tarrances, father and son, are together again in death.

There are those in Kentucky who would say their reunion must have taken place in Hell . . .

THE END

If you can use a pencil you can use a slide rule

For bookkeepers, accountants, salesmen (figuring commissions, cost, etc.), farmers, housewives, etc. For Armed Forces highly important. Men's most useful too. Easy to calculate instantly. Multiplying, proportions, divisions, extracting roots, etc. "High Vision" Clear View Slide. Full 10" Rule. A, B, C, D, C1 and K scales. FREE 28-page instruction book on how to get correct answers instantly without pencil or paper.

LARCH, 118 E. 28, DEPT. -V, New York 16

Free Book on Arthritis And Rheumatism

HOW TO AVOID CRIPPLING DEFORMITIES

An amazing newly enlarged 36-page book entitled "Arthritis-Rheumatism" will be sent free to anyone who will write for it.

It reveals why drugs and medicines give only temporary relief and fail to remove the causes of the trouble; explains a specialized non-surgical, non-medical treatment which has proven successful since 1919.

You incur no obligation in sending for this instructive book. It may be the means of saving you years of untold misery. Write today to The Ball Clinic, DEPT. 658 Excelsior Springs, Missouri.

Get GENUINE DIAMONDS

from New York's Leading Diamond Specialist

SAVE up to 50% And More

LIBERAL CREDIT TERMS TOO! 12 FULL MONTHS TO PAY. . . ONLY 10% DOWN
FREE CATALOG WITH YOUR BONDED GUARANTEE
VALUABLE ADVICE AND 10 DAY APPROVAL OFFER!

● NOW enjoy the thrilling excitement of owning genuine diamonds you have been waiting for at a bargain price. Kaskel's, New York's leading diamond specialist established in 1882, wants you to see his offers before you buy. You save up to 50% and more with this direct plan. You don't risk a single penny. You take no risk whatsoever because Kaskel's money back guarantee, if not satisfied, protects you 100%. You are furnished with a written, sworn bond that is actually notarized and sent to you with your selection. Here you have unmatchable bargains that defy competition. Here you have a choice of many types of brand new, artistic mountings in 14 Kt. gold or platinum. Kaskel's lay-away plan permits you to secure any size genuine diamond regardless of your income. Diamonds are acknowledged to be as good as money in the bank and when you buy them at Kaskel's low, low prices you have rich enjoyment, pleasure and protection all in one.

DIAMOND BARGAINS in Brand New 14 Kt. Gold Settings Like These Are Included!

These pictures give you an idea of the beautiful, brand new, 14 Kt. gold and platinum mountings for the first grade genuine diamonds Kaskel's offers you. Hundreds of diamond bargains to select from . . . they include diamond rings, diamond pins, diamond watches, diamond earrings, diamond bracelets . . . can be yours for $25. up to $5,000.

CASH or CREDIT. . . as you prefer

Send for FREE CATALOG of Bargains. . .NO OBLIGATION

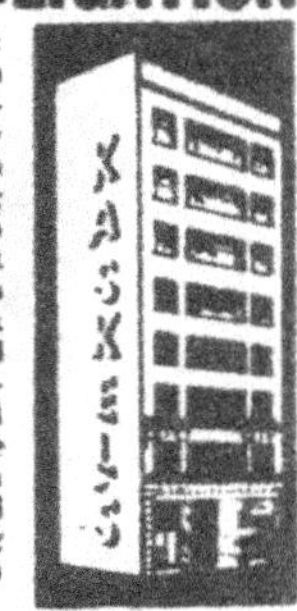

Send today for our big illustrated catalog just off the press. It is yours just for the asking and without obligation. It is not only crammed from cover to cover with the most exquisite and exciting settings you ever laid your eyes on . . . but it also contains important advice about diamonds that is priceless. You are also told about Kaskel's special lay-away plan and full details about the 100% protective money back guarantee and sworn written bond. Get these facts. They are free! Just sign your name to the coupon below and receive the most surprising catalog of diamonds you ever saw by return postpaid mail.

Our references: Your own bank or any mercantile agency.

KASKEL'S, Dept. 738-E
41 West 57th St., New York 19, N.Y.

Send me absolutely free, by return postpaid mail and without obligation, a copy of your big free catalog of genuine diamond bargains. Also send me the free advice about diamonds and the Kaskel plan. (No salesman will call.)

NAME ....

ADDRESS ....

CITY .... STATE ....

NOISY RADIO?

Distorted T.V. Picture?

Simple CLEARTONE plug-in condenser instantly filters humming, buzzing, noisy sounds and picture-distorting electric line interference at source. Only **$1**

On-Approval Money Back Trial Offer

No matter what make or model radio or T.V. set you have . . . old or new . . . when vacuum cleaners, electric hair dryers, furnace blowers, elevators, electric shavers and many other appliances and electric machines on the line spoil radio and T.V. enjoyment by creating disturbing sounds and noises and by streaking and distorting T.V. pictures, send for amazing CLEARTONE. So simple anyone can do it, you just plug cord from the appliance creating the disturbance into CLEARTONE CONDENSER . . . then plug CLEARTONE into wall socket. Or plug cord from radio or T.V. set into Cleartone and plug Cleartone into wall socket . . . see which works better. Filters both A.C. and D.C. current. Over 2½ million sold to Radio and T.V. Set Owners.

TRY 10 DAYS AT OUR RISK

If not delighted return for purchase price refund. Only $1 . . . 3 for $2.50 . . . 6 for $4 . . . 12 for $6.00. If C.O.D. postage extra. Cash orders add 25c and we ship postage paid. Don't put up with noisy radio or distorted T.V. pictures without first making CLEARTONE 10 day test. Rush order today.

Rapid Specialties Co., Dept. SE-1820 Grand Rapids 2, Michigan

EXCITING *LOVE NOVELS*

Originally these books sold for $2.00 and more each. Each book complete—packed with romance, passion and excitement. Now you can buy a complete season's reading pleasure of these popular, paper-bound books for less than cost of one regular novel.

Now Offered At These Special Prices:
4 for $1.00 | 12 for $2.75
8 for $2.00 | 23 for $5.00

1. A Little Sin
2. Beautiful Body
3. Dangerous Loves
4. Dance Hall Girl
5. French Model
6. Love Cheat
7. Love On Call
8. Love at a Price
9. Lust for Love
10. Loose Ladies
11. Made for Love
12. Pick-Up Girl
13. Reckless Girl
14. Resort Hostess
15. Raw Passion
16. Scandalous Affair
17. Seventh Wife
18. Street of Sin
19. Shameless Woman
20. Torrid Love
21. Unwilling Virgin
22. Wanton Blonde
23. Wayward Girl

PADELL BOOK CO., Dept. SMG-5
208 E. 46th Street, N.Y. 17, N.Y.
Please send me the books whose numbers I have circled below. I enclose $ in payment.
1 2 3 4 5 6 7 8 9 10
11 12 13 14 15 16 17 18 19 20
21 22 23
Name
Address
City State
check here—
☐ If you want books to be sent c.o.d. plus postage and c.o.d. fees, which amount to at least 48c above cost of books.

Don't *ENVY* the "Lucky" Fisherman...*Be One!*

Penetrates Water Up to 75 Feet to LURE FISH TO YOUR BAIT BY SMELL!

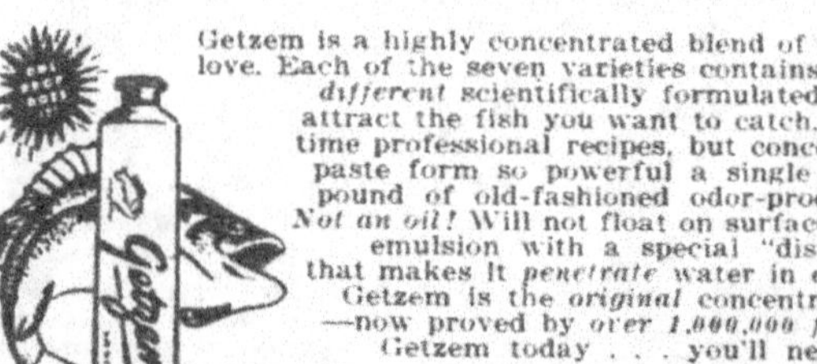

Getzem is a highly concentrated blend of food odors fish love. Each of the seven varieties contains from 17 to 34 *different* scientifically formulated ingredients to attract the fish you want to catch. Based on old-time professional recipes, but concentrated into a paste form so powerful a single drop equals a pound of old-fashioned odor-producing recipes. *Not an oil!* Will not float on surface. Getzem is an emulsion with a special "dispersion" agent that makes it *penetrate* water in *every* direction. Getzem is the *original* concentrated bait odor—now proved by *over 1,000,000 fishermen!* Try Getzem today . . . you'll never go fishing without it!

$1.00 TUBE **3 for $2.50**

tube catches dozens of fish. Only $1. (3 for $2.50.) Indicate odor: Trout, cat, carp. Fresh water, salmon, salt water, ice fishing. Postpaid except C.O.D.'s.
NORKIN LABORATORIES Dept. BD-87N
809 Wyandotte St. Kansas City, Mo.

Tiger Woman's Sweet Revenge

(continued from page 16)

not found in law books. She fell for him, and issued her own writ of *habeas corpus*. Within a week after they met, they were married.

The road to disillusionment was somewhat—but not much—longer. First, she discovered that his title was phony. And then, that he was. And he became violently nauseous at the mere mention of work. He considered Wanda the ideal bread-winner. But worst of all, he got her on morphine; a habit that she was to find more binding by far than the promises of Godfrey Barrington.

She met Barrington at a studio party of so-called Bohemians on Chicago's North Side. By then, she had renounced the Count.

Barrington appeared to be his complete antithesis: kindly as her father, interested in her career, catering to her every whim. What she failed to detect was the frustrated *avante-garde* artist, constantly apologizing for his phenomenal commercial success; the pretentious arty faddist who, despite an extremely acceptable wife, maintained a constant round-robin of affairs with women half his age. His wife, Susan Jerome Barrington, was a gifted cellist, who, it was rumored, "understood" her misunderstood" spouse because she had a perfectly blended affair of her own on the side with a young composer of unpublished operas. She was perennially about to divorce Barrington but, somehow, never did.

Soon, he and Wanda were accepted as an inseparable twosome. He bragged that she was the brainiest woman he had ever met, and neither was ever invited anywhere without the other. Susan treated her with generous, good-natured hospitality, and no one else gave a damn.

By now, Wanda had divorced the Count. It was her understanding that Barrington was divorcing Susan so that they would be married.

To her dismay and annoyance, she discovered not only that neither Barry nor his wife had instituted divorce proceedings, but that both still shared the same bedroom.

Far more disheartening to Wanda, she learned that her tender lover had gone through this cycle of extramarital romance many times previous. That when the ladies demanded to know his ultimate intentions, he always pleaded *nolo contendere* and figuratively retreated behind his wife. Wanda was lawyer enough to know that this barrier was legally, morally and socially impeccable. But as time, plus her continued obsession for Godfrey Barrington and the ravages of morphine wore on her, her sharp legal mind lost its focus. She could only think that Susan Jerome Barrington refused to give her husband a divorce. She took a leave of absence from her job in the United States attorney's office and went to Detroit, being careful first to let it be known to Godfrey Barrington that she was reconciling with her husband. Actually, she had no idea where the Count was, and didn't care.

Barrington stood it for three months. Every time he thought of her in the arms of the Count, he went nuts. Finally, he caught the first train to Detroit, and brought her back to Chicago.

By now, she was too far gone to seriously practice law. Morphine had damaged her mental processes. She was rapidly becoming incapable of supporting herself and, for the first time, Godfrey Barrington had to give her an allowance, to keep her as a paid mistress.

But in the dark, warped recesses of her troubled mind, she continued to blame all her woes on Mrs. Barrington. She wrote her letters, threatening her for refusing to give her husband a divorce, and demanding a showdown. It came at a conference with Barry and Susan.

Susan Jerome Barrington turned to her husband and inquired, "Do you wish a divorce, Barry?"

Barrington dropped his eyes. He turned to his wife. "Yes," he lied.

"And do you want to marry Wanda?"

This, in the presence of a witness, even his wife, was too much. For the first time in his life he told the truth to a woman. "No," he said.

Wanda screamed and lunged at Barrington's wife, her fingernails extended.

Barrington got between them, held her off from the older woman, and finally quieted her

He was full of soulful sentiments and pious regrets, but it all added up to his refusal to divorce his wife.

Nor did he suggest they continue their affair. But he did suggest an alternative.

"My dear," he began again. "Get away from the morphine, and from me. Go away where you can forget. Go to New York."

He offered to send her $150 a month till she could get a job and support herself. But subtly, he made it clear that if she stayed in Chicago he would give her nothing.

At the moment, the idea was not wholly unattractive to Wanda. She had always firmly believed that her talents, brains, beauty and charm were worthy of no less than the Big Town. Though she would not see Barry, she might meet someone else. And since she had absolutely no money and her former devoted lover left her no choice, she

DO YOU WANT POWER?
Power to make you victorious in all you undertake? Power to make people admire you? Power to earn money? Power to gain popularity—love? Power to make anyone follow you? I will send you information which is the result of scientific research. This information and directions will help you become more masterful and exert greater influence. You will be able to break prevailing misconceptions. IF YOU ARE NOT DELIGHTED, YOUR MONEY IMMEDIATELY REFUNDED. Just send your name and address. Pay on delivery $2.00 plus postage or send $2.00 cash or money order and I will pay postage.
FREE with every order: Talismanic Seal of Luck in blood-red ink on Egyptian mottled parchment.
SECULAR PRODUCTS, DEPT. 132-D
504 HICKSVILLE RD., MASSAPEQUA, N. Y.

EASIER WAY
Tints Hair
NATURAL-LIKE
Imagine—a remarkable TINTZ Shampoo in bar shape which colors hair as it washes out oil, dirt and loose dandruff. Dull, streaked or graying hair loses its drabness and gains new youthfulness, glamour and allure. Nothing like it on the market. It's old-fashioned to look mature. Today—get a bar of TINTZ. Glamourize—revitalize. TINTZ "Bar" Shampoo tints hair gradually—each application adds color, tone and sparkle. NO DYED LOOK. Won't hurt permanents. Full size cake only 50c—2 for $1.00 plus tax. Comes in Black, Dark Brown, Medium Brown, Light Brown, Auburn, Henna, and Blonde. Try it today on the guarantee of satisfaction or money back.
TRY AT OUR RISK. Just mail name, address and shade wanted with 50c for 1 bar or $1.00 for 2 bars, tax incl. We pay postage. Sorry no C.O.D.
TINTZ CO., DEPT. 426, 230 N. Michigan, Chicago 1, Ill.

help your heart fund

Get ORDERS and CASH from your mailmen—do work in SPARE TIME at home—or expand into FULL TIME business. Send coupon for Free facts about the newest and most fascinating of all home operated businesses. For the first time a simplified machine brings the fabulous profits of Plastic Sealing and Plastic Laminating within the reach of the small operator. Anyone can learn to operate the machine with a few minutes practice—then with our Magic Mail Plan can get mail orders pouring in daily with cash in every envelope. No canvassing—no selling. We even supply the circulars you mail to bring back cash and orders. Don't waste a minute. Rush your name. We'll send you FREE and postpaid pictures, prices, details, and all the facts you need to start. Mail coupon or send name on postcard. No charge.
WARNER ELECTRIC CO.
1512 Jarvis Av., Dept. L-79-J Chicago 26, Ill.

THIS MAN.. . . . is taking out of the machine a Plastic Sealing Job — ordered by mail—only 11c in material cost brings back $2.58 in cash by mail. Capacity of machine: $25.00 profit per hour of operation.

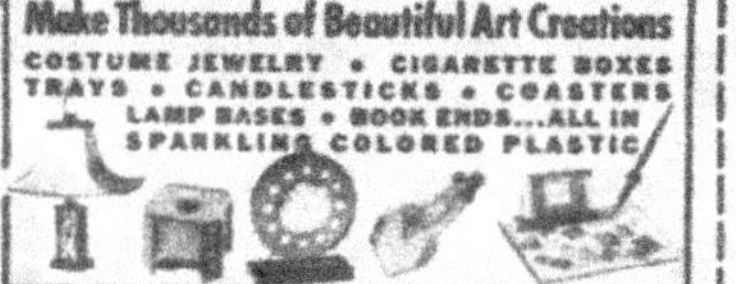

WARNER ELECTRIC CO., 1512 Jarvis Av.
DEPT. L-79-J, Chicago 26, Ill.
At no cost to me, please rush complete details postage prepaid. I am under no obligation.
Name
Address
City Zone State

LEARN **PLASTICS**

Complete LOW COST Shop Method
HOME TRAINING NOW AVAILABLE

Get in on Big Money opportunities in Plastic molding, casting, forming, carving, etc. Earn as you learn with Interstate's professionally prepared course. All plastic materials furnished.

WRITE FOR FREE BOOKLET **INTERSTATE TRAINING SERVICE** DEPT. C39 , PORTLAND 13, OREGON

HIGH SCHOOL DIPLOMA

You can earn a High School Diploma in your own home! Prepare yourself for a better job and more pay. Study in your spare time . . . No classes . . . all materials furnished. Certified teachers. Valuable diploma awarded.

WRITE TODAY FOR COMPLETE INFORMATION

SOUTHERN STATES ACADEMY
Box 144XK Sta. E, Atlanta, Georgia

FREE LESSON SAMPLE

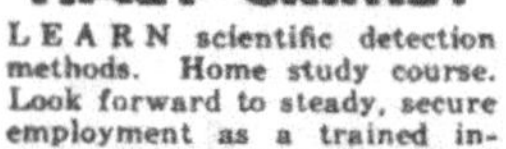

OUR 25th YEAR

LEARN HOW TO
HALT CRIME!

LEARN scientific detection methods. Home study course. Look forward to steady, secure employment as a trained investigator. Developed by former Federal Agent and Naval Intelligence official, reveals latest methods of detecting violations quickly, surely. Write today for free book & lesson sample. Special low rates now.

International Detective Training School
1701 Monroe St., N.E., DEPT. B-78, Washington 18, D.C.

SECRETS of the PSALMS

"Through a pious life and by a rational use of the Psalms, you may obtain the grace of God, the favor of Princes, and the Love of your fellow man." says the author.

Here are some of the amazing things he tells you about: Psalm to receive Instruction or Information through a Dream or Vision. Psalm to escape danger. Psalm to become safe from Enemies. Psalm to receive GOOD after committing a heavy sin. Psalm to make you fortunate in everything you try to do. Psalm to free yourself from Evil Spirits. Psalm to make peace between Man and Wife.

MIDGET BIBLE FREE

Now you can carry the Bible with you at all times. (Smallest Bible in the World.) Many people feel that this is of great value in obtaining things you desire.

SEND NO MONEY. Just send your name and address Today and pay postman only $1.49 plus postage on delivery. I positively GUARANTEE that you will be more than delighted within 5 days or your money will be returned promptly on request. Order now.

LARCH, 118 E. 28th, Dept. 545-K , New York 16

DANCE to ROMANCE

LEARN TO DANCE IN ONLY 1 WEEK

Become An Expert Dancer in Just Minutes a Day!

Yes! You Dance a New Step Each Evening for 7 Days or

DOUBLE YOUR MONEY BACK!

This new speed-method makes learning to dance so simple, quick and easy — you will amaze your friends in one single week! You'll be able to say "good-bye" to loneliness and "hello" to fun and romance. Of course, if you enjoy being a wallflower this easy, quick, self-teaching method is not for you. But, if you want to get out of your rut and start living — send for this Complete Dance Instruction Course on our DOUBLE YOUR MONEY BACK GUARANTEE! You have nothing to lose, and popularity and good times to gain, so act now! For your promptness, we include without extra charge, a wonderful book of Square Dances.

A picture of a dancing couple shows you each step and movement; easy follow-the-footprint drawings for every step of each complete dance. Simple-to-read instructions. All together, this new speed-method makes it easy and quick to learn to dance.

NOW— Start to DANCE Your Way to ROMANCE!

FOX-TROT RHUMBA SAMBA CONGA SQUARE DANCES WALTZ LINDY TANGO JITTERBUG

BE POPULAR . . . GET MORE FUN OUT OF LIFE

The good dancers have the best times . . . get the most invitations. Here's your chance to own this new, complete, Short-Cut Course to expert dancing. And, DOUBLE YOUR MONEY BACK if it isn't everything we say it is. The bonus book of Square Dances is yours.

COMPLETE COURSE of DANCE INSTRUCTION ONLY 1.98

BONUS for PROMPTNESS

DOUBLE YOUR MONEY BACK GUARANTEE!

You must learn to dance, in the privacy of ygur own home, in 7 days, or you may return the Complete Course of Dance Instruction for immediate refund of double your purchase price. The Bonus Book of Square Dances is yours to keep.
PICKWICK CO.
Box 463, Midtown Sta., New York 18, N. Y.

MAIL DOUBLE REFUND COUPON NOW!

PICKWICK CO., DEPT. 910-A
Box 463, Midtown Sta., New York 18, N. Y.

Send, at once, the Complete Course of Dance Instruction. For my promptness, include the Book of Square Dances. On delivery, will pay postman just $1.98 plus postage. If not delighted and thrilled within 7 days, may return the Dance Course for REFUND OF DOUBLE THE PURCHASE PRICE. The Book of Square Dances is mine to keep.

Name ....
Address ....
City .... Zone .... State ....

☐ SAVE MONEY: Send payment now, and we pay the 48c postage. No APO, FPO, or Foreign C.O.D.'s.

took the first $150 and departed for New York.

Quite characteristically, she settled in Greenwich Village; not realizing perhaps that there she would meet the same type of people and be drawn into the same type of life that she should avoid. She did make one start in the right direction by taking a job; in fact, she took several jobs simultaneously, apparently plunging into work in the belief she could forget her troubles.

From 9 to 5 she worked for the legal firm of Joseph P. Tumulty, noted former associate of Woodrow Wilson, and was able to make herself valuable. Partly to keep from thinking about Barry, partially to avoid morphine, and partly to fatten even further her now considerable income—for she continued to accept Barry's money without telling him she was working—she also worked nights helping to compile and edit a legal textbook.

And as if this were not enough she decided to become a writer, enrolling in a course in short story writing. She began to grind out plotless, subjective soul searchings for the literary quarterlies and other *avante garde* publications, all of which were speedily rejected.

Perhaps her sudden, hitherto undiscovered urge to express herself in immortal literature was derived from her new-found associates. She now was caught up in a whirl of the *literati* who disdained to prostitute their talent, if any, in commercial popular writing. But they were people with mnay interesting and advanced ideas that they never hesitated to spout in payment for imported Russian caviar, champagne and gin that Wanda ladled out at her parties.

She became famous throughout the Village as an open-handed, generous hostess. She met and frequently held brief, passing affairs, with a multitude of men. But none claimed her emotions as Barry. She thought none as charming as he, nor as able a lover. She could not forget him, and soon she was writing him regularly, though he rarely answered.

Soon she was lost again, entrapped by the mental image of her faraway lover. And again, she took to morphine.

She lost both her jobs and forgot about trying to write. She wandered sleepless nights through the Village streets, miraged with hallucinations of Barry. Finally with her pride and almost all her money gone, there remained not love for Barry but her obsession with love. She sat down and wrote him one more dreamy, unrealistic letter. It read:

> *I sincerely wish for your success and happiness more than anything and I feel that*

my attachment for you has become a sort of millstone around your neck; that you never intended it to reach the hectic state that it has. That is my fault. I am exceptionally romantic and you are romantic to me.

I know you love me but it is not a deep, integral part of yourself. You have not found yourself in love any more than you have in art; and I feel that my love for you is a real drawback to your finding yourself in art.

If I have known you so intimately for two years without being of assistance, but instead a bad influence, then my withdrawal should have the opposite effect. Therefore, I am withdrawing, and I am doing it in no halfway fashion this time, my dear. Go on with your little love affairs, if you like, without thought of what it may be doing to me. Only consider me as a friend.

Once a week I will go to your little house, put it in order, bring out your laundry, which I will have sent out, and on its return I will look over the clothes and mend them as may be necessary, replacing them in their proper drawers at some time not during your working hours.

At no time during the week, except on Saturday, when I shall change your linen and clean house for you, will I intrude upon you. I promise, however, to hold myself in readiness to come to you whenever you may wish.

Wanda never received a reply to her letter.

Illogically, she continued to blame Susan for all her troubles. At this time she kept a diary, in which she now ominously noted, "Paid Nick $250 for impregnated candy." She sent the box of chocolate creams to Susan and Barry.

But before mailing she extracted one, held it to await the news that the Barringtons had eaten theirs. Then she would eat hers, for each contained potassium of cyanide.

But it was Barry who opened the box. Although there was no return address, it was postmarked New York. He readily guessed who had sent it—and for what purpose. Fearing a public scandal, he threw Wanda's $250 box of chocolates into the garbage pail, and told his wife.

For the first time in her married life, Susan Barrington was afraid of another woman. She fully realized the deadly danger of Wanda's desperation. But she acceded to his wishes, and said nothing to anyone.

Wanda, failing to hear of the Bar-

Amazing Low Cost Precision Instrument Checks All TV And Radio Tubes!

MAKE MONEY! SAVE MONEY
Amazing ALL-PURPOSE-TESTER

SAVE DIRECT FROM MFGR. Reg. $7.95 Value only 4.95

TESTS ALL TV & RADIO TUBES

TEST and REPAIR | TV & RADIO SETS | APPLIANCES TOASTERS — LAMPS IRONS — BROILERS FANS — HEATERS ETC. | AUTO ELECTRICAL CIRCUITS & PARTS | MOTORS WIRING FUSES

PAYS FOR ITSELF THE FIRST TIME YOU USE IT!

Now you can own a precision instrument tester that will save you money and make you money! Your repair bills for TV, Radio, Appliances, Auto circuits and parts . . . will be cut down 90%! You'll earn extra money in your spare time, doing these repairs for your friends, neighbors, and customers. All-Purpose-Tester will pay for itself the first time you use it. You can make from $50 to $100 a week alone on TV repairs. Over 85% of TV & Radio troubles are due to bad tubes. You can now test these tubes in a jiffy and locate the trouble! We'll also tell you how to buy the TV & Radio tubes, at the wholesale price!

A COMPLETE TUBE AND ELECTRICAL TESTER FOR ONLY $4.95

COMPLETE WITH
- ★ 5 special sockets that take 4000 types of TV & Radio Tubes (including picture tube.)
- ★ Neon Test Indicator.
- ★ Two 16 inch test probes.
- ★ Cord Set.
- ★ Internal precision electronic components assembled, in a beautiful steel case. READY TO USE.

FREE BONUS

Order today, and at no extra charge, you will receive bonus listing of TV & Radio Tubes and parts, that permits you to buy wholesale. Once again you both save money and make money!

SIMPLE TO USE NO EXPERIENCE NEEDED

This is a professional model which anyone can operate. You simply plug the extension cord in to any outlet AC or DC, and for TV or Radio tubes, you just insert the tube into one of 5 special sockets provided. If the tube is good the All-Purpose-Tester Neon Indicator lights. If the Neon Indicator doesn't light, the tube is bad! That's all there is to it! And these special five sockets will take any one of 4000 tube types made, including the big TV Picture Tube!

A special pair of test probes are provided for testing appliances, toasters, irons, fans, outlets, auto wiring, capacitors, spark plugs, motors, electric circuits, and 1001 other electric devices. You follow simple instructions. Instantly the Neon Light Indicator gives you the answer!

FREE TRIAL

TUBE WHOLESALERS CO. DEPT. RP-8
31 West 47th St., New York 36, N. Y.

Please rush me my amazing "All-Purpose-Tester." I may use it for 30 days and if not completely satisfied I can return it for a full refund. Enclosed find $4.95 (plus 50¢ for handling charges). Be sure to send me my Free Bonus!

NAME ______ PLEASE PRINT
ADDRESS ______
CITY ______ STATE ______

EXCITING COURSE REVEALS NEW BUST CONTOUR METHODS

COVER GIRLS — MOVIE STARS — MODELS — GLAMOUR GIRLS — WOMEN IN ALL WALKS OF LIFE . . . HERE'S HOW YOU MAY BE ABLE TO DEVELOP A GLAMOROUS BUST CONTOUR!

• Yes, it is the woman with a beautiful alluring bust contour who most often wins the admiration, popularity and affection every woman desires. And there can be no complete feminine beauty without a warmly rounded, lovely bust contour, symbol of woman eternal. Look through history, look around you today . . . it is the woman with the graceful, appealing figure lines who enjoys social and romantic triumph. Yes, as often happens, wit, charm and friendliness fall by the wayside when competing with the natural law of man's attraction to beauty fulfilled completely.

52 Features and Contour Techniques,
128 Photographs, Charts and Pictures

THE BONOMO RITUAL for Beautifying the Bust Contour is aimed to help those with unsatisfactory Bust Contours who, through prescribed exercise, diet, correct posture and support, may be able to improve the handicap of un-appealing figure lines. Improved, fully revised, the BONOMO RITUAL, through the simple Photo-Instructor Method, shows how to apply, in the privacy of your home, the prescribed techniques which may mean the difference between loneliness and thrilling, romantic fulfillment! This course, complete in book form, is yours for the special offer price of — only $1.00!

formerly $2.00 SPECIAL OFFER PRICE ONLY $1.00

Money-Back Guarantee! Don't let skepticism or discouragement deny you the opportunity for happiness. Fill in the coupon below and mail with your remittance today. If after 30 days, you are not satisfied — for any reason — return the course for a full refund. But don't delay. Be fair to yourself — to your future as a woman. Send for your copy NOW!

IN PLAIN PACKAGE

PARTIAL LIST OF CONTENTS

This is Joe Bonomo Speaking (A heart-to-heart talk with the Author.) Bust Contour . . . Know Yourself . . . Structure and Function of the Breast . . . Four Types of Breasts . . . Muscles for Support . . . With the Stars of Stage and Screen . . . Secrets of Allure . . . The Commandments of Loveliness . . . The ABC's of Brassieres . . . Other Methods of Bust Control . . . Creams, Lotions, and Massage . . . Plastic Surgery . . . The Worshipper and the Supporter . . . The Rounder and the Latissimus Dorsi . . . The Pectorals and the Chesters . . . Ritual (First to Third Day) . . . Ritual (Fourth to Sixth Day) . . . Caloric Diets

INTIMATE BOOKS CO. Dept. SKM
1841 Broadway, New York 23, N. Y.

INTIMATE BOOKS CO. DEPT. SKM
1841 Broadway
New York 23, N. Y.

Please send the BONOMO RITUAL, in plain wrapper, by return mail. (Special price: $1.00) Enclosed is my ☐ check ☐ money order ☐ cash. You pay postage. It is understood that after 30 days, if I am not satisfied for any reason, I may return the course for full refund.

name ______ (Please print plainly)
address ______
city ______ zone ______ state ______

(Canada and Foreign—$1.25 cash in advance. Same 30-day return privilege applies.)

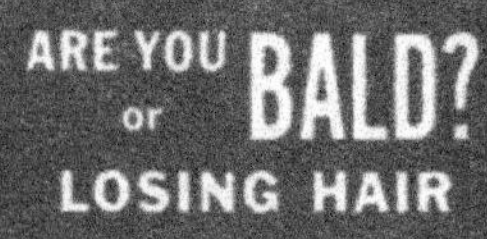

BEFORE

Today you have new hope for hair regrowth for it has been proved that, even though you are bald, the hair roots may still be alive to produce new hairs. Thousands *have accomplished this* with the amazing Brandenfels System. See "before" and "after" pictures at left! Write now for full FREE information!

AFTER

Carl Brandenfels
BOX 7X21 St. Helens, Oregon

ringtons' death by poison, and realizing that her plans had gone astray, felt an overpowering, manic urge to satisfy her own ego, to achieve at least a partial triumph by gloating over her deed. She wrote Barry, "It is quite fitting that I should send poisoned sweets to the man who has ruined my life with poisoned sweetness."

Barry's failure to answer her, even to reproach her, or to show fear by threatening to go to the police, goaded her to even greater fury. She wrote, saying that she was coming to Chicago for a final showdown. When he again refused to answer, she tried to phone him. He refused to accept the call. It was then that Wanda made her decision.

She issued invitations to all her acquaintances in the Village to one last, grand party; a "giveaway" party she called it, because she planned to give away all of her possessions.

Someone finally thought to inquire of her why this sudden, unprecedented generosity; why she was giving away all she owned.

She replied, "I'm leaving for Chicago in the morning. I've got unfinished business coming due. I have to kill a woman—and maybe a man, too." Everybody laughed uproariously.

The next morning, Wanda awoke with a splitting headache. She lay in her bed, the last remaining piece in the apartment, trying to recollect how much she had told; half hoping, half fearing that somebody might have notified the police. She fumbled under her pillow and, reassured by the cold steel of the .38 automatic she had purchased the day before, she stumbled into the bathroom, vomited and took a cold shower. She dressed, reached Grand Central, and boarded the *20th Century Limited.*

Outside the station in Chicago, at 7 A.M. Thursday morning, she engaged an ancient taxicab. Though she had not chosen the aged touring car with black window curtains deliberately, Fate could not have been more kind. For nobody could see into the cab and the driver had that very day lost his rear license plate.

Since Wanda last had been in Chicago, the Godfrey Barringtons had moved. They had rented a rambling, clapboard house on 89th Street in Palos Park, far out in the suburbs. Wanda had learned the address and so directed the taxi driver.

Henry Manning had left the Barringtons just 10 minutes before. Manning had been their man-of-all work for many years and knew all about Wanda, and the affair. Throughout it, he had remained devoted to Barry and Susan.

Barry was at work at the studio in the city. Susan was alone in the house in Palos Park, in bed and seri-

There is an art in knowing how to gain love and affection. How to hold it so that happiness can last for a lifetime. Here within the pages of TRUE LOVE GUIDE you can discover — from the experience of successful lovers—many proven ways to find and hold a mate. You get secrets of technique . . . confidential information on how to avoid heartbreaking mistakes. All in simple, easy-to-understand language. TRUE LOVE GUIDE — which can be so vital to your personal happiness — is yours at the low, low price of $1.98 on 5-day free examination. Act promptly and we send you FREE of extra charge the ART OF KISSING and MODERN LOVE LETTERS. Remember, you can woo and win . . . if you know how!

TRUE LOVE guide

ONLY $1.98

PLUS THESE 2 VALUABLE FACT-PACKED BOOKS FREE OF EXTRA CHARGE

1. ART OF KISSING
The greatest lovers of all times agree that correct kissing is one of the most important steps in wooing and winning. To master this art is to enjoy life. "The Art of Kissing" explains and discusses 23 kinds of kisses.

MODERN LOVE LETTERS

2. MODERN LOVE LETTERS
Complete instructions for writing letters on love, courtship, and marriage. 47 effective model letters for any situation, together with poems and thoughts of love which you will find very helpful in your correspondence.

RUSH THIS FREE-TRIAL COUPON!

PICKWICK CO. Dept. 734-A
Box 463, Midtown Sta., New York 18, N. Y.

Rush TRUE LOVE GUIDE plus the Art of Kissing and Modern Love Letters to me in plain wrapper. I enclose $.......... (cash or money-order). If not completely delighted, can return the 3 books within 5 days for prompt refund of purchase price.

Name....................
Address....................
City....................State..........

( ) If C.O.D. preferred, mark X in box, mail coupon and pay postman $1.98 plus postage. Canadian orders 20% additional — cash with order.

No C.O.D. to APO, FPO, or outside Continental U. S. A.

ously ill with influenza. Manning had left the house in search of a locol girl who had promised to sit with her while he shopped for groceries. A registered nurse had been engaged to arrive late that day.

Thus Susan Barrington was alone and ill with a high fever when Wanda arrived. The girl told the driver to wait for her and, firmly grasping her pocketbook containing the gun, skittered up the front porch steps and rang the doorbell. Only a woman who was tending the front garden saw her.

Susan Barrington believed it was the local girl sent by Manning, and wrapped herself in a woolen dressing gown and answered the door.

"Why, Wanda," she said, surprised. "What are you doing here?" Then her fever-flushed face went deadly white with fear; she knew.

Wanda pushed her way in through the door. Susan, without knowing that the girl had a gun, realized that she was in deadly peril. In her present condition she would be unable to defend herself. Her only hope lay in gaining Wanda's sympathy, and she quickly lied. "I may die," she said. "I've got pneumonia." And she retreated back to her bedroom, and climbed into bed. Wanda followed her, laughing and warned, "You're going to die, anyhow."

But the girl was in no hurry. She wanted this woman to suffer, to know the slow, growing chill of terror; to grovel and beg tearfully for her life. Then she'd kill her.

It was a heady experience for Wanda, too precious to waste. She thrilled to its sweet power, indulged herself in the luxury of a long, rambling recital of all the wrongs committed against her.

Since Wanda had entered the house the woman in the flower garden, Susan's neighbor, had gone downtown. She met Henry Manning still looking for the local girl to sit with Mrs. Barrington.

"I suppose then it must be the nurse who came," she told Manning after mentioning the young woman she had seen.

Manning grew excited, asked, "What did she look like?" And before the neighbor could finish describing her, he rushed off toward the Barrington home. He knew now who had come. And why.

Meanwhile, the beautiful Pole paced the sick room, waving the revolver and larding her endless harangue with imminent threats. Susan cowered, trembling violently beneath the blankets, certain that every moment was her last. But, frightened as she was, she refused to admit it, to grovel in abject terror. And finally Wanda, enraged by the refusal of her rival to beg for mercy or to cry out, moved close to the bed and aimed the revolver. Susan Barrington still refused to cry, and at that moment Henry Manning's key was turning in the front door.

He rushed down the hallway and burst into the bedroom.

Startled, she whirled. "Get out, or I'll kill you, too," she said. Henry Manning stopped in his tracks.

But he didn't stop thinking. He was 69 years old, going on 70, and not as fast nor as strong as he used to be; yet, somehow, he must get that gun. He tried to wheedle Wanda. Yet it did no good. Slowly, he began to edge forward, toward her. She watched him and warned, "Your next step will be your last, mister." Henry Manning knew it, too; yet he had to take the chance. And, suddenly, he leaped.

He grabbed her gun wrist, wrestled with her for possession of the .38. And then it went off—twice.

Henry Manning staggered back several feet, two bullets in his heart. He fell dead. Wanda whirled toward the bed, determined now to kill Susan. But Susan hadn't waited,

MEAT CUTTING OFFERS YOU SUCCESS And SECURITY

In The Best Established Business In The World • PEOPLE MUST EAT!

TRAIN QUICKLY in 8 short weeks for a job with a bright and secure future in the vital meat business. Trained meat men needed. Good pay, full-time jobs, year-round income, no lay-offs— HAVE A PROFITABLE MARKET OF YOUR OWN!

LEARN BY DOING

Get your training under actual meat market conditions in our big modern cutting and processing rooms and retail meat market. Expert instructors show you how—then you do each job yourself. Nearly a million dollars' worth of meat is cut, processed, displayed and merchandised by National students yearly!

PAY AFTER GRADUATION

Come to National for complete 8-weeks course and pay your tuition in easy installments after you graduate. Diploma awarded. Free employment help. Thousands of successful graduates. OUR 35th YEAR!

FREE CATALOG—MAIL COUPON

Send now for big, new, illustrated National School catalog. See students in training. Read what graduates are doing and earning. See meat you cut and equipment you work with. No obligation. No salesman will call. Send coupon in envelope or paste on postal card. Get all the facts NOW! G. I. APPROVED.

National School Of Meat Cutting, Inc.
Dept. B-27 Toledo 4, Ohio

NATIONAL SCHOOL OF MEAT CUTTING, INC., Dept. B-27, Toledo 4, Ohio

Send me FREE 52-page school catalog on LEARN-BY DOING training in PROFITABLE MEAT CUTTING, SUCCESSFUL MEAT MERCHANDISING and SELF-SERVICE MEATS at Toledo. No obligation. No salesman will call.
(Approved for Training Korean Veterans)

Name.. Age..........

Address..

City.................... Zone.......... State..........

and was dashing across the back-yard to a neighbor's house.

Wanda took careful aim and fired twice. But Susan kept running. Wanda shrugged, turned and sauntered casually from the house, and drove away in the waiting cab.

Susan Barrington and her next-door neighbor, Mrs. George Hermanson, wife of the police chief of Palos Park, could swear that the rear of the getaway car contained no license plate. Mrs. Hermanson immediately phoned her husband, and informed him what had happened. He alerted the Chicago police.

Sick as she was, Susan Jerome Barrington refused to go to bed until she had warned her husband that he was probably next on Wanda's list. Then she collapsed into Mrs. Hermanson's bed. Somehow, she knew that at last her marriage had been reborn. Smiling, she fingered the two bullet holes in her pajamas.

Chief Collins ordered the Chicago police to throw a cordon of cops around Godfrey Barrington's studio, and to watch the railroad stations in New York, Chicago and Detroit. Guests at her last party in the Village told of her threats to kill Mrs. Barrington.

The police began to hunt for the murder car. The newspapers ran front-page photos of Wanda.

The taxi driver saw the photos simultaneously with the discovery of the loss of his license plate, and notified the police. He explained, "I did not hear the shots in the house, and had no idea of what she had done. She came out so casually that I never would have guessed she had just committed murder."

She had ordered him to drive to the Illinois Central Railroad Station, he said, instead got out of the cab at 20th and Michigan Avenue, eight blocks from the terminal.

The police, unable to find her in Chicago, believed she had taken an Illinois Central train, anyhow, and notified all way points and terminals to watch for her.

Ben Thornton, of Indianapolis, was sitting in the lobby of the *Hotel Statler* in Detroit, reading his paper. He glanced up, his eyes following the strikingly beautiful girl crossing the lobby. Startled, he looked at his newspaper again, at the photograph of the girl on the front page. By now, the girl had inserted a letter in the mail chute, and had reentered the elevator.

Thornton rushed over to a desk clerk, guesturing at the photo and talking excitedly. Detectives Wilson and Roach were summoned. Guided by Thornton's description and the desk clerk's knowledge of his guests, they checked the hotel register.

Up in her room, Wanda had written her mother a note, sealed it in

CHRONOGRAPH WRIST WATCH
Lifetime Guarantee
(EXCLUSIVE OF PARTS)

3 DIALS
5 HANDS
2 BUTTONS
$7.90 Plus Tax
Multi-purpose watch that measures distance, speed, time, moving objects. Used as Stop Watch or Timepiece. Has Sweep-Second Hand for full 60 Second count. Second Dial records up to 45 minutes. Third Dial then records up to 6 hours. Seconds—Minutes—Hours, all recorded automatically.
INDEPENDENT MOVEMENTS
For sportsmen, professional men and women—timekeeper works when other hands and dials are stopped—separate movements permit dual use at same time.
RUGGED CONSTRUCTION
Precision workmanship and shock resistant features are added to enhance the value of this watch. Sold everywhere for as high as $17.00. Our low introductory price is only $7.90 plus 10% tax. (Total $8.69.) Send check or money order and we prepay postage. Or sent C.O.D. plus charges. LIMITED STOCK!
MARDO SALES CO., 480 Lexington Ave., DEPT. W-41, N.Y. 17, N.Y

FREE! to prove that in Only 15 Minutes you can start to

PLAY PIANO
with BOTH hands . . . this Marvelous New Way
Send for free Sample Lesson today! I will include 5 simple "play-at-once" songs— a Note Selector for your right hand—and my Patented Automatic Chord Selector to strike simple bass chords instantly with your left hand. No "tricks" in my tested, proven method. You actually learn by playing simple single note melodies with one hand, while striking beautiful simple resonant bass chord accompaniments with the other. No tedious scales. No boring exercises. No dreary practice. Just delightful enjoyment. Simply send name, address, and 10c for postage and handling to: DEAN ROSS, 45 West 45 St., Studio A-1701, New York 36.

AFRAID?
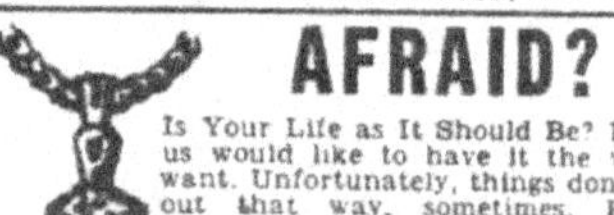
Is Your Life as It Should Be? Most of us would like to have it the way we want. Unfortunately, things don't work out that way, sometimes. Perhaps something is missing! FAITH-HOPE-? Then you need our Genuine Rhodium Plated Holy Cross, to look at . . . think of . . . and pray to. Comes in a STUNNING BLUE VELVET BOX, AND IS FULL OF FIRST QUALITY SIMULATED DIAMONDS on a BEAUTIFUL CHAIN, to WEAR CLOSE TO YOU AT ALL TIMES. The LORD'S PRAYER is in the center of our CROSS. Wonderful as a GIFT to your loved ones. DON'T BE AFRAID TO BELIEVE IN IT AND YOU WILL BLESS THE DAY THAT YOU BOUGHT IT. Only $3.00 with order (C.O.D. $3.50) Money Back in 7 days if not satisfied. BELADOR, 125 BROAD ST., DEPT. 134-C, NEW YORK 4.
FREE with every CROSS, a copy of one of the smallest Bibles in the World, to fit your purse or pocket.

POEMS WANTED
To Be Set To Music
Send one or more of your best poems today for FREE EXAMINATION. Any Subject. Immediate Consideration.
Phonograph Records Made
CROWN MUSIC CO., 49 W. 32 St., Studio 626, New York 1

CARDS, INKS, etc.
FREE CATALOGUE tells all about odds and percentages. Everything in club supplies.
O. C. NOVELTY CO. Dept. 3
1311 W. Main, Okla. City, Okla.

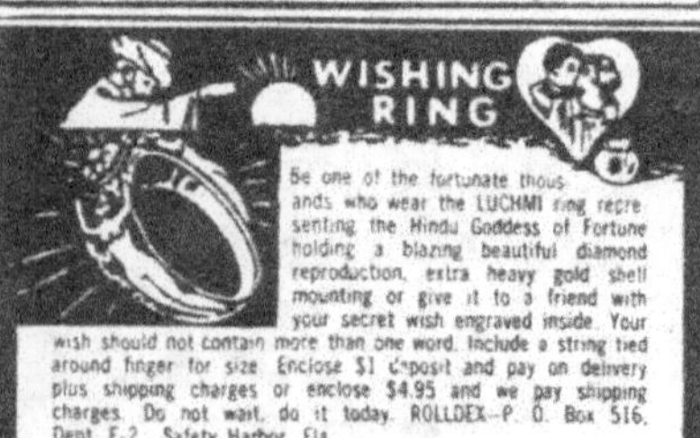

an envelope with her few, remaining possessions: $150 in cash, a 1,000 mark Polish government bond, and a $200 insurance policy made out to her mother. After mailing the envelope in the lobby, she began final preparations.

Downstairs, the desk clerk pointed excitedly at a signature on the guest register. "That's her. That Missus Ted Glaskoff," he said.

Wilson ordered the desk clerk, "Call her, and keep her on the telephone until we get up there." Then, with an assistant manager and the house dick, they started up in the elevator.

Wanda picked up the ringing telephone. "I'm ill," she moaned without asking who it was.

At the sound of the master key in her door, the receiver dropped from her hand. She turned, then crumpled in a heap on the floor. She was dead.

She had committed suicide by swallowing the chocolate bon-bon containing the cyanide of potassium, Coroner Charles Earle stated. The police examined her pitiful possessions: a diary detailing her great love for Godfrey Barrington and the resulting agony of the injustice she felt done her; a few story manuscripts with the reject slips still attached; in her handbag was the .38 with four discharged cartridges. Ballistics later proved it to be the murder weapon.

The body was removed to an undertaker's on Third Street. The Henry Manning murder was solved.

Susan took a new lease on life, and recovered. Although it had cost the life of Henry Manning, the murder proved the healing balm to the last wound in the Barrington's marriage. They lived happily, if somewhat less eventually, forever after.

EDITOR'S NOTE: *To protect persons innocently involved in this case, the names Godfrey and Susan Jerome Barrington and Ben Thornton are fictitious as used here.*

THE END

Sex Killer's Deadly Desires

(continued from page 21)

them. He promised to report his findings to the Rockland authorities the next day.

The following morning, Stern and Mock received the report. It indicated beyond all doubt that Mason was lying when he said that he was innocent of the double murder. But obtaining a confession from the shy, sensitive youth was another thing. The veteran officers knew this

Amazing 100 Year Old Mysteriously Scented Gypsy Fish Bait Oil

Makes Catfish Go Crazy!

"I am enclosing pictures of 2 different catfish we caught using Gypsy Fish Bait Oil on our bait! We fish the Fox River at Mineral Springs, Ill. where we have a summer cottage. One fish my brother is holding weighed 8½ pounds and the other one weighed 7¾ pounds." Miss Dorothy Gribing, 6052 S. Fairfield—Chicago 29, Ill.

Here Are Genuine Reports about Catching Smell Feeding Fish

19 INCH CATFISH

"Gypsy Fish Bait Oil does everything you say! I caught a 19 inch channel catfish and 1½ pounds bull heads."
Mrs. D. Loring, Box 352
Elmhurst, Ill.

DOUBLE STRENGTH BEST YET

"I just tried the new double strength Gypsy and it is the best yet. I caught 20 pounds of smell feeding fish including some big cats the first time out."
L. C. Beasley—2751 W. Warren
Chicago, Ill.

11 POUNDS OF CATFISH

"Gypsy Fish Bait Oil is sure wonderful. I caught 2 flathead cats, weight 11 pounds."
Robert D. Whitlock
11 N. Jackson St.—Danville, Ill.

FOUR CHANNEL CATS

"Gypsy is hard to beat! We caught 13 including four channel cats 3½ to 12 pounds. Incidentally over 100 people have written us after seeing our names in your ad."
Ruby and Allen Wilkerson
Box 240—Iola, Kansas

EVER CATCH FISH LIKE THIS?

"I have been using Gypsy Fish Bait Oil 2 years now and have never found anything to compare with it. A group of fishermen were sitting along a stone crib in the Portage River. They were using night crawlers for bait and weren't catching anything. I cast my line in on the other side of the crib and before the sinker hit the bottom I had a 6 pound silver catfish. And I repeated this 4 times before any of the others caught a fish. I showed them my worms and to this day they couldn't figure how I can catch big fish right where they only got nibbles and a few small bullheads. They don't know I used Gypsy on my bait and they didn't. Last night another party and I caught 24 catfish on rods and reels in 5 hours using Gypsy. Rush this order as I am about out. The big catfish run is starting and I am nearly out of bait and I would not know what to do without it."

Ray Hathaway, 226 E. 6th St., Port Clinton, Ohio

Like Sharks Are Attracted To Smell of Blood...

Fishing experts are just learning what wandering Romany Gypsies found out 100 years ago . . . many kinds of the best eating fish such as catfish, snappers, bull-heads, carp, often feed along the dark bottom are attracted to bait by their acute sense of smell. Gypsies invented this mysteriously scented oil and it makes these smell feeding fish literally go crazy. It excites them through the thousands of smell organs that cover their bodies. Like a shark goes wild at the smell of blood, so these smell-feeders go crazy at the first whiff of the new double strength Gypsy Fish Bait Oil. Send the coupon and try double strength Gypsy Fish Bait Oil at our risk. If yours isn't the biggest catch in your entire party, your money back.

FREE! Fisherman's Pouch without Extra Cost

With every bottle of Gypsy Fish Bait Oil . . . a large waterproof plastic pouch. Ideal for lunches, tobacco, matches, etc. Yours to keep even if you return Oil for money back.

Simple Easy Way To Fish

Use your regular bait . . . plug, minnow, worm, fly, night crawler . . . fish your regular waters . . . rivers, creeks, lakes, ponds, or the ocean . . . fish your usual way . . . still fish with pole and bobber, cast, troll, spin . . . all you do is dab a drop or so of the new double strength GYPSY FISH BAIT OIL on the bait. It's just that easy. And North or South, East or West . . . let them get one whiff of your bait while feeding and smell feeders all streak madly for your bait and usually the biggest one wins. You keep hauling 'em in to everyone's envy and amazement!

SEND NO MONEY

You fish "On-Approval"

Be as skeptical as you like . . . go ahead and say we're crazy. But mail coupon or write for your trial of the new improved double strength Gypsy Fish Bait Oil that's making experts out of amateurs all over America for catching smell feeding fish. On arrival put up as deposit $1.98 for one or $4.98 for 3 bottles plus C.O.D. postage thru postman. Use the next time you go fishing and if you aren't delighted return what's left for money back. Send cash and we pay postage. Don't wait. Mail coupon.

WALLING KEITH CHEMICALS, INC.
Dept. 270-K—Birmingham 1, Ala.

MAIL THIS COUPON

Walling Keith Chemicals, Inc., DEPT. 270-K
Birmingham 1, Alabama.

☐ Send one bottle double strength Gypsy Fish Bait Oil and Free Fisherman's pouch. I'll pay $1.98 plus C.O.D. postage on arrival on guarantee I can return Gypsy after first test trial for money back and keep pouch for my trouble.

☐ Send 3 Gypsy (3 Free pouches) . . . $4.98 ☐ Remittance enclosed. Send postage paid.

Name ____________

Address ____________

City ________ Zone ____ State ________

ONLY Truss In The World For

ONLY 3-Legged Man In The World

READ THIS!

"Brooks is the ONLY Appliance I can wear comfortably." Frank A. Lentini
ULETA, FLORIDA

THIS IS NO "GAG"

If an unfortunate man with three legs can wear a Brooks comfortably, why not you? Clip Coupon below NOW for Free Booklet on Rupture and Proof of Results. Every Brooks is made to order and Sold on Trial. Amazing Air-Cushion invention is simple, sanitary, and satisfying.

Made to Measure - Sent on Trial!

Where Is Your Rupture?

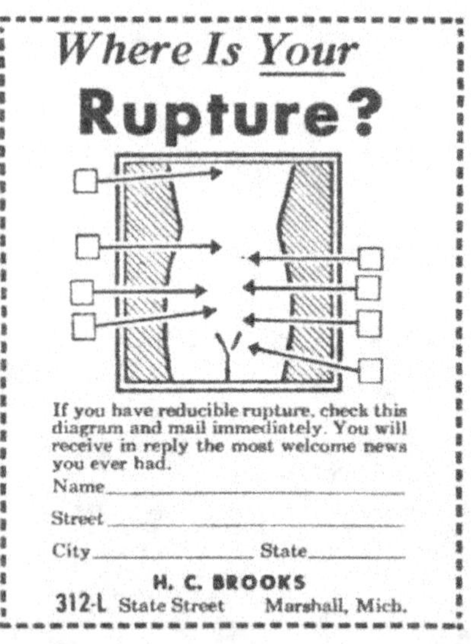

If you have reducible rupture, check this diagram and mail immediately. You will receive in reply the most welcome news you ever had.

Name__________

Street__________

City__________ State__________

H. C. BROOKS
312-L State Street Marshall, Mich.

would take careful handling.

Sheriff Mock decided the best approach was to talk about high school basketball. Mason, a student at the Spring Valley High School, like all older children who lived at the Lakeside school when they passed the eighth grade, had seen the sheriff's son playing on the Nyack High School junior varsity team.

With this rapport established between sheriff and suspect, the other officers eased from the room. After a little more friendly talk from Mock, the boy's eyes welled with tears and he offered to lead him to the hidden knife.

"I was lying when I told you I lost the knife Sunday afternoon," Mason said with a sob. "Come with me and I'll find it for you."

Mock and Deputy Sheriff Henry Beers accompanied Mason into the woods. All carried flashlights. Mason bent over and poked around the ground in several spots. At one place, Mason retrieved the knife and deftly palmed it, unseen by the officers. He apparently had a belated change of heart.

But a little farther on, Mason appeared to stumble beside a swamp hole. Mock and Beers were quick to detect the ruse. The deputy's flashlight was trained on the water when the knife hit it with a splash. Quickly the officers fished it out, while Mason hung his head and wept bitterly.

Taken back to the school, Mason still refused to admit he had killed Esther Nagy with the weapon. District Attorney Shaken, Chief Stern and Sheriff Mock continued to question him in an office of the administration building until, shortly before midnight, Mason confessed.

The slim, brown-haired boy told the officers that he had killed both girls in a panic after luring one of them to the wooded area from the school playground. He said his principal interest, a sexual one, was in Marjorie. Esther apparently lost her life because she insisted on tagging along with Marjorie, her constant companion.

The district attorney's investigator, William F. Sterns, quoted the boy as saying:

"I told Marjorie the house mother wanted to see her. Esther was with her. I told Marjorie that the house mother was waiting down at the corner behind a large pile of brush.

"I couldn't get rid of Esther. When we got down there (the brush pile) I told Marjorie to go around the pile—that the house mother was waiting on the other side.

"Esther started to cry and I tried to chase her away. I didn't know what to do. I was angry, panicky, so I took out my knife and put it in her back.

"I went around the pile and met Marjorie. She hadn't found the

ENDS GRAY HAIR

WORRIES IN 5 SECONDS

$1.00 PLUS TAX

Quick, easy Tintz Touch-up Pencil colors gray, faded hair at roots, parting, temples. Like lipstick. In metal swivel case. Won't rub off, but washes out. TRY AT OUR RISK. Send $1.10 tax included on guarantee of satisfaction or Money Back. Sorry no C.O.D.

State shade: Black, Dark Brown, Med Brown, Light Brown, Auburn or Blonde. Mail order now to:
TINTZ CO., Dept. 425, 230 N. Michigan Ave., Chicago 1, Ill.

SPARKLING 8 x 10 ENLARGEMENT ONLY 49¢

FREE! On orders of 2 or more we will send you one sparkling wallet size print FREE.

Mail us any photo, snapshot or negative and receive, postpaid, your enlargement on double-weight paper. Original returned unharmed. Nothing else to pay. If beautiful hand-coloring is desired add 50c for each print. C.O.D.'s accepted on orders of 2 or more, plus C.O.D. charges. Satisfaction Guaranteed.

QUALITY VALUES, Studio 2-B
5 BEEKMAN STREET New York 38, N. Y.

HOW to PRAY

and get RESULTS

The true way to mastery will open for you when you know how to ask for and how to accept the gifts that GOD has stored up for those that love and obey Him. Learn

THE MAGIC FORMULA for SUCCESSFUL PRAYER

Here are some of the amazing things it tells you about: When to pray, where to pray, How to pray; The Magic Formulas for Health and Success through prayer; for conquering fear through prayer; for obtaining work through prayer; for money through prayer; for influencing others through prayer; and many other valuable instructions that help you get things you want.

5-DAY TRIAL—SEND NO MONEY

Just send your name and address today and on delivery simply deposit the small sum of only $1.49 plus postage with your postman. I positively GUARANTEE that you will be more than delighted with RESULTS within 5 days or your money will be returned promptly on request and no questions asked. Order At Once.

LARCH, 118 E. 28, Dept. 645-K, New York 16

SEWS LEATHER

AND TOUGH TEXTILES LIKE A MACHINE

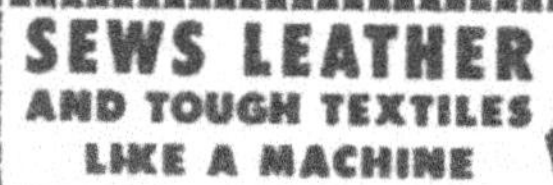

With SPEEDY STITCHER Automatic Sewing Awl, anyone can quickly and skillfully sew or repair anything made of LEATHER, CANVAS, NYLON, PLASTIC, or other heavy materials. Sews firm, even lock-stitches like a machine. Gets into hard-to-reach places. Specially made for heavy duty sewing on LUGGAGE, FOOTWEAR, RUGS, AWNINGS, SAILS, SADDLERY, UPHOLSTERY, OVER-ALLS, AUTO-TOPS, SPORTS GEAR, and other tough sewing jobs. Here's the handiest tool you'll ever own. Will save you many times its small cost. Comes ready for instant use complete with bobbin of waxed thread and 3 different types of diamond-pointed needles. Easy-to-follow directions will make you an expert in minutes. Extra needles and waxed-thread always available. Save money, send $1.98 for postpaid delivery. If C.O.D., $1.98 plus postage. MONEY BACK GUARANTEE.

ONLY 1.98

SPORTSMAN'S POST
366 Madison Ave., Dept. A-132, New York 17

GIRLS

GET YOUR MAN

and make him yours FOREVER. Why take chances against other women who may be using mysterious charms? This is your chance to learn and use Secrets of Sex Appeal so powerful that even bad women can keep good men while good girls go without.

HOW TO WIN AND HOLD A HUSBAND

contains the very essence of confidential advice that a great Love and Marriage Expert has given to thousands of women—all reduced to a simple set of rules—an easy formula that you can learn to use to WIN YOUR MAN. 10-DAY TRIAL—Just send your name and address today and on delivery deposit only $2 plus postage with your postman. (Or send $2 with order to save C.O.D. and postage.) Use for 10 days. I positively GUARANTEE that you will be more than delighted or your money back promptly and no questions asked. Order At Once.

LARCH, 118 East 28 St., Dept. 445-K, New York 16

Now! A Tranquilizing Pill Without A Doctor's Prescription

Released to you for the first time! An entirely different kind of "Calm-Down Pill"—that helps you FIGHT NERVOUSNESS...FIGHT TENSION...FIGHT AGGRAVATION, HEADACHE AND ANXIETY like nothing you have ever tried before without a doctor's prescription!

Think of it! Right now—today—the wonder-working ingredients in these pills are being recommended by leading specialists all over America, in cases of nervous headache . . . in cases of migraine-like headache . . . in cases of stomach upset or sleeplessness caused by nervous tension! They are used to fight the terrible, frantic depression caused by constant anxiety! They are given in almost every clinic, hospital, and doctor's office in the world—to men and women of all ages, who need *doctor-prescribed help* to break the continuous chain of worry, tension and anxiety that is ruining their life today!

And now these exact same capsules are yours to try in your own home — WITHOUT a doctor's prescription — and without risking a penny!

Here is all we ask you to do! Simply take one of these tiny capsules the next time you are twisted with anxiety . . . the next time you are bent double with worry . . . the next time nervous tension tears apart your life! Take these tiny capsules — *and they must help you open the door to a whole new world of peace and calmness that you never knew existed within you before*— they must help you *relax*, no matter how great the temporary strain — OR EVERY CENT OF YOUR MONEY BACK! You try them entirely at our risk! Act TODAY!

Nervous Tension Can Kill You – Fight it Today!

Be honest with yourself for one moment! How many times in the past month have you literally been "sick with worry"? How many times have you come home in the evening — completely exhausted — not from work, but from constant aggravation! How many times have you sat down at your dinner table — so tense, so irritated, so nervous that you couldn't even enjoy your own food!

Yes, and how many times have you spent an entire evening with your stomach tied up in a knot — with the muscles of your arms and shoulders and legs "as stiff as boards"! How many times have you told yourself: "I shouldn't worry" — "There's no reason to be nervous" . . . and then fell right back in the same old killing pattern of nervous tension that's been torturing you before!

Would it be worth one minute of your time to help break that Chain of Nervous Tension! Would it be worth one minute of your time to help prove that you CAN relax . . . that you CAN live in peace and tranquility . . . that you CAN fight that nervous excitability AS EASILY AND QUICKLY AS YOU'D TAKE AN ASPIRIN!

Doctors Give You The Answer!

Doctors believe that the answers to these questions are YES! Doctors know that the *mere symptoms* of Nervous Tension cripple thousands of Americans every month! They have seen patient after patient come into their offices, *with actual permanent physical damage to their bodies — caused by tension, and tension alone!*

For years, doctors and scientists and pharmaceutical researchers have been working on MEDICAL RELIEF for you — tiny capsules that would knock this tension right out of your body . . . that would soothe that constant irritation . . . that would help give you the tranquility and peace of mind that you've been searching for for years! In case after case they have succeeded beyond their fondest dreams! Medical wonder drugs such as Meprobamate and Rauwolfia have literally transformed the entire practice of medicine!

But all of these drugs had to be given by doctor's prescription! They could only be taken under a doctor's constant care! And millions of men and women — who desperately needed their help — couldn't tolerate them at all!

This is the reason for this announcement! To bring you an entirely different kind of Calm-Down Pill — that will give you this same kind of blessed relief — WITHOUT THESE RESTRICTIONS! Yes! A tiny, harmless capsule that you can take anywhere, anytime, according to simple directions — AND TAKE SAFELY — AS MUCH AS TWO TO FOUR TIMES A DAY — WITHOUT THE SLIGHTEST FEAR OF FORMING A HABIT!

Not One – But FOUR PROVEN SEDATIVES Give You Startling Relief!

The name of this product is TR-34. It is an almost-magic blend of proven Daytime Sedatives—ingredients that help calm your nerves . . . soothe your tensions . . . drain off the pain caused by constant irritation—*but are NOT intended to make you sleepy, or "dopey," or drowsy!*

Every one of these ingredients has been tested and proven and written up in the medical literature of every country in the world! Any one of them — if it were given to you by itself — could bring you startling relief! *But blended together — adding one proven calming effect to another, and another, and another — they become SO effective, and yet SO gentle and SO mild THAT WE ASK YOU TO TRY THEM ENTIRELY AT OUR RISK — WITH THIS AMAZING FULL-MONEY-BACK GUARANTEE!*

1. **This amazing Formula — TR-34 — must start to work in your body in as little as fifteen short minutes — OR EVERY CENT OF YOUR MONEY BACK!**

2. **If you now suffer from nervous tensions or anxieties caused by business, or financial worries, or family troubles — this product must help you *relax* in the face of all these temporary strains . . . must help you clear your mind so you can meet and solve these problems . . . must help your body prevent permanent damage caused by these tensions — OR EVERY CENT OF YOUR MONEY BACK!**

3. **This product must help *drain off* the pain and discomfort of nervous headaches . . . migraine-like headaches . . . dizzy headaches — OR EVERY CENT OF YOUR MONEY BACK!**

4. **This product must help you fight the constant *strain and tiredness* — caused by nervous tension — that is now draining your energy and health . . . and actually help you *regain* that energy — OR EVERY CENT OF YOUR MONEY BACK!**

5. **And above all — this product must help you *Fight Nervousness . . . Fight Tension . . . Fight Nervous Depression, Headache and Anxiety*, EVERY DAY THAT YOU MEET THEM—OR EVERY CENT OF YOUR MONEY BACK!**

Try It Entirely At Our Risk!

The price of TR-34 is only \$2.98 for the full 30-capsule supply — *or less than one-half* the cost of similar products! Or if you wish, you may buy the 60-capsules size — twice as much — for only \$4.98 — *a saving of one dollar!* Or, you may buy the economy size of 90 capsules — THREE TIMES as much — for only \$5.98! This is a saving of THREE FULL DOLLARS! *And the same money-back guarantee is yours — for thirty full days — no matter which size you try!*

You have nothing to lose! This product must work for you! Act TODAY!

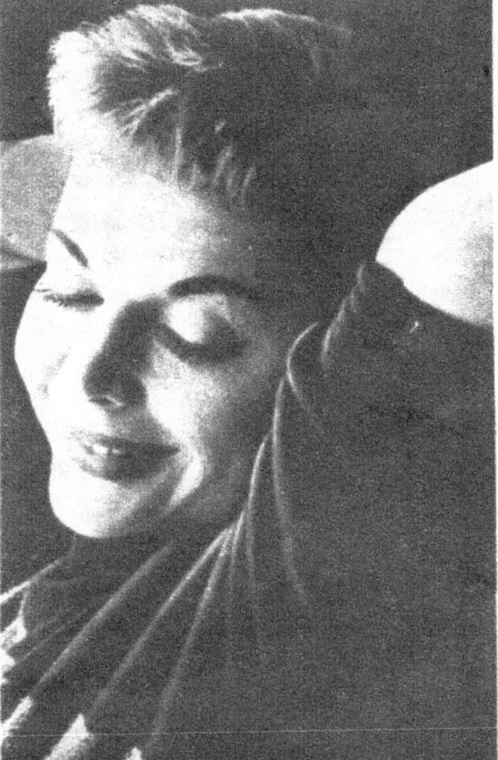

IMPORTANT NOTICE On this page, you will learn about an entirely different type of "Tranquilizing Pill," released for the first time in this magazine. It is the opinion of a leading nerve specialist — connected with one of the largest hospitals in the world — that this pill will give you the same kind of blessed relief as Tranquilizers now sold only through doctor's prescriptions — *and yet this product is now released to you without prescription of any kind!* We believe that it is so important that you try this product — in your own home — that we ask you to test it ENTIRELY AT OUR RISK — WITHOUT YOUR GAMBLING A CENT! Read the thrilling details on this page! ACT TODAY!

MEDICAL PROOF!

From the Files of One of America's Leading Nerve Specialists!

Here are case histories of men and women like yourself — who were actually rescued from despair by TR-34, *even after every known tranquilizer had completely failed them!*

Case #1: J.A. — 54-year-old married salesman. Suffered from never-ending anxiety. Plagued by continuous tension so strong that his arms and legs ached at night — that he felt as though someone was sitting on his chest — that he could hardly sleep. *This patient had received almost every sedative known to medical science — with only moderate and temporary results!*

On January 11, 1957, he was placed on TR-34. *Since that time, he has not suffered from a single attack of anxiety!* His muscle tension is greatly relieved. He sleeps much better and is filled with a sense of well being, gratitude, new hope and vigor! All this from the very first week of treatment! *And there were no disturbing side effects reported from TR-34!*

Case #2: G.M. — A thirty-year-old single woman, with a five year history of repeated tortuous headaches. These psychosomatic headaches always occurred behind the right eye. They were so painful, and throbbed so much, that they woke the patient nightly from her sleep. She was forced to walk the floor for one full hour until the attack left her. *In past years, she had been given several kinds of sedatives, analgesics, antihistamines, vasal constrictors and tranquilizers with absolutely no effect.*

On January 7, 1957, she was given TR-34. *This amazing medication relieved almost all attacks WITHIN 10 MINUTES after being taken! This relief was reported from the very first night!*

Case #3: S.D. — a 56-year-old divorced secretary. Had been suffering for the past six years from repeated bouts of severe melancholy — during which she felt life had "left her behind" . . . during which she neglected her home and personal appearance . . . lost appetite and sleep . . . and felt that she was unable to do her work. She complained of deep-seated pains in her stomach and head. *None of the tranquilizers used in the past could effectively help her fight off the violence of these moods — nor could they help her eliminate the pain!*

On January 7, 1957, patient was placed on TR-34. *The beneficial effect was immediately noticed by both patient and physician!* She was able to "face" life and "work things out." Her attacks of anxiety and excitement began to subside immediately. Her pain was immediately lessened, and she enjoyed restful sleep. *No harmful side effects were reported!*

Case #4: R.L. — a 24-year-old married housewife, mother of two. She had become increasingly more despondent — giving way to frequent crying spells — suffering from feelings of inadequacy, unworthiness and guilt. She was terrified by repeated nightmares — which had grown more and more frightening during the past few weeks. *Her family physician had tried to curb these symptoms with the aid of barbiturates and tranquilizers — but without results.*

On January 28, 1957, patient was instructed to take one capsule of TR-34 after breakfast . . . one capsule after supper . . . and two capsules before retiring. *The effect was almost immediate!* When seen a full week later the patient reported immediately that she has not had a single repetition of these nightmares—and that generally she feels much more calm, pacified and even-tempered. *No harmful side effects of any kind were reported!*

Try it at our risk! Act TODAY!

MAIL NO RISK COUPON TODAY!

NORTH AMERICAN STEVENS CORP., DEPT. RP-8
31 WEST 47th STREET, NEW YORK 36, N.Y.

Yes, I want to try your amazing new Formula, TR-34, entirely at your risk. I understand that these amazing new capsules must help me fight tension . . . fight nervousness . . . fight agitation, nervous headaches, and anxiety — or my full money back! I will pay the postman only the low introductory price checked below, plus C.O.D. charges. I also understand, if I am not completely delighted, that I may return the used package within one month and get a FULL REFUND. No questions asked!

☐ I want the full 30-capsule supply for only \$2.98.

☐ I want the big 60-capsule supply for only \$4.98. This is a saving of \$1.00.

☐ I want the giant economy supply, 90-capsules for only \$5.98. This is a saving of a full \$3.00.

NAME ____________________

ADDRESS ____________________

CITY ____________ ZONE ____ STATE ____________

☐ SAVE MORE! *Send cash, check or money order with coupon, and we pay all postage charges! Saves you as much as .98! Same money-back guarantee of course!*

©*Entire Contents Copyrighted by North American Stevens Corp., 1957*

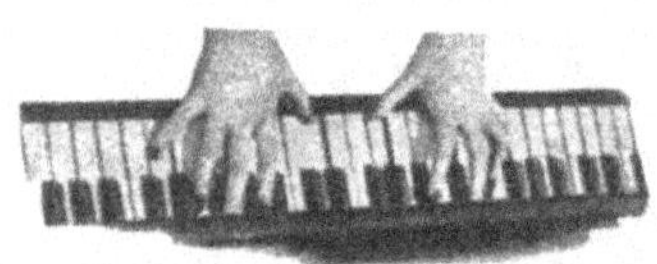

BE YOUR OWN MUSIC TEACHER

Send For Free Book Telling How Easily You Can Learn Piano, Guitar, Accordion, ANY Instrument This EASY A-B-C Way

NOW IT'S EASY to learn music at home. No tiresome "exercises." No teacher. Just START RIGHT OUT playing simple pieces. Thousands now play who never thought they could. Our pictured lessons make it easy as A-B-C to learn to play popular music, hymns, classical and any other music. On easy-pay plan, only a few cents a lesson. Over 900,000 students! (Our 59th successful year.)

Stop Cheating Yourself of These Joys!

Popularity! New friends. Gay parties. Good times. Career. Extra Money. Understand, appreciate, and converse about music. Learn lives and compositions of modern and great masters . . . . Relax! Banish worries and frustrations. Satisfy self-expression, creative urge. Gain self-confidence.

MAIL COUPON FOR FREE BOOK. Find out why our method can teach you quickly, easily, inexpensively. Write for 36-page illustrated Free Book. No obligation. Mention your favorite instrument. Just mail coupon below today!

U. S. SCHOOL OF MUSIC
Studio A3038
Port Washington, N. Y.

U. S. SCHOOL OF MUSIC
Studio A3038, Port Washington, N. Y.

Please send me your 36-page illustrated Free Book. I would like to play (Name Instrument).

Instrument.................... Have you Instrument?..................

Name.. (Please Print)

Address..

City...................... Zone.... State..........

SCANDALOUS CONFESSION

Scandalous confession rocked the marriage bed! A second husband, he was jealous of his predecessor and wanted to know what was none of his business. She, poor thing, desired only to please, and so made a natural mistake . . . You must read this story for one of the intimate and exciting revelations in MARRIAGE MISCHIEF.

SINGLE OR MARRIED, you'll go for this saucy "undress" view of bride and groom. MARRIAGE MISCHIEF is brand new, devilishly indiscreet, with original full page cartoons. Featuring: What Every Bride Should Know . . . Counsel for the Bewildered Groom . . . The Wedding Daze . . . The Bachelor Dinner . . . Hazards of the First Night . . . Honeymoons, Conventional and Otherwise . . . From Smoker to Bedroom . . . The Truth About Trousseaux . . . And many more provoking topics to keep you gagging. An ideal wedding or anniversary gift.

TRY MARRIAGE MISCHIEF 10 DAYS AT OUR EXPENSE. Money back if not satisfied. C.O.D. pay postman 98¢ plus postage. If you send 98¢, we pay postage.

PLAZA BOOK CO. DEPT. A-778
109 Broad St., New York 4, N. Y.

house mother. She saw the bloody knife sticking out of my pocket. She screamed. I couldn't stand her screams. I don't know why, but I picked up a rock and hit her over the head with it."

Throughout the confession, Mason denied that he had assaulted either of the girls sexually. But Dr. Moses' earlier announcement that both girls had been violated by a sex pervert was confirmed in the autopsies performed by Dr. William R. Strutton, pathologist at Rockland State Hospital.

Coroner Moses said that "Mason is the coolest kid I ever saw. Throughout the questioning, he was cool as ice."

Wright, the school's director, was momentarily speechless with shock when informed that Mason had signed a confession to the slayings. "It's unbelievable," he gasped.

Officials of the high school Mason attended said his conduct was good. He had an I.Q. of 76, regarded as very low, and was in his second year as a freshman after flunking English and social studies the last term.

There were other indications, however, that young Mason had been mentally ill for some time. At home, in New York City, he had become so unmanageable in 1950 that his mother had him committed to Bellevue Hospital for observation. He was in and out of children's shelters and temporary asylums on at least three occasions. When he was released from Bellevue, his home situation was so precarious that psychiatrists refused to send him back to his mother, who also had a history of psychiatric disturbance.

Mason was ordered transferred, instead, to the Queensborough Society for the Prevention of Cruelty to Children. From there, in January, 1951, he was sent to the Lakeside school. At first he had been "sullen, insecure and withdrawn," according to the school's social worker, but lately he had "levelled off beautifully. He made remarkable progress. He became communicative and even friendly."

Then, on Sunday, March 8th, something snapped. He suddenly, and without warning, committed what Dr. Frederick Wertham, noted psychiatrist, called "a horrible, frightful act of violence."

Meanwhile, Carlton Mason re-enacted the crime in front of movie cameras while the officers watched. He was then arraigned on charges of first degree murder and remanded to the Rockland County Jail at New City, without bail, to await action of the grand jury.

He was sentenced on June 22nd, 1953, to a term at Elmira Prison of from 60 years to life for second degree murder. Sick in mind, Carl-

SONGWRITERS

LARGE RECORDING COMPANY WANTS NEW SONGS! Your song may be chosen for recording on ROYALTY BASIS. NATIONAL SALES, PROMOTION, DISTRIBUTION if selected. Send songs, song poems for FREE examination. NO CHARGE FOR MELODIES.
MUSIC MAKERS, Dept. SM-11 Box 2507, HOLLYWOOD, CALIF.

DETECTIVE TRAINING

Robert B. Phillips, Sr., founder 35 years' detective experience. Former U. S. Government special agent. Our course is very reasonable and easy to master. Careers for men and women, young and old. For free information write to Phillips Secret Service System. 1917-R North Kenneth Ave., Chicago 39. Illinois.

GIVE UNITED CEREBRAL PALSY

GIVE TO YOUR C/P LOCAL AFFILIATE

DICE•CARDS

Perfect Dice, Magic Dice, Magic Cards—READ THE BACKS—Inks, Daubs, Poker Chips, Gaming Layouts, Dice Boxes, Counter Games, Punch Boards. WRITE FOR FREE CATALOG TODAY!

K. C. CARD CO., Room 528
831 S. Wabash Ave., Chicago, Ill.

FUN WITH AMAZING NEW MAGIC DICE

Here's a special pair of fun dice that certainly can do wonders. It's amazingly easy to predict numbers, perform amusing tricks. No one can guess the hidden "secret" unless you tell them! Display amazing "control" yet the real reason is cleverly concealed from everyone. Fun and fascination! Easy directions explain details. Perform many "magic" tricks! Price only $2.98. Get a pair today. Send no money. Just name and address. On arrival, pay postman only $2.98 plus postage.

Address HOLLISTER WHITE CO., Dept. 593-D
3016 W. Van Buren St., Chicago 12, Ill.

LUCKY LODESTONES?

MAGNETIC LODESTONES are truly ANCIENT. Romans and Greeks used them in BIBLICAL TIMES. We offer our ANCIENT BRAND of highly MAGNETIC LODESTONES, the same type the ANCIENTS may have used. Our ANCIENT BRAND of highly MAGNETIC LODESTONES come to you in a red flannel bag, together with a so-called Talismanic Seal of Luck No. 20, as shown in the 6th and 7th BOOK OF MOSES by Louis de Claremont. All FOUR items for only $2.00 postpaid or $2.50 C.O.D. We make no claims and sell them only as curios.

ANCIENT PRODUCTS, DEPT. 234-C
504 Hicksville Road Massapequa, N. Y.

Up to 9 Miles More Per Gallon! Up to 20 More Horsepower!

All From One Simple Change in Your Car!

YES! In the next two minutes I'm going to show you how you can get up to 20 MORE HORSEPOWER from your car . . . how you can save enough gas in a single year to drive up to A FULL THOUSAND MILES . . . how you can eliminate most of the ignition knocks and pings that are driving you crazy now . . . how you can get battery-saving, sure-fire starting even in below-freezing weather—and do it without buying one single complicated gadget —without paying a mechanic a penny! How? SIMPLY BY CHANGING THE COLOR OF YOUR SPARK PLUGS!

By ED MITCHELL

Let me say this at the start. What I'm offering you on this page is a very simple investment. I want you to try the most fantastic spark plug in the world, entirely at my risk! A spark plug that costs *only a few pennies* more than the old-fashioned model that's on your car today. A spark plug that lasts up to 10 *times as long* as that old-fashioned model . . . that gives you the *full blazing horsepower* that that old plug is robbing you of today . . . and that actually saves you enough gas *to drive half way across America*, every single year that you use it!

Does this sound impossible? *It's been proven a thousand times this year!* Here is a small sample of that proof.

This Is Why Your Car WastesGas,LosesPower

Some day, if you ever have a spare moment, *lift one of the spark plugs out of your car!* Look at the bottom of that plug. In 10 seconds, you'll learn more about gas waste than any book could teach you in a year.

If that plug has been in your car a thousand miles or more, then what you'll see on the bottom of that plug is *FILTH!* The Firing Point of that plug — the most important single point in your car—*will be choked to death with BLACK, FILTHY CARBON! Carbon that robs your car of as much as 20 vital horsepower every time your engine fires!*

Now, wipe that filth away. And look at the Firing Point itself. This is the *POWER POINT* of your car . . . the pin-head of electricity that turns raw gas into 200 horsepower of driving energy! And what is the condition of that Point? *CORRODED . . . PITTED . . . SCARRED . . . AND WORN!* Hardly able to deliver half the spark it should! Wasting gas . . . wasting money, every time you put your foot down on the pedal!

Yes! You pay $2000 . . . $3000 . . . $4000 for your car. *And a single 98c part robs you* of the real power and enjoyment of that car.

At Last A Plug So Smart That It "Thinks"

Now look at the new plug—the *jet-finish "POWER-FLASH"* plug that I send you—*for only a few pennies* more than you're paying today!

Here is a plug that has not only *ONE* firing point—but hundreds of firing points! That fires so fast, so effectively, so often that it actually *ELIMINATES THAT DEADLY CARBON . . . BURNS IT UP . . . THROWS IT AWAY . . . KEEPS ITSELF SPARKLING CLEAN, ON EVERY SINGLE STROKE!* The full, blazing horsepower that was there when your car was brand-new, is *still* there 30,000 miles later.

But that's just the beginning! *This plug actually gives you the different firing power* you need for every driving condition — smooth, dependable power for city stop-and-go driving . . . effortless horsepower for the parkway . . . blazing reserve power for super speeds! No more missing, sputtering, knocking when you want to pull ahead of other cars at high speeds! No more groaning take-offs at the lights! *FULL POWER 24 HOURS A DAY* . . . or we send you a new set *Free*.

And that's still just the beginning! Best of all — this is the toughest, strongest, longest-lasting plug ever made! *YOU COULD ACTUALLY POUND IT AGAINST A CONCRETE WALL WITH A HAMMER, WITHOUT EVEN DENTING IT — AND THIS AMAZING PLUG WOULD STILL FIRE CLEAN AND HOT FOR 30,000 MILES!* Yes! These fantastic plugs give you such terrific, consistent, long-lasting service that

See The Amazing Difference Yourself!

This new "Power-Flash" Hi-Compression Power Plug (on the left) is guaranteed to be the most powerful longest lasting Spark Plug ever made! Here's why:

1. Only "Power-Flash" gives you an unlimited number of firing points — plus a guaranteed minimum of 800% more spark action than ordinary plugs! Higher compression, longer engine life, more mileage, power and pep!

2. Only "Power-Flash" gives you automatic heat and gap control! Actually thinks for itself! Gives you faster, wider spark for smoother performance, instant starting, faster pick-up even in freezing weather!

3. Only "Power-Flash" gives you exclusive self-cleaning action! Actually forces plug to clean itself. Plugs run cleaner, cooler, longer! No more fouling "ping" or power loss!

4. Only "Power-Flash" gives you toughest insulators made! Lifetime guaranteed — diamond-like hardness! Gets rid of deadly heat up to 30 times faster than ordinary insulators!

Plus this startling guarantee. Satisfaction guaranteed for two full years or 30,000 miles . . . or a new set free! Act today!

we can afford to make *one of the most amazing guarantees you ever heard!*

Try It at My Risk, Today!

What have you got to lose? These amazing jet finish "POWER-FLASH" plugs cost only $1.45 each — or $8.70 for a complete set for six-cylinder cars, and $11.60 for a complete set for eight-cylinder cars. *They cost only a few pennies more than ordinary old-fashioned plugs—and they can save you up to $100 this year!*

Here is my guarantee to you. Put these plugs in your car yourself. No mechanic needed. Nothing to adjust. From the very first moment that you get back in that car and drive, you must notice amazing new power and pick-up —or I'll send you a new set free!

You must notice new gas savings . . . you must eliminate most ignition knocks and pings . . . you must get instant carbon-free, cold weather starting . . . and you must get this thrilling, new-car performance year-in and year-out — *FOR TWO FULL YEARS, OR 30,000 MILES* — or I'll send you a new set — *FREE!*

You have nothing to lose! *BUT THE SUPPLY OF THESE PLUGS IS STRICTLY LIMITED. THE NICKEL ALLOY WHICH MAKES UP THEIR ELECTRODES IS HELD IN SHORT SUPPLY BY THE UNITED STATES GOVERNMENT. THIS WILL BE ABSOLUTELY THE LAST TIME WE CAN MAKE THIS OFFER! ACT TODAY!*

FREE BONUS!

Sensational, Nationally Advertised, Car Book Saves You Up To $250 On Repairs This Year Alone!

Over a quarter-of-a-million drivers have paid up to $3.00 for the same exact money-saving handbook! But now IT'S YOURS FREE!

The legendary Car Book that made history by showing millions of economy-minded car-owners how they could save up to $250 a year in costly gas and repair bills. The sensational book that ripped the lid off all the professional tips and tricks known by the nation's trouble-shooters and ace mechanics! Here, are all the eye-opening, money-saving secrets that save you dollar after dollar in costly car upkeep and repairs.

Here are simple tips that show you how to add amazing mileage to your car — without touching a tool — without even lifting the hood of your car! Here's a fantastic 30-second trick that gives you up to 2-3-4 miles more per gallon! Another secret shows you how to switch one single wire and save up to 50 gallons of gas in your winter driving . . . how you can add up to 10,000 more miles to your tires . . . how to get your "dead" battery started in just one minute — without a push or a tow!

Yes, professional tips that can save you hundreds of dollars a year! And it's all yours — *FREE!* How would you like to get power to zoom away from other cars at the lights . . . to drive up to 5,000 miles—without changing your oil! Other ingenious tips show you how to remove rust from your chrome . . . make dents and scratches disappear for good . . . to stop steering wheel "play" . . . how to adjust your own brakes and save $5 . . . to repair your clutch yourself and save $13 . . . to fix a leaky radiator and save $20!

Yes, all this and more is yours—absolutely *FREE* — our *BONUS GIFT* to you with your purchase of the amazing new *"POWER-FLASH" PLUGS* which are absolutely guaranteed for two years or 30,000 miles of the most fabulous spark plug service you've ever enjoyed! But if you want this special *FREE BONUS* — the sensational book "How To Double The Performance Of Your Car" — you must order your *"POWER-FLASH" PLUGS* today! Our supply of this free, Final Edition of the Car-Book is limited! So act *NOW!*

HERE'S PROOF!

Users Report Fantastic New Mileage — Breathtaking New Power!

"Your Power Plugs are well on the way to paying for themselves. So far have saved about $8.00 a month on my gasoline bill. As far as I can figure, I am getting 9 miles more per gallon of gas than I used to get.

"Although I did have a new set of spark plugs in my car before replacing them with your Power Plugs, the old plugs made my engine spit and gallop. Now it really runs smooth and starts a lot better, too."

R. O., Duluth, Minn.

"I bought your plugs for my '54 Ford some time ago . . . as far as I can tell I am getting at least 8 miles per gallon better mileage. Also my Ford has far better pickup and horsepower. I have driven about 12,000 miles since purchasing the plugs and they are in as good condition as ever."

C. M., Avilla, Indiana

"I replaced the equipment-type spark plugs in my Lincoln Continental with yours. With the old style plugs, I was getting approximately 15 miles to the gallon. During the first thousand miles of operation with Power Plugs, my mileage increased to 22 miles per gallon. This was an increase of 7 miles per gallon. In addition to the increased mileage, I was happy to notice much better idling and absolutely no stalling. Hills which I formerly took in second gear now present no problem in climbing with high gear. My heavy Continental used to lope away from signals, now it dashes away."

D. C. W., President Exporting Co.

A BOSS MECHANIC SAYS:

"I earn my living repairing automobiles. As a master mechanic I have installed all kinds of spark plugs over the past 18 years. You boys really have something. I have never seen a plug before that fires so true and hot and on our test equipment, every installation has shown a big increase in horsepower; as much as 20% in some cases. For the boys who want more power and better pickup, you have the answer."

J. C., Magnolia, Arkansas

"Your plugs have been in my car now for three or four months, and I must say it's running better than it ever did before, and I am getting a lot better mileage out of it. At least as much as the 15% you claim."

"I'd say your plugs are well worth the price you ask, especially as I do not expect to have to buy a new set as long as I have my present car—a 1953 Mercury."

R. H. D., Chicago, Ill.

33,000 MILES WITHOUT A SINGLE ADJUSTMENT

"I have just disposed of the car in which your spark plugs were installed. The following facts may be of interest to you.

"Speedometer reading, mileage at installation—27,756—mileage at this date — 61,334. No replacement nor adjustments since installation and plugs giving perfect service."

G. K. H., Indianapolis, Indiana

AMAZING MONEY-BACK GUARANTEE!

Clip this guarantee section out of this page. It authorizes you to try these amazing POWER-FLASH Spark Plugs *entirely at our risk!* First — test them for one full month for *surging power, thrilling new driving performance, breathtaking gas savings alone!* During that very first month alone:

1) These plugs must give you up to 9 miles MORE per gallon — INSTANTLY — *or every cent of your money back!*

2) These plugs must give you up to 20 MORE horsepower — INSTANTLY — *or every cent of your money back!*

And 3) — as an *extra added assurance* — These plugs must *continue* to give you this power, performance and gas savings — FOR TWO FULL YEARS—*or we will send you a brand-new set, ABSOLUTELY FREE!*

You have nothing to lose! This is probably the most amazing guarantee in car history! No strings! No questions asked! Act TODAY!

© Entire Contents Copyrighted by Eugene Stevens, Inc., 1956

Mail No Risk Coupon Today!

EUGENE STEVENS, INC.
31 WEST 47th STREET, NEW YORK 36, N. Y.
DEPT. RP-8

IMPORTANT: Please fill in the entire coupon. PLEASE PRINT!

Gentlemen: Yes, I want to try your amazing "POWER-FLASH" jet finish Spark Plugs entirely at your risk! I will pay postman only amount checked below plus low C.O.D. charges:

☐ $8.70 for a matched set of six "POWER-FLASH" Spark Plugs ☐ $11.60 for a matched set of eight "POWER-FLASH" Spark Plugs.

I understand that these "POWER-FLASH" Plugs must give me more power, tremendous new performance, amazing gas savings . . . must actually do everything you say for a period of 2 FULL YEARS or 30,000 MILES, or I may simply return them for a NEW SET FREE!

Also send me as your Extra Gift Premium, the Free nationally advertised car-book, "How To Double The Performance Of Your Car." This book is mine to keep as a Free Gift even if I return the plugs.

MAKE OF CAR________ YEAR________

MODEL________ NO. OF CYLINDERS________

NAME________

ADDRESS________

CITY________ ZONE________ STATE________

☐ CHECK HERE AND SAVE MORE! Enclose check or money order and we pay all postage and handling charges. You save as much as $1.00!

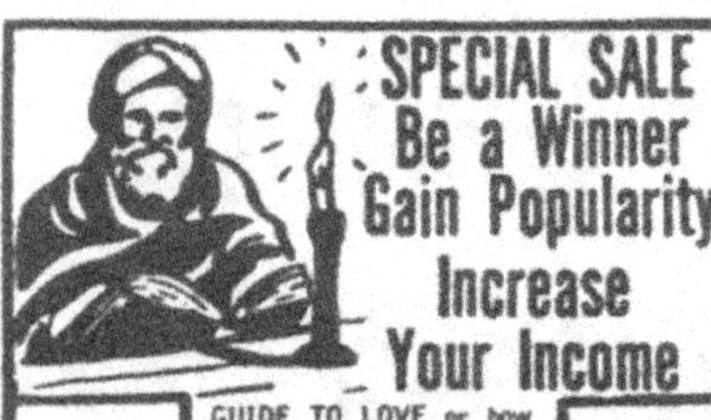

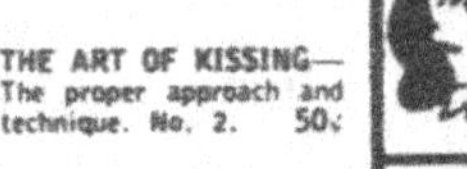

GUIDE TO LOVE or how to win and hold the man or woman of your choice. No. 1. 50¢

THE ART OF KISSING—The proper approach and technique. No. 2. 50¢

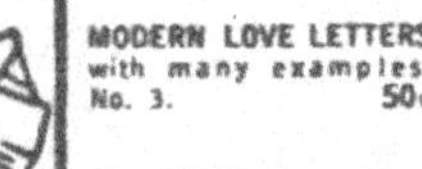

MODERN LOVE LETTERS with many examples. No. 3. 50¢

JU-JITSU for personal defense and counter attack. No. 4. 50¢

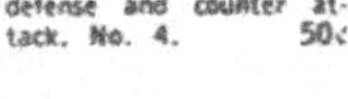

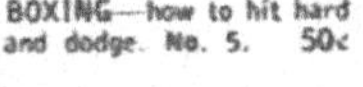

BOXING—how to hit hard and dodge. No. 5. 50¢

TOUCH TYPING in four hours with keyboard chart. No. 6. $1.89

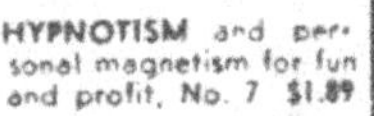

HYPNOTISM and personal magnetism for fun and profit. No. 7 $1.89

ALPHABET SHORTHAND—learn quickly and increase your income. No. 8. $3.89

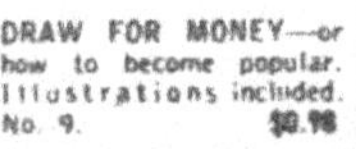

DRAW FOR MONEY—or how to become popular. Illustrations included. No. 9. $0.98

FOREIGN LANGUAGES—Spanish, French, Italian, German, Polish. No. 12. Each 50¢

VENTRILOQUISM—Secrets revealed, easy to learn. No. 16. 98¢

EXPERT AT CARDS—Surprise your friends with your ability to win. No. 17. 50¢

BUILD MUSCLES—Learn how, ideal for beginners. No. 18. $1.89

FORTUNE TELLING—by Cards. Nothing like it to cheer up a party, become popular. No. 19. 50¢

WRESTLING AND SELF DEFENSE—Teaches you how to overcome stronger opponents. No. 20. 50¢

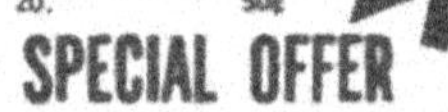

SPECIAL OFFER

$1-free in books for every $5 order
$3-free in books for every $10 order
(No COD's for less than $1.)

ROLLDEX

P. O. BOX B-7 Safety Harbor, Florida

Please send me the books I have circled:

1 2 3 4 5 6 7 8
9 12 16 17 18 19 20

☐ I enclose ______ and you pay all shipping charges.

☐ Please send C.O.D. plus shipping charges.

My Order of ______ entitles me to a
☐ $1-free in books ☐ $3 free in books

Name ______

Address ______

City ______ State ______

He looked pitiful standing there alone, without a real home, without a family, but he had snuffed out the precious lives of two small, defenseless girls. Sick in mind, Carlton Mason will probably never fully realize what he has done, but he will never again be in a position to repeat his horrible crime.

THE END

Kill Her by the Next Full Moon!

(continued from page 31)

choking the barracks phones. Broadfield, himself, sat glued to his desk, and personally answering each call. Almost every man and woman in the area, it seemed, was suspecting his neighbor. Targets for the bulk of the suspicion were those who either owned or drove trucks, despite the fact that many of the vehicles in question failed to conform to the description of the stake model.

"Our only hope is that stake truck," he told the troopers. "But if it wasn't a local one, we might as well call it quits. Tomorrow, for better or for worse, we'll try to get a list of all such trucks owned by persons living in the Adirondack area and we'll take it from there."

Sergeant Woolsey sat up with a sudden inspiration. "That gives me an idea," he said. "We've been taking it for granted that those cigarettes were available here in the immediate vicinity. But since they're not, first thing in the morning I'll phone the tobacco distributors over at Plattsburg and Yatertown and find out from them exactly who retails those smokes in this whole area."

Back on the job the following morning, Broadfield's first move was to get in touch with the Motor Vehicles Bureau at Albany, with a request for a list of the residents of that area who were registered as owners of stake trucks.

"Practically all stake trucks are manufactured by the same company—the Chevrolet division of General Motors," the bureau superintendent informed him. "We'll put a crew of girls to work checking the truck registrations for Chevrolets, and we'll phone you the minute the list's ready.

At two o'clock, the promised report from Albany was being relayed to Broadfield. The list contained a score of names and the owners in question were widely scattered throughout the general area. Broadfield lost no time assigning troopers to begin checking the names.

By noon of the following day, the list had been exhausted but without success. None of the truck owners,

To be really popular, you should know how to do many different things and do them well. An expert dancer is always in demand socially. A man who can box or wrestle is always liked and respected. People like you if you know how to entertain. And the man or girl who knows the art of love is REALLY desirable. These books tell you how.

LOVE AND ROMANCE
45. The Art of Kissing ....50¢
46. True Love Guide ....50¢
47. Modern Love Letters ....50¢

SELF-DEFENSE
24. Police Jiu-Jitsu ....50¢
25. Police Wrestling ....50¢
26. Scientific Boxing ....50¢
11. How to Fight ....50¢
12. American Judo ....50¢

DANCE INSTRUCTION
30. How to Dance ....50¢
31. Swing Steps ....50¢
32. Tap Dancing ....50¢

FORTUNE TELLING
8. Fortune Telling by Cards ....50¢
10. Astrology—Horoscopes. ....50¢

DREAMS AND THEIR MEANING
3. Prince All Dream Book ....50¢
19. What Your Dream Meant ....50¢
20. Dictionary of 1,000 Dreams ....50¢
4. Alleged Lucky Numbers Gypsy Dream Book, Formerly $1 ....50¢

CARD TRICKS
1. Herman's Card Tricks ....50¢
2. Thurston's Card Tricks ....50¢
63. Thursday's Card Tricks ....50¢

LANGUAGES SELF-TAUGHT
6. French Self-Taught ....50¢
7. Spanish Self-Taught ....50¢
15. Italian Self-Taught ....50¢
16. German Self-Taught ....50¢
17. Polish Self-Taught ....50¢

HYPNOTISM
40. 25 Lessons in Hypnotism ....50¢

MAGIC
65. Magic Made Easy ....50¢
64. Easy Card Magic ....50¢

TOASTS AND SPEECHES
55. The Big Toast Book ....50¢
56. Ready-Made Speeches and Toasts ....50¢

HUMOR
60. Joe Miller's Joke Book ....50¢
5. Famous Cowboy Songs ....50¢
9. Famous Poems and Recitations ....50¢
22. Famous Old Time Songs ....50¢
61. How To Be The Life Of The Party ....50¢
62. One Hundred Amusements ....50¢

SPECIAL OFFERS

Any Three Books.......$1.00
All 36 Books.......Only $11.00

WE PAY ALL WRAPPING AND POSTAGE COSTS IF MONEY IS SENT WITH ORDER

Money Back Guarantee

You must be satisfied . . . we know you will be. Examine for 5 days and if not delighted return for full purchase price refund.

How to Order

Pick out the books you want in this list. Fill out the coupon below, placing a circle around the number of each book you want, and mail the coupon to us now!

FILL OUT THE COUPON NOW!

PICKWICK CO., Dept. 810-A
Box 463, Midtown Sta., New York 18, N. Y.

I enclose $ .... (in cash or money order for which send me the books checked below.

45	30	1	40	60
46	31	2	65	5
47	32	63	64	9
24	8	6	55	22
25	10	7	56	61
26	3	15		62
11	19	16		
12	20	17		
	4			

Name ....

Street ....

City & Zone .... State ....

☐ If C.O.D. preferred mark X in box, mail coupon and pay postman, plus postage.
Canadian orders 20% additional—cash with order.

Medical TABLET *Discovery*

NEW *Effective* TREATMENT

FOR UNSIGHTLY SCALES, CRUSTS, PATCHES OF

PSORIASIS

TROPISAN

HERE'S WHAT PSORIASIS SUFFERERS SAY ABOUT TROPISAN AND THE BLESSED RELIEF THEY GET FROM EXTERNAL SYMPTOMS

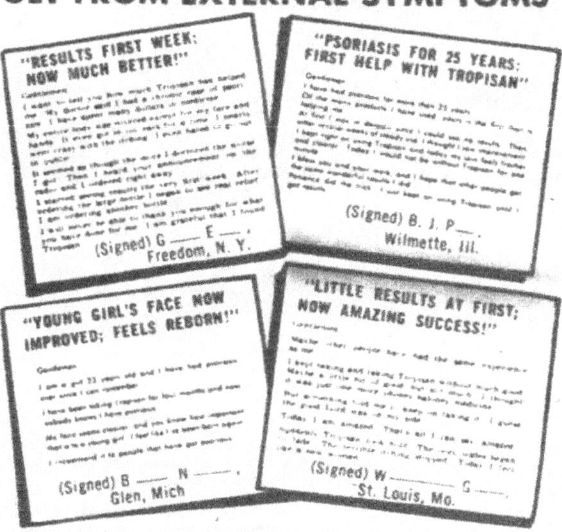

Start Living a Normal Life. No More Unsightly Bandages To Mar Work or Play. No More Mess or Fuss

Tropisan tablets are odorless and tasteless. Just pop a few into your mouth before each meal or snack. Keep tablets with you in any small handy container. Now at last you may say goodbye to smelly greasy oils or salves, to unsightly bandages that mark work or play. Taking Tropisan is as inconspicuous as taking aspirin. No one need ever know you're taking something for psoriasis.

MAKE THIS NO RISK HOME TEST: Here is your guarantee of satisfaction. Try Tropisan for the prescribed period. If you are not completely overjoyed with Tropisan, your purchase price will be cheerfully refunded. Accept this no-risk offer. Order Tropisan today!

SEND NO MONEY: Just name and address for generous home trial offer. On arrival pay postman $1 plus C.O.D. charges on guarantee of complete satisfaction or money back.

NEW HOPE FOR CRUSTS, SCALES — NO MESS, NO FUSS, SIMPLE SAFE EASY TABLET!

Proven "Effective Treatment"

Tropisan tablets taken as directed have proven to be an effective treatment for the relief of external psoriasis symptoms in many thousand cases. Many of these psoriasis sufferers had tried ointments, ungents, lotions and external applications with little success. Now Tropisan tablets have proven themselves to be an "effective treatment" in the relief of external psoriasis symptoms.

Every Reported Case Stated That Tropisan Tablets Relieved Symptoms To Some Degree With Continuous Use

Even people who had suffered disappointment after disappointment with almost every type and variety of treatment . . . people whose crusts and scabs would not fade with other medications . . . now found Tropisan tablets relieved symptoms. Yes, the itching stopped, the crusts, scales, oozing faded so no one need ever know you're taking medicine.

Strikes Internally To Relieve The External Symptoms Of Psoriasis

Almost all medical doctors believe that psoriasis occurs because of internal causes, possibly faulty fat metabolism. Tropisan is designed to strike and give relief of the external psoriasis symptoms through the blood stream—not just to act as a messy sticky goo for surface application.

Mail This Coupon Today

TROPISAN DRUG COMPANY **DEPT. 802**
2630 E. 75th St.
Chicago 49, Ill.

Please send me generous Home Trial Offer of Tropisan on guarantee of complete satisfaction or money back.

- ☐ Send C.O.D. I will pay postman $1 per package plus postage.
- ☐ Cash enclosed, ship prepaid.
- ☐ Send 2 packages for $2.00.

Name ______

Address ______

City ______ State ______

A WICKED EYEFUL!

That's what confronted *this* lucky male! "He forgot that he was a porter and had only one eye . . . He availed himself of those rights which his calling gave him to act like a brute. Brutal he was accordingly — and happy!" . . . Thus begins a gay evening session of THE PLEASURE PRIMER. Thousands are now enjoying *Rollicking Bedside Fun,* and you will too, when you possess this ideal bedside companion. Here's entertainment for open minds and ticklish spines. Here's lusty, merry recreation for unsqueamish men and women. Here's life with apologies to none. Collected, selected from the best there is, this zestful Primer is an eye-opener . . . YOU ARE INVITED TO EXAMINE THE PLEASURE PRIMER 10 DAYS AT OUR EXPENSE. IT IS GUARANTEED TO PLEASE OR YOUR PURCHASE PRICE WILL BE REFUNDED AT ONCE!

10-DAY TRIAL OFFER

PLAZA BOOK CO., DEPT. P-678
109 Broad St., New York 4, N. Y.

Please send THE PLEASURE PRIMER on 10-day trial. If I'm not pleased, I get my purchase price refunded at once.

☐ Send C.O.D. I'll pay postman 98c plus postage.
☐ I enclose $1. You pay all postage.

Name...
Address...
City.................Zone..........State..........

it developed, had been anywhere near Bloomingdale on the day of the crime.

Meanwhile, Woolsey and Rosbrook were meeting with equally disappointing results in their canvass of tobacco shops. Furnished with the desired list of their retail outlets by the tobacco distributors, the pair had talked to a good many steady smokers of Cubebs but without encountering anyone who drove a stake truck or answered to Betty Freen's description of the man who had yelled out his invitation to her on the road. And they were fast running out of retailers when, late in the afternoon of June 20th, the pair entered a small shop on a back street in Saranac Lake.

Informed of their errand, the man behind the counter nodded. "Yep, I usually stack 'em but I haven't had any in a month. Funny thing you should ask about 'em, 'cause I've had some calls lately from kids over at the CCC camp at Lake Barnum when they've been in town. They get 'em at the camp canteen, from what they told me."

Half an hour later, the two troopers were at the Civilian Conservation Corps camp at Lake Barnum, approximately 15 miles to the north.

"Do you have any stake trucks around here?" Woolsey asked.

The director nodded. "We have three Chevrolet trucks," he replied, "and they're all stake models."

"Any with diamond-shaped tire treads?"

"Yes. All of them. You see, everything we have around here is government issue, so the trucks and the tires they're equipped with are identical."

Woolsey rubbed his chin. "That's the reason we haven't been getting anywhere," he said, turning to Rosbrook. "We've been checking on privately owned vehicles, not figuring it was a government truck we were after."

The camp director raised his eyebrows. "Something wrong?" he asked.

The State Police sergeant shrugged. "We have no proof," he said, "only the fact that a stake truck was mixed up in a crime. Where were your trucks on the morning of June 23?"

The director squinted at a calendar. "That was a Saturday," he said, half to himself. "It would be our day for picking up supplies . . ."

He turned to the office records and soon produced an entry. "All three of those trucks were in Saranac Lake that morning. They took on loads at the Delaware and Hudson Railroad depot."

"Who were the drivers and did they get back together?" Woolsey asked.

When the director told him, Woolsey asked how they stacked up.

"All good boys, far as I know,"

LUGER AUTOMATIC WHOLESALE **$2.98**

6.50 mm.
10 Shot Magazine
DESIGNED by MASTER Craftsmen from the FAMOUS GERMAN FAST SHOOTING AUTOMATIC LUGER.
Be the Proud owner of this EXCITING AUTOMATIC model and the envy of your friends! Finished in SLEEK Blue-Black of High Impact #475 Styron and FANCY Polished-Chrome-type steel trigger!!
SHARP LOOKING—simulated knurled IVORY GRIPS!! Not an air or CO_2 gun. FIRES 10 SLUGS IN RAPID FIRE!!

NO C.O.D.'s

FREE—FREE SURPRISE PACKAGE!! PLUS 100 slugs with order of 2 LUGERS at $5.95. ORDER NOW—while they last. BE A TWO-GUN MAN!!
LOOK TERRIFIC SPECIAL!! SUPER HI-POWER Binoculars. Just IMPORTED! Terrific BUY! Just think—only $4.98. FREE Case and Surprise Pkg. First come, first served. Going Fast at THIS price. Few left. HURRY! HURRY! NO C.O.D.'s.
Krieger Labs., SK-1708 N. McCadden Pl., H'wood 28, Cal.

BORROW BY MAIL

PRIVATE $50 to $500

You can get the cash you need **immediately** . . . entirely by mail. **No co-signers** or endorsers required. No inquiries of employers, relatives, or friends. Convenient monthly payments to fit your income. **Men** and **women** with steady income eligible, anywhere in U. S. If you need $50 to $500 extra cash for **any purpose**, mail the coupon today; we'll rush **free** application blank to you.

Licensed by NEBRASKA BANKING DEPARTMENT

FREE Application Blank sent in Plain Envelope

AMERICAN LOAN PLAN
City National Bank Bldg.
Omaha 2, Nebraska . . . Dept. SM-8

Amount Wanted $

NAME...
ADDRESS...
CITY.............................STATE..............
OCCUPATION.......................AGE...............
Husband or Wife's OCCUPATION.........................

I'll Send You These Products FOR FREE TRIAL

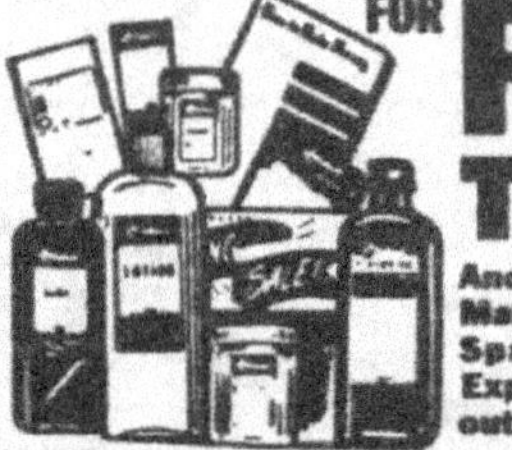

And Show You How to Make Money in Full or Spare Time without Experience and without Putting Up a Penny

Just send me your name and I'll rush you PREPAID these full-size packages of famous Blair Home Products: Cosmetics, Flavorings, Foods, etc. Make money introducing to friends, neighbors. Special bargains, valuable premiums, spectacular offers put you into a successful business of your own overnight. You don't need experience, and I give you credit. Assortment of full-size products for FREE TRIAL ready! Send no money. Write today.
BLAIR, Dept. 534-J, Lynchburg, Virginia

HANDS TIED?

—because you lack a HIGH SCHOOL DIPLOMA

• You can qualify for an American School Diploma *in spare time at home!* If you have left school, write or mail coupon for FREE booklet that tells how. No obligation of any kind.

OUR 60th YEAR

AMERICAN SCHOOL, Dept. HC12
Drexel at 58th, Chicago 37, Illinois

Please send FREE High School booklet.

Name...
Address...
City & State....................................

Complete Canadian Courses available. Write American School, Dept. HA12, 6083 Sherbrooke St. W., Montreal.

IMPORTANT Medical Facts For Every Man Who Has Passed His 40th Birthday

Men, Too, Go Thru "Change of Life"

DOCTORS CALL IT "MALE CLIMACTERIC"

WE MEN PAST FORTY HATE TO ADMIT IT! But—it's True! And, Thank Goodness, a Safe, New Discovery is Now Available (Without Prescription) To Us When We May Need it Most.

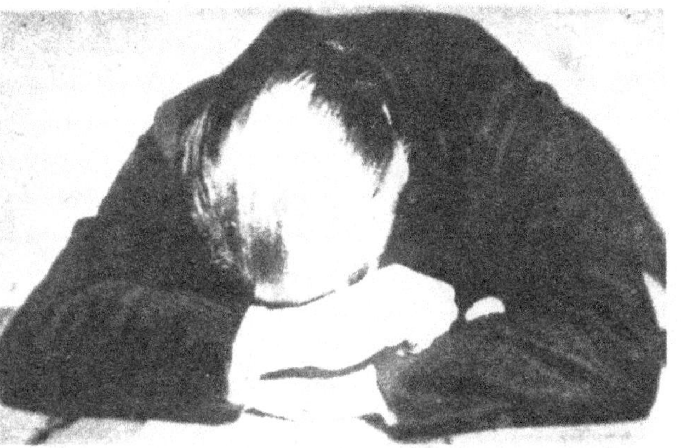

Doctors know it, employers know it . . . and many men past forty "feel" something is happening, but usually don't know what it is . . . After the first forty years, the human body undergoes important normal changes. But, men think that "change of life" occurs only in women! This "change" happens in MEN as well as women! You can be in perfect health and still go thru "change of life"... because it is a change that may occur in anyone over forty. Don't take my word for it . . . ask your doctor. During "male climacteric" or as we call it "change of life"... it is more important than ever that your body be at its strongest and not deficient in vital vitamins and minerals during this period. Yes, your body needs not just "any" vitamin or mineral . . . but a combination of nutritional supplements created especially for the needs of older men and women. If you've read this far, you are sincerely interested . . . please continue on for facts that will absolutely amaze you.

Amazing Health in a Capsule Discovery You've Long Heard Was Coming!

Recently, a well known scientist perfected this all new After 40 Capsule vitamin and mineral formula . . . he created it especially for men and women past forty. Yes, he combined a special group of essential vitamins and minerals that his years of study revealed were most needed, often lacking by folks approaching the late years when "change of life" usually occurs. Common sense and your doctor will tell you your body often requires a supply of different vitamins and minerals in different amounts during the older years than they did during your younger years to function at their best. Perhaps as a child you took cod-liver oil . . . you don't take it now. During your older years you are more interested in maintaining your body . . . during younger years the main interest was in growth. That's why the special AFTER 40 Capsule formula is so important . . . it was created for the exclusive needs of older folks . . . for YOU, and no one else. TRY AT OUR EXPENSE!

I've Said it . . . You've Said It Too,

"When I was Younger I Could Eat Anything . . . But Now . . ." It's An Old Story When You Get Past Forty!

You can fool yourself . . . but you can't fool Nature. As we grow older usually our appetite is smaller and our digestion isn't as good. We can't eat everything we should eat to maintain our best health. If we wear plates, or have missing teeth (which is common during the later years) we can eat only certain foods. It's no fun, I know. Just when we are at a time of life when we need every bit of nutritional help we can get . . . Nature seems to be working against us by making it more difficult to eat the foods we need most. During "change of life" we should be more careful than ever not to suffer vitamin or mineral deficiencies which may well aggravate or prolong our suffering. Don't take needless and foolish risks during this important time of your life. MAIL HOME TRIAL COUPON TODAY. SEE WHAT AN AMAZING DIFFERENCE AFTER 40 CAPSULES MAY MAKE IN **YOUR** LIFE!

ELMORENE CO., DEPT. G-393
230 N. Michigan Ave., Chicago 1, Ill.

Don't Surrender to Vitamin & Mineral Deficiency Until You've Made Sensational "No Risk" Home Trial Offer!

What Is Climacteric? . . .
Medical dictionaries tell us "climacteric" is the time of life when the body undergoes a radical change. First, usually between 12-17, when boys become men and girls women . . . and again usually between 40-50.

Whom Does Climacteric Affect?
Both men and women. In women it is called "menopause" or "change of life" . . . in men, doctors call it "Male Climacteric".

What Can Be Done? . . .
During the late years, it is more important than ever that your system isn't deficient in the very nutrients nature created to help your body in times of need. After 40 Capsules supply the body with a special combination of vitamins and minerals that are often lacking in older folks during these important years. SHOW THE AFTER 40 FORMULA TO YOUR DOCTOR . . . *he will tell you what an excellent one it is!*

"MIDDLE AGED" FOLKS, Please Read Carefully!

A famous scientist stated that nutrition is one of the greatest problems in preventative medicine. With After 40 Capsules you are taking the first step to keep your health from falling below par by supplying your body with essential vitamins and valuable minerals. These are absolutely necessary as your doctor will tell you to attain a healthier body and a better outlook on life. After 40 Capsules are especially designed for people over forty to combat vitamin and mineral deficiencies that may often lead to disease.

The vitamins and minerals found in After 40 Capsules are essential for body building and functioning. Inadequate supplies of vitamins and minerals may lead to illness and deficiency diseases which may be quite serious when you are over forty.

Each AFTER 40 Capsule Contains These 20 Important Ingredients Needed By "Middle-Aged" Folks

Vitamin A, Vitamin D, Vitamin E, Vitamin B1, Vitamin B2, Vitamin B12, Vitamin D, Niacinamide, Vitamin B6, Calcium Pantothenate, Rutin, Inositol, Defatted Wheat Germ, Choline, Iodine, Calcium, Phosphorus, Manganese, Copper & Iron.

—SEND NO MONEY . . . Just Mail "Home Trial" Coupon!—

Try After 40 Capsules at Our Expense. Just fill in coupon and mail to address below. On arrival of FULL MONTH'S SUPPLY of After 40 Capsules, pay postman only $5.00 and regular C.O.D. postage. Take as directed. You be the judge. If results are not to your entire satisfaction in every way, return label within one month from date of purchase for prompt, cheerful refund. Fair enough? (Save C.O.D. postage, send $5.00 cash, check or money order, After 40 Capsules sent prepaid. Same guarantee.) MAIL TODAY!

NAME________________

ADDRESS________________

CITY________________ZONE____STATE________

ELMORENE CO., Dept. G-393, 230 N. Michigan Ave., Chicago 1, Illinois

SHE'LL LOVE YOU FOR 'EM

Here is the nite time garment inspired by the fashions of the palaces of the near East, where often hundreds of women compete to attract one man.

YOU'LL LOVE HER IN 'EM

Just notice how the soft lace of the top caresses her bare shoulders, softly encloses to conceal yet reveal. Then watch how the harem pants fall in sheer curves and folds from the hips to the ankles, teasingly caressing the thighs with each little movement, ever revealing startling new aspects of charms. Made of nylon in sheer bewitching black or daring, fiery, filmy red. Only $6.95. Shipped in plain wrapper. State bust and waist size. **Send no money.** Order C.O.D. and pay postman on delivery plus postage. Save by sending payment. We pay postage.

Smoothee Co., Dept. HP-6, Lynbrook, N.Y.

was the answer. "Right now they're over to Union Falls on a job. They'll be back around noon."

"We'll wait for them," Woolsey said.

Rosbrook drew the sergeant aside and told him about an idea that had just come to him. "We've got a chance to look over their clothing while they're gone," he said. "If one of them killed that girl, he'd be pretty sure to have got his things bloodstained. And he wouldn't be apt to be wearing them around."

Woolsey nodded and swung back to the director. "Where do those fellows keep their clothes?" he asked.

Explaining that the camp provided lockers, the director led the two troopers to the other end of the barracks. A minute later, he was pulling up in front of a double row of lockers and producing a set of keys from his pocket.

In the first two lockers they inspected, Woolsey and Rosbrook found nothing. But on looking into the third, the two troopers found a collection of pornographic pictures concealed there.

"Who uses this locker?" Woolsey demanded.

The director consulted his records. "Thomas Showers," he replied.

"He's the fellow we want to talk to," Woolsey said.

Around noon, when the three trucks pulled into the yard, Showers' machine was pointed out. The officers approached the vehicle and saw a tall, slim youth who answered, in every detail, to the description Betty Freen had given of him. A cigarette dangled from his lips.

"We want to talk to you," Woolsey said.

Showers blew out a cloud of smoke. "What about?" he drawled.

"We think maybe you can tell us about a girl who disappeared from home on June 23rd."

The youth looked back, the cigarette poised halfway to his lips. "What would I know about that?"

Woolsey did not answer directly. "Is that a Cubeb you're smoking?" he wanted to know.

"Yeah," Showers replied. "What about it?"

"This about it," the sergeant told him. "We're taking you back to Malone with us."

At Malone, surrounded by Captain Broadfield, Prosecutor Harold Main, Coroner Cargill, Herrick, McCann, McGinnis and Woolsey, the suspect turned all questions aside with blunt refusals to answer.

"I ain't done nothin'," he said finally, "and I don't like the idea of being here answering questions. If you think I'm the guy who did it, get ready to prove it."

Broadfield signalled an end to the interrogation. "We'll do just that,"

MAGNIFYING GLASSES

FOR FOLKS OVER 40

NOW.—magnifying lenses for elderly folks who don't wear glasses regularly, who do not have astigmatism or diseases of the eye, and who have difficulty reading newspapers, the Bible and doing fancy work. It's no longer necessary to struggle and squint with an old-fashioned magnifying glass which has only one lens, because Precision Magnifying glasses bring you a magnifying lens for each eye and help stop eyestrain and discomfort. Permit restful reading hour after hour like you never did before. Try them at home on a five day trial plan that leaves no room for doubt.

PRECISION MAGNIFYING GLASSES

A Blessing for Elderly Folks

Lenses are scientifically (not Rx) ground and polished, then fitted into a frame of simulated zylonite. Truly they add to your looks, and, for reading purposes they're wonderful. Complete satisfaction guaranteed. Best order a pair today.

SEND NO MONEY

Just mail name, address and age. On arrival pay postman only $4.00 plus C.O.D. postage. Wear them 5 days, then, if you aren't more than satisfied return for refund of purchase price. If you remit with your order, we ship prepaid, same guarantee. Order from:

PRECISION OPTICAL, INC.

Dept. 654-J **Rochelle, Ill.**

CORNS·CALLOUSES

Lift Right Off in 30 Minutes

Say goodbye to laming corns and callouses that make you limp around in torture. New easy safe painless liquid discovery called Half-Hour Cornmaster removes even stubborn corns and callouses in 30 minutes! Just dab on, let set, lift off. No cutting, no pads. Removes soft corns between toes just as easy. Not in stores. Send $1 for enough to get rid of 25 corns and callouses. Postpaid. Special 3 for $2.50. If C.O.D. postage extra. $1 deposit on C.O.D. orders. Be delighted in 30 minutes or return for money back. Write to

TINTZ CO., DEPT. 427 230 N. Michigan Ave. Chicago 1, Ill.

LOSE WEIGHT

WHILE YOU SLEEP!

Don't let EXCESS WEIGHT hinder your social and business life. TRIM THOSE E-X-T-R-A POUNDS off your body—WHILE YOU SLEEP—with our revolutionary NEW secret method.

NO CALORIE COUNTING — NO EXERCISING!

R. W. of Toronto, Canada, says: "I lost 23 pounds in 2 short weeks." J. H. of New York City, states: "Your new scientific method took off 47 pounds of excess weight. I now enjoy myself as never before, and find it easy to make new friends."

Take advantage NOW of this new, EASY road to personal happiness and success. Don't delay—in ONLY 10 DAYS you can have a NEW, TRIM FIGURE! FEEL AND LOOK BETTER. For COMPLETE kit, with fully described instructions, rush only $3.00 to Dept. 18, North-West Research Institute, South 11 Altamont Street, Spokane, Wash. THE SUPPLY IS LIMITED!

YOU MUST BE COMPLETELY SATISFIED OR YOUR MONEY REFUNDED IN FULL.

SIGN PAINTING

Teaches you commercial sign painting and sign building as it is being done TODAY in leading shops all over the country. A good practical course for self-instruction. Shows latest methods of doing truck lettering, office doors, wood letters, reflecting signs, plastics, sprayed signs, gold leaf, silk screen process, alphabets, etc. Includes money-making business information. Full price only **$4.95.** Satisfaction guaranteed! Just circle **No. 101** in coupon.

SHOW CARD WRITING

Practical training for beginners and tricks-of-the-trade for those already in the field. Very complete teaching plan takes you through each step of the trade from fundamentals of lettering to how to run your own show card studio successfully. Tells you where and how to begin in this field, teaches alphabets, layout, spacing, color application, etc. All fully illustrated with actual commercial work as practical examples. Complete price only **$4.95** Circle **No. 102** in the coupon. Satisfaction or refund!

MACHINE SHOP Practice

Unusually complete study of all the standard operations performed on lathe, drill press, shaper, planer, milling machine, grinding machine, etc. Also includes practical information on layouts, measurements and the use of machinists' hand tools. Shows you step-by-step how to read a blue-print, how to do practical machine shop work. Full price only **$3.97** postpaid. Satisfaction or your money back. Circle **No. 121** in coupon below.

HOW TO DRAW FUNNY PICTURES

Complete—practical—and easy-to-follow. A short course in cartooning containing more than 200 original illustrations! Tells you exactly what materials you need to start with. Then carefully instructs you every step of the way through caricature, illustrated jokes, sports cartooning, chalk talking, political and editorial cartooning, etc. Begins with the simplest kinds of sketches to teach you how it's done! Full price only **$3.97.** Just circle **No. 125** in coupon below.

CONCRETE CONSTRUCTION

Complete illustrated instructions! Teaches you the best methods—as used TODAY. Includes proper procedure for building forms and pouring concrete. Details on materials to use and how to mix different kinds of concrete. You'll learn the tricks-of-the-trade for doing sidewalks, driveways, steps, etc. What tools to use and how to use them, how to make columns, walls, etc. Price is only **$3.97.** Satisfaction guaranteed. Circle **No. 113** in coupon below.

PRACTICAL ELECTRICITY

A short course in one handy volume. Teaches you how to understand and use electricity. How to do wiring for light and power, repair small motors, how to work on circuits, dynamos, generators, electroplating, heating, etc. Simple enough for beginners! Price **$2.97.** Circle **No. 115** in coupon.

How to Have a BETTER HOUSE

How to Build . . . Buy . . . Remodel

A priceless guide for prospective owners! Tells you in detail how to plan a new home from selection of the lot to arrangement of the furniture. Gives you a wealth of practical help on improvements and remodeling jobs. Instructs you on the art of getting the most for your money—how to select an architect, builder, contractor, material dealer. How to finance at lowest cost. Includes actual photographs and floor plans! Price only **$3.97.** Satisfaction or refund. Circle **No. 116** in coupon.

The HUMAN BODY!

Teaches you how your body is constructed, how it works. Big 640-page course explains EVERY part of the body with hundreds of excellent illustrations. Learn about your nervous system, blood pressure, sex and reproduction, stomach, heart, lungs, digestion, muscles, brain, skin, the five senses, etc. You will be fascinated with the expert recent information about cancer, pernicious anemia, emotional disorders, blood transfusion, wonder drugs, vitamins, etc. Learn what makes you tick . . . and learn how you can make the most of what you've got! Bargain price, only **$4.98.** Satisfaction or refund. Circle **No. 107** in coupon below.

PLUMBING MADE EASY

Practical one-volume short course. Written especially for the beginner in the trade and for the handy man home-owner. Shows you how to plan, install, maintain common plumbing systems economically and without violating regulations. Everything you want to know simply explained and well illustrated. Includes details on traps, drains, vents, stacks, water supply, valves, pipe fitting, joints, hot water supply, care, emergency repairing, etc. Latest printing! Price only **$2.98.** Satisfaction or your money back. Circle **No. 108** in coupon below.

IT'S EASY TO ORDER In coupon draw a circle around the number of each course you want us to send you. Print your name and full address clearly, then mail coupon right away. Send full payment with your order and we'll prepay all postage charges—on C.O.D. shipments you pay charges. Satisfaction or refund guaranteed . . . you take no risk.

FREE!! Select two or more courses from this page and we will include an **EXTRA** educational item as a special bonus . . . without any additional cost to you! You may keep this excellent Dividend Item, as your own, even should you send back for refund the courses you order. We reserve the right to withdraw this unusual offer when present limited stock is gone. Don't lose out—**mail coupon today!**

NELSON-HALL CO. *(Established 1909)*
210 S. Clinton St., Dept. 2GT-87 Chicago 6, Ill.

SPRAY PAINTING

A real good how-to-do-it text! For both industrial and Commercial use. These practical instructions teach the fundamental principles of spraying technique, together with the latest developments and practice of this craft. Arranged as a self-instruction course for spraygun operators in industrial concerns and commercial studios such as sign shops, interior and exterior decoration, etc. Includes excellent sections on flock and suede finishes, automobile work, etc. Unusually complete and well illustrated! Full price, only **$3.97** postpaid. Satisfaction guaranteed or your money back. Order "Spray Painting." Circle **No. 122** in coupon at bottom of page.

Only $3.47 COMPLETE SLIDE RULE MANUAL

Self-instruction text with logarithmic tables, including 10-place tables. Explains practical use of the slide rule for all purposes as employed by draftsmen, engineers, electricians, mechanics, business men, merchants, etc. Shows you how to solve nearly all problems with ease, speed, accuracy. Learning the slide rule is an investment in time that will pay you big dividends if you have figuring to do in any form. Latest edition. Price only **$3.47.** Order "Complete Slide Rule Manual." Circle **No. 104** in coupon below. Satisfaction or refund.

Blacksmithing & Horseshoeing

Useful instruction fresh from the anvil. Written by a successful working blacksmith—not a school teacher. Here is the everyday how-to-do-it information you need on shop equipment, tools, methods of horseshoeing, Wagon wheels and axle repair. Plowshares, hardening, pointing, sharpening, setting. Boiler work. Hoisting hooks. Horse diseases and treatments, etc. Good clear helpful illustrations. Full price only **$3.47** postpaid. Satisfaction guaranteed! Circle **No. 118** in coupon.

DIESEL ENGINES

Not technical—written for the average mechanically-minded man. Practical instructions on the care, operation and adjustment of all common Diesel engines. Excellent sections on the principles and construction of Diesel engines—and also the care and operation of electrical power equipment in connection with Diesel engines. Very complete and helpful lessons! Hundreds of illustrations. Full price only **$3.98.** Circle **No. 126** in coupon.

Learn SHEET METAL WORK

Virtually a self-instruction course complete in one handy volume. Practical, usable information on pattern drafting and construction work, in light and heavy gauge metal, including sky-lights, roofing cornice work, patterns for forced air fittings, etc. Air conditioning is creating wonderful opportunities for ambitious men in the sheet metal field. This big illustrated treatise is the latest revised edition! Price only **$3.97.** Satisfaction or refund. Circle **No. 106** in the coupon.

WELDING COURSE Latest information in this fine one-volume course covering arc, spot, butt and flash electric welding; gas welding and cutting; hand forging; thermit welding; brazing and soldering, etc. Explains materials required for each kind of weld, then lists equipment and tools required, then gives you step by step instructions on how to complete each job satisfactorily. Price only **$3.47.** Circle **No. 112** in coupon.

FINGERPRINTING

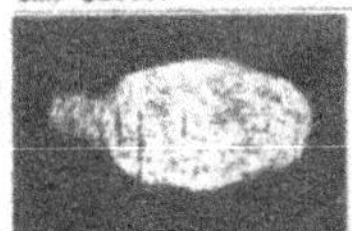

Well-illustrated simplified course in one handy volume. Teaches you the science of reading, classifying and identifying fingerprints. Includes many sample prints enlarged for easy study. Also includes questions and answers for self-instruction! Full price only **$3.47.** Satisfaction guaranteed. Circle **No. 127** in coupon.

HANDYMAN'S CYCLOPEDIA

SHOWS YOU HOW TO SAVE HUNDREDS OF DOLLARS AROUND YOUR HOME EVERY YEAR! Like having a dependable hired man around your place 24 hours each day. Tells everything . . . shows everything . . . repairing, remodeling, modernizing . . . carpentry, painting, decorating . . . plumbing, heating, electric wiring and appliance repairing, furniture repairs, etc. Wonderfully illustrated—every operation pictured! Will save you time, trouble and money . . . and will make you the smartest handy man on your street. Full price only **$4.97.** Satisfaction or refund. Circle **No. 114** in coupon.

ELECTRIC APPLIANCE SERVICING

Practical guide to job and business success in this big and important new field. Illustrated how-to-do-it information on repairing all common household appliances: food mixers, sewing machines, vacuum cleaners, washing machines, ironers, roasters, waffle irons, chimes, percolators, toasters, etc. Valuable self-instruction lessons for the handy man who wants information fast and hates to waste time! Full price only **$3.97.** Circle **No. 103** in coupon.

How to Mix COLORS and PAINTS

Expert up-to-date information for interior decorators, house painters, artists and craftsmen. Full list of easy-to-follow formulas. Extra color charts included. Also includes full information on white lead, paint oils, thinners, driers, paint mixing methods, color theories, matching secrets, aluminum paints, color harmony, color schemes, etc. Newest edition. Price only **$3.49.** Order "Colors & Paints." Circle **No. 105** in coupon below. Satisfaction or money back!

CARPENTRY LESSONS

Fully explains and illustrates practically every step from selection of proper tools, how to use them, and how to do hundreds of kinds of finished jobs. Will instruct the beginner and the practical home-owner how to do professional work. Show you through clear illustrations how to hang doors, sharpen tools, use steel square, make window and door frames, floor and ceiling work, boxing, sidings, roofing, screens, heavy timber framing and reinforcing, how to use power tools, etc. Full price only **$3.98.** New edition. Satisfaction guaranteed! Order "Carpentry." Circle **No. 110** in coupon.

TELEVISION SERVICING

Instructions on the more basic fundamentals which do not change from one model to the next. Teaches you practical trouble shooting. Easy-to-follow, well-illustrated information for the handy man. Full price only **$4.97.** Circle **No. 45** in coupon.

PAPER HANGING

Self-Instruction Text—Only $3.97

Thoroughly illustrated, step-by-step, one-volume course for self-instruction. Complete enough for vocational training and simple enough for the average home-owner. Each job, each step is explained in detail. Easy to follow and get perfect results.

SELF-INSTRUCTION TEXT—Only $3.97

Teaches you about paste-table work, hanging patterns, hanging side-wall and ceiling paper, hanging tonal paper, etc. Complete price only **$3.97.** Satisfaction or refund. Just circle **No. 124** in the coupon below.

PAINTING & DECORATING Complete Cyclopedia

ONLY $3.98

Professionals in the trade use this handy one-volume course as a reference to keep abreast with the latest methods. But it is written so simply and illustrated so thoroughly that the average home-owner and beginner in the trade finds the lessons easy to understand and practical to follow. You will find everything from A to Z at your finger-tips—nothing left for you to guess at.

347 STEP-BY-STEP ILLUSTRATIONS!

Shows you how to do ceilings, with paint, paper, whitewash, calcimine, etc.; shows you how to do floors and steps; how to do walls, inside and outside, what tools to use, what materials you need, how to prepare surfaces to simplify your work, how to stain, paint, varnish, marble, enamel, fume; complete detailed instructions on how to do a thousand and one jobs! Full price only **$3.98** postpaid. Satisfaction guaranteed. Circle **No. 123** in coupon.

AUTO REPAIRING

Trouble shooting guide. Sound up-to-date. Complete illustrated instructions on operation, maintenance and repair of your car. Includes ignition, transmission, steering, body, tune-up, etc. Easy to understand! Complete price only **$2.98.** Circle **No. 47** in coupon.

REFRIGERATION

Practical service manual—like a self-instruction course—teaches you the newest professional methods of repairing and taking care of electric refrigerators and refrigeration systems. Up-to-date! Complete price only **$3.47.** Circle **No. 119** in coupon.

REAL ESTATE BUSINESS

Train yourself for a profitable career in this booming profession! Practical lessons on appraisals, valuations, management, investments, real estate operating low-cost housing, the law on real estate transactions including legal forms, salesmanship, etc. Strictly up-to-date! Complete price only **$9.95.** Satisfaction guaranteed. Circle **No. 31** in coupon.

STEEL SQUARE Complete practical study of the steel square and how to use it. Teaches you which of your craft problems can be solved by a steel square—and shows you step by step how to solve them! Valuable to anyone in the building trades as well as the practical home-owner who wants to do professional-looking work. Hundreds of helpful illustrations. Full price only **$3.47.** Circle **No. 111** in coupon.

HEATING, COOLING and AIR CONDITIONING

Especially prepared by experts *for the amateur*. Combined reference manual and instruction text. Ideal for the home-owner, as well as the ambitious man who wants to get into these fine growing trades. Illustrated practical information on how to select, install and operate all standard types of equipment. Contains extra section on radiant heating. Very valuable one-volume course! New revised edition. Price only **$4.98** postpaid. Satisfaction guaranteed. Circle **No. 120** in coupon.

Mail This No-Risk Coupon Today

NELSON-HALL COMPANY, DEPT. 2GT-87 P
210 South Clinton Street, Chicago 6, Ill.

Please rush me the practical concentrated courses I have circled below. I understand each is complete and this is the full price, nothing more for me to pay. I have the right to examine everything you send me for 10 full days. Then if I am not more than satisfied in every way I will return the material and you guarantee to make complete immediate refund, without question or quibble. (Draw a circle around the number of each course you want.)

31	45	47	101	102	103	104	105	106	107
108	109	110	111	112	113	114	115	116	117
118	119	120	121	122	123	124	125	126	127

☐ I enclose $.............................. in full payment. Ship entirely postpaid.
☐ Ship C.O.D. for $.............................. plus postage.

NAME..

ADDRESS..

CITY.......................................STATE...............

☐ Check here if above order is for two or more numbers. In this case we send you, **without extra charge**, a fine educational volume as a bonus. You'll be delighted with this excellent gift. And it is yours to keep, free, even if you return the courses after inspection. MAIL this coupon NOW—this special bonus offer is subject to cancellation when our present stock runs out.

READING GLASSES ONLY $2.95
FOR PEOPLE OVER 40
See Fine Print

GET THE FINEST PLANO-CONVEX LENSES AND SAVE UP TO $12 OR MORE

You will bless the day you read this ad! No longer need you strain or squint to read small type. CLEARVISION MAGNIFYING SPECTACLES make small type you could hardly read jump up clear and large. Now you can read fine Bible print, find telephone numbers and read newspapers with ease never before possible.

30 DAY FREE TRIAL—SEND NO MONEY

CLEARVISION READING GLASSES use lenses which are ground and polished to high standards of precision. You could pay up to $18 for glasses and not get greater usefulness or satisfaction. They are set in attractive, shock-resistant optical frames designed for years of service and they cost you complete only $2.95. If you have eye disease or astigmatism, consult your physician to be sure you will be helped by ready to wear magnifying spectacles.

GUARANTEED PERSONAL SATISFACTION OR MONEY BACK

Order today. Send your name, address, age and sex. We will rush your Clearvision Reading Glasses to you. Send $2.95 purchase price plus 25c for shipping and handling. Or send no money, order COD—you pay postman same charges plus COD postage. If you are not completely satisfied just return them within 30 days. We will refund the full purchase price promptly.

NULIFE PRODUCTS, DEPT. P-11
COS COB, CONN.

KISS and Cry No More!

Your "sexcess" depends on *when, where, how, how much, with whom*—and a lot more. It calls for the *right line* and the *sure touch*. And what you don't know can hurt you!

EVERY DETAIL PICTURE-CLEAR

Lay questions, doubts and fears to rest. Get straightened out and "cued up" with the best-selling FROM FREUD TO KINSEY, now in its ninth large printing. All the answers you need in plain man-and-woman talk—every detail picture-clear! Exciting entertainment from cover to cover!

MONEY BACK GUARANTEE

Order FROM FREUD TO KINSEY in plain wrapper now. If not pleased, return it for refund of purchase price. Don't go another night without it!

10 DAY FREE TRIAL • MAIL COUPON NOW

PLAZA BOOK CO., Dept. K-138
109 Broad St., New York 4, N. Y.
Rush FROM FREUD TO KINSEY in plain wrapper for 10 DAY FREE TRIAL. If not satisfied, I get my purchase price refunded at once.
☐ Send C.O.D. I'll pay postman $1.98 plus postage.
☐ I enclose $1.98. You pay all postage.

Name.............................. Age.....
Address......................................
City.................. Zone..... State......
Canada & Foreign—No C.O.D.—Send $2.30

he told Showers. "And while we're doing it, you're going to stay right here."

At the commandant's instructions, Woolsey and Rosbrook went back to the camp and talked with the men who had driven the other trucks on the fatal day.

"Was Showers' truck with you all the way down and back?" the sergeant asked them.

The pair took time out to think back; then both shook their heads. Showers, they said, had trailed them down Route 3 to a point about halfway to Saranac Lake. Then suddenly, he had swerved off to a side road running between Onchiota and Vermontville.

Later, they said, when they were fully loaded at the Saranac Lake depot, Showers showed up and begged them to wait for him. "I don't want to get in a jam with the CO." he said. That was the reason, the pair explained, that all three trucks arrived back in camp practically together.

From Showers' locker the police officers seized a jumper and dungarees that had been recently washed. At the canteen, the manager told them Showers was a steady buyer of Cubeb cigarettes.

Back at Malone with their evidence and testimony, Woolsey and Rosbrook learned that the tires of Showers' truck had been found to match the roadside tracks and that his shoes fitted into the casts of the footprints.

With the case against him apparently clinched, the CCC worker continued to hold out, though not with such vehemence as before. His chin now trembled as he answered questions, and with each new piece of evidence produced, he slumped lower in his chair.

"There's just one thing more," Captain Broadfield said, reaching into his drawer. "When that girl struggled with you, she pulled some of your hair out by the roots. I have that hair here and I'm sure . . ."

Showers put his hands up to his face. "Never mind," he said. "I'll tell you. I did it, but it was an accident."

The youth then proceeded to relate one of the most fantastic stories the police in that region had ever heard.

"She was walking along the road," he said, "when I drove up alongside of her. I yelled something and she must have become frightened. She slipped and fell under the back wheel of the truck and I ran over her.

"I could see she was badly hurt. I got panicky. I put her in my truck and headed toward Bloomingdale. She was moanin' all the way. Finally I stopped and carried her into the woods. It was one of those things," he said. "She looked so pretty. And the moon was full.

Help Your BACK Feel Years Younger!

Even Pounding Vibration loses much of its power to wear you out when you guard your back with Pi Peer BACK-EASER.

Pi Peer BACK-EASER®

Rests and Massages Back Muscles As you Work and Walk

Work more rested!—Feel, look and act more comfortable, guarded against needless soreness and tiredness in that weary, strained or weak back. Even despite a pounding, back-jarring job . . . standing all day . . . lifting, etc. That's the promise of the makers of new Pi Peer BACK-EASER. You'll get all these blessings—or GET YOUR MONEY BACK!

Not Like Others!

Don't think of Pi Peer BACK-EASER as any other "back rest," "back belt," etc. It's different and better, from its muscle-engineered sacroiliac cushion (which massages the back as you move) to its balanced-pull belt. This last advanced design keeps equalized support on pelvis and sacroiliac; can't twist itself; can't twist **you**! Yet it's light, soft, completely washable and easy to wear as your shorts.

Why You Feel So Much Better

Actually Pi Peer BACK-EASER works like "extra back muscles" to "hold you together." You look better, too, because Pi Peer BACK-EASER helps flatten sagging belly muscles, makes it easier to breathe deeper; meantime "massage-action" spinal cushion stimulates circulation.

We'll Prove It at Our Risk!

Don't just take our word for it—(and do nothing!). Accept our challenge and find out how much more **rested**—more **youthful**—yes, more **healthy** you can feel, wearing Pi Peer BACK-EASER. Order from us on this daring offer: We'll send you the BACK-EASER. Try it 10 days. If you're not convinced, send it back, and we'll refund every cent of your money! Very little money, too, for so much comfort — we send Pi Peer BACK-EASER under our solid guarantee, for only $5.95 postpaid (cash, check or money order). Use coupon below to order. Mail it today!

Piper Brace Co., DEPT. BD-87B
811 Wyandotte St., Kansas City 5, Mo.

ORDER NOW!

Piper Brace Co., DEPT. BD-87B
811 Wyandotte, Kansas City 5, Mo.

Send ...... Pi Peer BACK-EASERS at $5.95 each. My measurement around hips is ...... inches.

Name
Address
City, State
$.......... ☐ money order enclosed ☐ cash ☐ check

"Never mind!" Broadfield, revolted, ordered. "Go on with your story."

It dawned on Showers that he would be in for a bad time of it if the girl lived and identified him. Accordingly, he had ripped off a piece of sapling and proceeded to beat her until she died.

"Then I got the hell out of there," he wound up his sordid story.

In the absence of even the slightest medical evidence that Cleo Tellstone had been run over by a truck, Showers' entire story was branded a lie by the officers.

Indicted three weeks later, on November 27th, 1939, the smirking twenty-year-old killer went on trial. Speedily found guilty, he was promptly sentenced to life imprisonment at Clinton Prison, Dannamora, for his crime.

EDITOR'S NOTE: *To protect a person innocently involved in this case, the name Betty Freen is fictitious as used here.*

THE END

Touch of Death

solution to puzzler on page 8

A typewriter – Marie's typewriter – had begun to glow. And the darker the evening grew, the more vivid and radiant the typewriter keys became.

Radium! Somebody had put radium on the keys of Marie's typewriter. As she struck away at the keys, the dread poison, invisible in the day time, was entering her body through her finger tips.

As soon as the doctors were informed of this new development, they began to treat Marie for radium poisoning and she began to respond. But the question remained –who had perpetrated such a fiendish plot? Who had tried to do away with pretty Marie through her fingertips?

The would-be killer turned out to be a deformed laboratory worker named Josef Kopriva. He had fallen madly in love with the attractive stenographer but Marie refused to encourage him. When it became clear that she would never have anything to do with him, he'd decided to arrange his revenge.

After prolonged but effective treatment, Marie finally recovered –and Josef Kopriva was sent to prison.

THE END

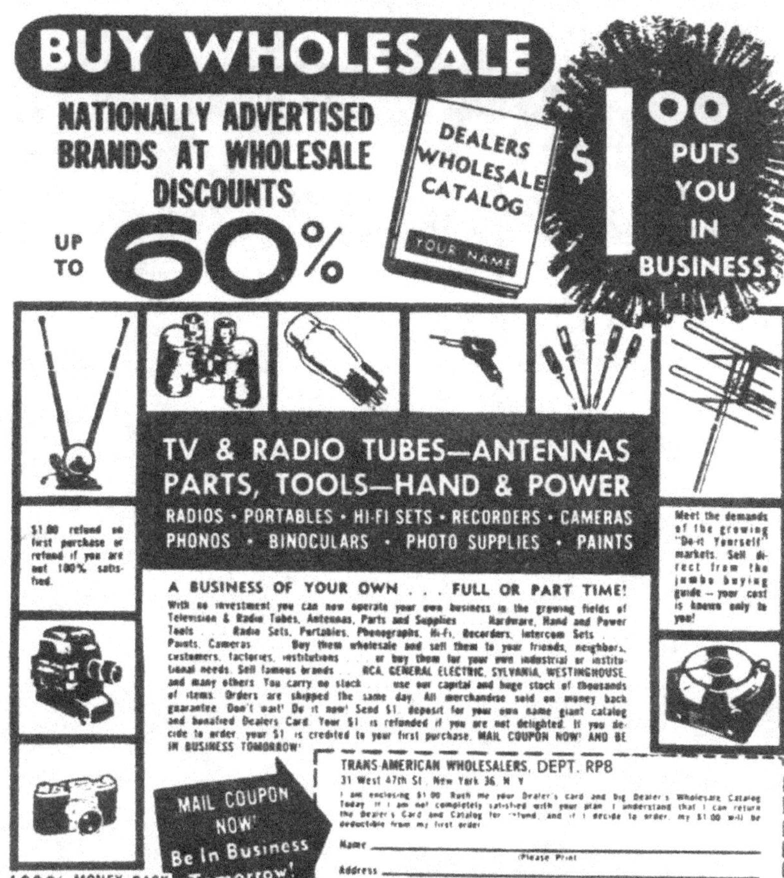

OPPORTUNITIES FOR EVERYBODY

Publisher's Classified Department (Trademark)

For classified advertising rates, write to William R. Stewart, 9 South Clinton Street, Chicago 6 (Men's Bi.-June-July) 7

EDUCATIONAL OPPORTUNITIES

COMPLETE YOUR HIGH School at home in spare time with 60-year-old school. Texts furnished. No classes. Diploma. Information booklet free. American School, Dept. XA18, Drexel at 58th, Chicago 37, Illinois.

FREE! "TALENT APTITUDE Test" Learn acting at home for TV, radio, theater, movie career. Hollywood Royal Academy, Studio F5, 5880 Hollywood Blvd., Hollywood 28, Calif.

LEARN WHILE ASLEEP! Details free. Research Association, Box 610-PE, Omaha.

CPA, ACCOUNTANT, BOOKKEEPER, Train at home. Free Information. Kitlow Business Institute, Alma 8, Nebraska.

LOANS BY MAIL

BORROW $50 TO $500. Employed men and women, over 25, eligible. Confidential no co-signers no inquiries of employers or friends. Repay in monthly payments to fit your income. Supervised by State of Nebraska. Loan application sent free in plain envelope. Give occupation. American Loan Plan, City National Bldg., Dept. BC-6, Omaha, Nebraska.

BORROW UP TO $600 By Mail. Employed men and women can borrow $100 to $600 from privacy of home. Speedy, easy and entirely confidential. No signers. No fees. No deductions. Money Request form sent Free, in plain envelope. State age, occupation and amount wanted. Postal Finance Co., 200 Keeline Bldg., Dept. 641K, Omaha, Nebraska.

SALESMEN WANTED

MAKE EXTRA MONEY. Cash commissions. Everybody buys easy-to-sell Advertising Book Matches. Union label. Big variety Glamour Girls, Scenics, Hillbillies. Powerhouse selling kit free. Steady repeat business. No experience necessary. Superior Match Co., Dept. G-657, 7528 S. Greenwood, Chicago 19.

ADD $20.00 TO $200.00 per week to your income with Miracle Bowls! Sell door to door and store to store. Just add water and watch them grow. Write for free literature now. Miracle Bowls, Dept. 161, Littleton, Colorado.

DETECTIVES

LEARN CIVIL AND Criminal Investigation at home. Earn steady, good pay. Inst. Applied Science, 1920 Sunnyside, Dept. 13A, Chicago 40, Ill.

LEARN DETECTIVE WORK at home. National Institute, 810 Holland Bldg., St. Louis, Mo.

BUSINESS OPPORTUNITIES

60 MONEY-MAKING Ideas, Catalogue Free. Universal, Box 1076-ME, Peoria, Ill.

$60 WEEKLY, SPARE time easy! Home Venetian Blind Laundry. Free book. Burtt, 2434DD, Wichita 13, Kansas.

MOVIE FILMS & EQUIPMENT

SAVE FILM $$$$. Fresh 8mm, 16mm, B&W, color film. Home Processing Equipment. Free Catalog. Superior Bulk Film Company, 446 North Wells St., Chicago 10.

INSTRUCTION

HYPNOTISM FULLY EXPLAINED. Free literature. Neval, Box 86, Myrtle Beach, South Carolina.

MUSIC & MUSICAL INSTRUMENTS

POEMS WANTED FOR New Songs. Send Poems. Free Examination. Immediate Consideration. Songcrafters, 2724 Arcade Station, Nashville, Tenn.

SHARE $29 MILLION dollars yearly for New Songwriters, songpoets. Information, appraisal Free from Nordyke, 6000 Sunset, Hollywood 28P, California.

SONGS SONG POEMS wanted by large recording company. Music Makers, Box 2507-D Hollywood, Calif.

FOREIGN & U.S.A. JOB LISTINGS

ALASKA, OVERSEAS, U.S., California Jobs! Men, Women. Transportation paid. To $400. Weekly. Free applications, information. International, Box 16, San Diego 12, Calif.

HIGH PAYING JOBS: Foreign, USA. All trades. Travel paid. Information, Application forms. Write Dept. 21D National, 1020 Broad, Newark, N.J.

MONEY MAKING OPPORTUNITIES

MAKE $25-$50 Week, clipping newspaper items for publishers. Some clippings worth $5.00 each. Particulars free. National 81-H, Knickerbocker Station, New York.

EXTRA MONEY PREPARING Mailing Postcards, Gul, 1815 Meyers, Lombard, Illinois.

MAKE YOUR TYPEWRITER Earn Money. Send $1.00. Hughes, 7004B Diversey, Chicago.

PERSONAL

"HOW TO HYPNOTIZE And Self-Hypnosis" fully illustrated, six methods to Hypnotize (including "Instant Hypnosis-also by Telephone"). Satisfaction guaranteed or money-back within 7 days. Only $1.98 (Sorry no C.O.D.) Ralph Slater, Dept. L-X, 155 West 72 St., New York 23, N.Y.

HOME SEWERS OPPORTUNITIES

$200. MONTHLY POSSIBLE, Sewing Babywear! No house selling! Send stamped, addressed envelope. Babygay, Warsaw 13, Indiana.

SEW BABY SHOES at home! $40 week possible. We contact stores for you. Tiny-Tot, Gallipolis 15, Ohio.

LAND BARGAINS

TEXAS RESORT-SITE, at Falcon Lake, adjoining city. Excellent fishing! Full price $149.50. Payments of $7.50 per month. Utilities, including City Water. Ideal vacation or retirement. Write for Free Photos. Dean Matlock, Box 7487, Fort Worth, Texas.

BOOKS & PERIODICALS

FREE ILLUSTRATED HYPNOTISM Catalogue. Write: Hypnotist, 8721 Sunset, Hollywood 46W, California.

DISPOSAL SALE: EXTREMELY interesting Books 12 - $1. Samples Free. Persil, 436 N.Y. Ave., Brooklyn 25, N.Y.

INVENTIONS WANTED

INVENTIONS NEEDED IMMEDIATELY for manufacturers. For additional information write Kessler Corporation, 12-JB, Fremont, Ohio.

Are You Giving Your Wife The Companionship She Craves?

YOU may be giving your wife all the love and care you are able to. You may have given her a good home, security, many of the conveniences all women yearn for. But is she completely satisfied? Are you giving her what she most expected on the day that you married her? *Are you giving her the full companionship of the man she loves?*

Or are you always "too tired" at the end of a day's work? Do you come home from work with only the "left-overs" of your vitality for your wife and family? Is time catching up with you *too fast* . . . at work, at play?

If so, your condition may simply be due to a common vitamin and mineral deficiency in your diet. Yes, *you may be well-fed, but poorly nourished.* The food you eat may just not contain the necessary amounts of vitamins and minerals to keep you healthy and vigorous. You owe it to yourself to find out whether a food supplement such as VITASAFE capsules can restore the youthful feeling you'd like to have. And you can find out at *absolutely no cost* by taking advantage of this sensational free offer!

EACH DAILY C. F. CAPSULE CONTAINS:

Choline Bitartrate	31.4 mg.	Vitamin B_2	2.5 mg.	Iron	30 mg.
Inositol	15 mg.	Vitamin B_6	0.5 mg.	Cobalt	0.04 mg.
dl-Methionine	10 mg.	Vitamin B_{12}	1 mcg.	Copper	0.45 mg.
Vitamin A	12,500 USP Units	Niacin Amide	40 mg.	Manganese	0.5 mg.
Vitamin D	1,000 USP Units	Calcium Pantothenate	4 mg.	Molybdenum	0.1 mg.
Vitamin C	75 mg.	Vitamin E	2 I.U.	Iodine	0.075 mg.
Vitamin B_1	5 mg.	Folic Acid	0.5 mg.	Potassium	2 mg.
		Calcium	75 mg.	Zinc	0.5 mg.
		Phosphorus	58 mg.	Magnesium	3 mg.

COMPARE THIS FORMULA WITH ANY OTHER!

FREE 30 DAYS SUPPLY HIGH POTENCY CAPSULES

LIPOTROPIC FACTORS, MINERALS and VITAMINS

Safe Nutritional Formula Containing 25 Proven Ingredients: Choline, Inositol, Methionine, 11 Vitamins (Including Blood-Building B-12 and Folic Acid) Plus 11 Minerals.

TO prove to you the remarkable advantages of the Vitasafe Plan . . . we will send you, without charge, a 30-day *free* supply of high-potency VITASAFE C.F. CAPSULES so you can discover for yourself how much healthier, happier and peppier you may feel after a few days' trial! Just one of these capsules each day supplies your body with over *twice* the minimum adult daily requirements of Vitamins A, C and D . . . *five times* the minimum adult daily requirement of Vitamin B-1 and the *full concentration* recommended by the National Research Council for the other four important vitamins! Each capsule contains the amazing Vitamin B-12 – one of the most remarkably potent nutrients science has yet discovered – a vitamin that actually helps strengthen your blood and nourish your body organs.

POTENCY AND PURITY GUARANTEED

There is no mystery to vitamin potency. As you probably know, the U.S. Government strictly controls each vitamin manufacturer and requires the exact quantity of each vitamin and mineral to be clearly stated on the label. This means that the purity of each ingredient, and the sanitary conditions of manufacture are carefully controlled for your protection! And it means that when you use VITASAFE C.F. CAPSULES you can be *sure* you're getting exactly what the label states . . . and that you're getting *pure* ingredients whose beneficial effects have been proven time and time again!

WHY WE WANT YOU TO TRY A 30-DAY SUPPLY – FREE!

We offer you this 30-day free trial of valuable VITASAFE C.F. CAPSULES for just one reason. So many persons have already tried them with such astounding results . . . so many people have written in telling us how much better they felt after only a short trial . . . that we are absolutely convinced that you, too, may experience the same feeling of health and well-being after a similar trial. In fact, we're so convinced that we're willing to back up our convictions with our own money. *You* don't spend a penny for the vitamins! All the cost and all the risk are *ours*. A month's supply of similar vitamin capsules would ordinarily cost $5.00 retail

AMAZING NEW PLAN SLASHES VITAMIN PRICES IN HALF!

With your free vitamins you will also receive complete details of an amazing new plan that provides you regularly with all the vitamins and minerals you will need. This Plan actually enables you to receive a 30-day supply of vitamins every month regularly, safely and factory fresh for exactly $2.00 – or 60% lower than the usual retail price. BUT YOU DO NOT HAVE TO DECIDE NOW – you are under no obligation to buy anything from us whatsoever. To get your free 30-day supply and learn all about this amazing new Plan, be sure to send us the coupon today – the supply is limited.

Have you been spending up to $5.00 and more each month for your vitamins? Have you been "vitamin - hopping" from one formula to another, in a desperate search for the kind that will restore the youthful feeling you want to have? Well, *stop* right now! *Look* at this amazing opportunity! And *read* this remarkable offer!

Mail Coupon Now

VITASAFE CORP. DEPT. 321-2
43 West 61st Street, New York 23, N. Y.

Please send me free a 30-day supply of the proven VITASAFE CF (Comprehensive Formula) Capsules, and full information about the VITASAFE plan. I am not under any obligation to buy any additional vitamins, and after trying my free sample supply, I may accept the benefits and substantial savings offered by the VITASAFE Plan, or if not fully satisfied will reject them. In any case, the trial month's supply of 30 VITASAFE Capsules is mine to use free.

I ENCLOSE 25¢ (coins or stamps) to help pay for packing and postage.

Name..

Address..

City.............................Zone.....State..........

This offer is limited to those who have never before taken advantage of this generous trial. Only one trial supply per family.

VITASAFE CORPORATION, 43 West 61st St., New York 23, N.Y.

STONE-FIELD CORPORATION, Dept. L-775,
532 S. Throop St., Chicago 7, Ill.

YOUR OWN SUITS WITHOUT 1¢ COST!

Our plan makes it easy for you to get your own personal suits, topcoats, and overcoats without paying 1¢—in addition to your big cash earnings. Think of it! Not only do we start you on the road to making big money, but we also make it easy for you to get your own clothes without paying one penny. No wonder thousands of men write enthusiastic letters of thanks.

JUST MAIL COUPON You don't invest a penny of your money now or any time. You don't pay money for samples, for outfits, or for your own suit under our remarkable plan. So do as other men have done—mail the coupon now. Don't send a penny. Just send us the coupon.

STONE-FIELD CORPORATION, Dept. L-775,
532 S. Throop St., Chicago 7, Ill.

Dear Sir: I WANT MONEY AND I WANT A SUIT TO WEAR AND SHOW, without paying 1¢ for it. Rush Valuable Suit Coupon and Sample Kit with actual fabrics ABSOLUTELY FREE.

Name.. Age......

Address ....

City.............................. State...................

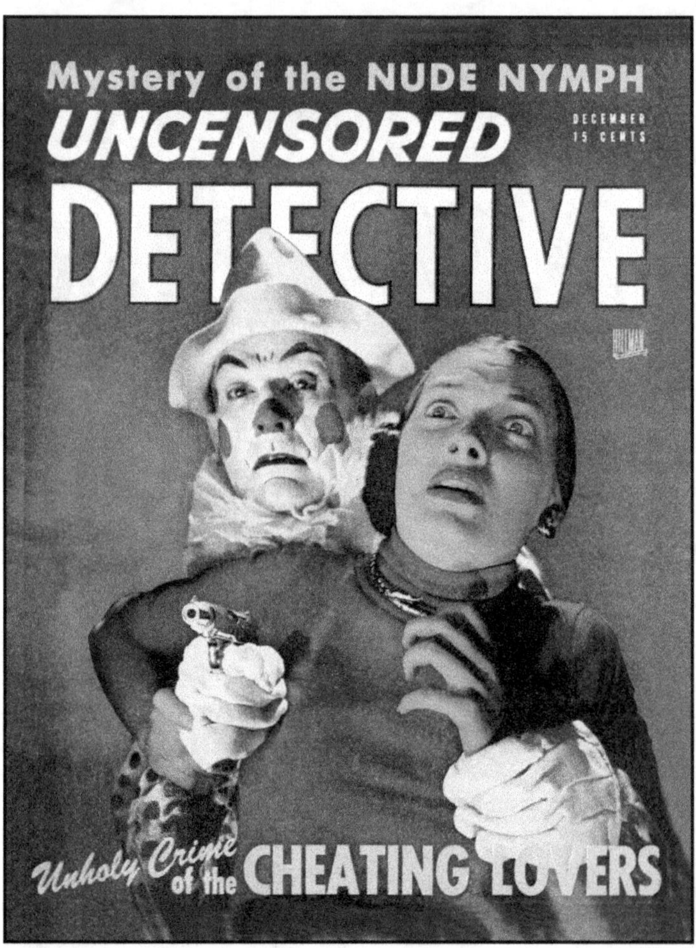

TRUE DETECTIVE MAGAZINE REPLICAS
www.FictionHousePress.com

www.ingramcontent.com/pod-product-compliance
Lightning Source LLC
LaVergne TN
LVHW061255100826
845148LV00008B/1126

* 9 7 8 1 6 4 7 2 0 3 6 2 7 *